DEMOCRACY IN ALBERTA

⋙ Democracy in Alberta ⋘

SOCIAL CREDIT AND THE PARTY SYSTEM

By

C. B. MACPHERSON

Professor of Political Science
University of Toronto

SECOND EDITION

UNIVERSITY OF TORONTO PRESS

Printed in the United States of America

TO MY WIFE

Foreword

꘏꘏

THIS is the fourth of a series, sponsored by the Canadian Social Science Research Council, relating to the background and development of the Social Credit movement in Alberta. Here Professor Macpherson has undertaken to provide an explanation for the distinctive kind of democratic system which has grown up in Alberta as represented by the United Farmers of Alberta and Social Credit experiments in government. His analysis constitutes an important contribution to an understanding of western Canadian political development and of the forces shaping democratic government in the modern world.

However far one may be prepared to go in accepting Professor Macpherson's explanation of developments in Alberta, there can be little question of the significance of these developments in relation to the general problem of democratic government. Within the political philosophies of the United Farmers of Alberta and of Social Credit there was a far-reaching questioning of accepted principles of political organization. Something new was tried; something, it was claimed, which was more truly democratic, more expressive of the real interests and needs of the population. How far these experiments have succeeded in establishing a radically new system of democratic government, Professor Macpherson has endeavoured to show. To him what has emerged is a distinctive type of party system—what he has chosen to call a quasi-party system. Such a development has not been confined to Alberta. It has been evident as well in the political organization of other Canadian provinces and in the Canadian federal state.

The thesis is a challenging one, argued with all the brilliance and force of a keen student of political theory. Not all Professor Macpherson's readers will accept his conclusions, but this is not the place to question the arguments put forward. Professor Macpherson has struck out on a new, bold approach to the study of Canadian politics. What he has done cannot fail to stimulate examination of the development and nature of democratic government in Canada.

S. D. CLARK

Preface to the Second Edition

->>)(((-

ANY party system is apt to be taken for granted while it works as
expected; only when it falters do we become aware that it exists and
that it may be precarious. The Canadian federal election of June 1962,
disarraying the accustomed system, has brought this awareness to
publicists and public alike. What had been a familiar, though it was
never a simple, party system has become something strange and un-
certain, to be looked at afresh. This new edition of *Democracy in
Alberta* is offered as a contribution to the reappraising which is likely
to go on for some time now at various levels. While the book deals
primarily with the party system in one province, it has something to
say about the possible directions and limits of the party system in
Canada. The method of analysis used, and the propositions offered
about the relation of party systems to social and economic structures,
may be thought to add a new dimension to the discussion.

The first edition carried the subtitle *The Theory and Practice of a
Quasi-party System*; that subtitle is still accurate enough, though it
may have misled some into expecting (or fearing) a more esoteric
theoretical work than is actually presented. The book does indeed deal
with theory as well as practice. It deals with the theories which two
Canadian political movements worked out about democracy and the
party system, and with their own practice of democracy and party
politics; it presents also a theory about their theory and practice, and
about the relation of both theory and practice to certain peculiarities
of Canadian society (in the first instance, but not exclusively, western
Canadian society).

The longest-lived of the two political movements, Social Credit,
spread beyond Alberta and has now shown sudden animation in the
distant province of Quebec. Indeed, the unexpected emergence of
Social Credit as a strong party there, in the federal election of June
1962, did as much as anything else to upset the Canadian image of
the party system, and to make it a matter for astonished rethinking.
It is appropriate therefore that this book, which deals largely with what

the Social Credit movement has thought about the party system, what it has done about it, and what it might do about it, should now appear with the subtitle *Social Credit and the Party System*.

I have to thank Mr. J. A. Franklin for pointing out a misleading statement (on p. 156) about the non-compulsive nature of the original English Social Credit proposals; this has now been corrected. The text of the first edition is otherwise, except for the correction of a misprint, unchanged. The analysis is not of the sort which needs continually to be brought up to date; it deals with fundamental limiting and directing forces which have not seriously changed.

When the book was first published, the concluding paragraphs attracted more attention than the rest of the book; in them, the replacement of the normal party system by a quasi-party system, in Canadian federal politics, was forecast as probable. Neither the federal elections of 1957 and 1958, which together routed the Liberal party after 22 years of office and put in its place a group of unknown men under a leader of considerable populist appeal, nor the election of June 1962 which virtually rejected them in turn and gave an indecisive balance of power to a still newer populist group—the Social Crediters of Quebec, who had risen from nothing within a year or so—neither of these seems to me to call for any alteration in that long-range forecast.

C.B.M.

September 6, 1962

Preface to the First Edition

→»«←

NOT every design for political change undergoes the test of practice. When a people takes up and tries with some success to put into effect, within a few decades, two new theories, each demanding abandonment of the orthodox party system, their action invites attention by the student of political theory and government. The present work began as an inquiry into the two apparent deviations from the British and Canadian tradition of democratic government in one Canadian province. As the work proceeded it appeared that there were uniformities of some importance underlying the two new theories and systems, which might therefore be considered not as a sequence of temporary deviations but as a new and persistent species of democratic government.

In trying to understand its emergence and significance it became necessary to go beyond the geographic-economic interpretation that has been predominant in Canadian political economy. It has been customary to look, for formative influences, mainly to the geographical and economic attributes peculiar to the northern part of the North American continent. The results obtained by directing attention to these features have been so impressive that an apology seems required now for using, in an analysis of Canadian phenomena, concepts which are primarily European. This applies particularly to one concept used extensively in the final chapter. Nobody likes to be called *petit-bourgeois*; and the term is especially opprobrious in North America, where there is a disposition to hope or believe that we are immune from those class forces that operate plainly enough in Europe. But the rapid spread of the European and urban doctrine of social credit into an agrarian and economically colonial province of Canada would be enough to suggest, if nothing else did so, that the political economies of Europe and Canada have similarities as important as their differences.

The emergence of the new political system, and its limits, are here traced to the needs of a society that is politically and economically a subordinate part of a mature capitalist economy, and whose people, at the same time, have preponderantly the outlook and assumptions of small-propertied independent commodity producers. Such a society is, in certain circumstances, led to reject the orthodox party system. But the party system characteristically performs a function that is indispensable for democracy within a mature capitalist economy: it moderates and contains the opposition of class interests. A society imbued with the independent producer's attitude towards property, and so accepting the basic tenets of capitalist enterprise, cannot dispense with the party system without providing a substitute competent to perform that essential function. Such a substitute appears to have been found in what I have called the quasi-party system, and I have suggested that it is appropriate to more than the one area in which its emergence is here traced.

The reader will find, in chapters IV and V and part of chapter VII, a rather fuller account of the English social credit doctrine and movement than would have been appropriate in this volume had there been any comprehensive account already available. There is also, in chapter I, a lengthy statistical analysis, which might more prudently have been put in an appendix: the reader is invited to treat it accordingly.

The description of the Alberta developments owes much to the kindness of many members and leaders of both the U.F.A. and Social Credit movements and governments, who have been generous with their time and their records. I am particularly indebted to the officers of the U.F.A. for allowing me to use their minute books, and to the Provincial Librarian of Alberta for her unfailing helpfulness in securing scarce early printed material. To the Canadian Social Science Research Council, which made the study possible, thanks are due for forbearance over an extended period. I have benefited much from discussions with Professor S. D. Clark at every stage of the work. My obligation to Professor H. A. Innis for constant and critical encouragement is greater than I can say.

Part of the analysis of the political theory of Social Credit was first published as an article in the *Canadian Journal of Economics and Political Science*, and I have to thank the editors for permission to make use of it here.

C.B.M.

September 1952

Contents

➤➤》《《◄

DEMOCRACY IN ALBERTA

CHAPTER ONE

Delegate Democracy and Political Economy

-»>«<-

§ 1. *Alberta's Political Experimentation*

Two major experiments in popular democracy have been worked out in the last thirty years in the province of Alberta. Each was based on a novel theory of democratic government, and each was carried into effect by a popular movement broader than a political party. The first theory was built directly from the experience of the organized farmers, though not without assumptions taken over from more general currents of reformist social thinking, and not without a belief that in meeting their own needs they would be solving the problem of democracy for all. It was put to the test of practice from 1921 to 1935, when the province was governed by the United Farmers of Alberta (or U.F.A., to give the movement its more usual name). When it proved inadequate, the U.F.A. as a political organization was superseded by another popular movement, Social Credit, with quite a different theory of democracy. The new theory had been developed in another country, and not by farmers. But since it was in rebellion against the same oligarchic tendencies as were the farmers, and made similar assumptions about the nature of society, it was acceptable to them; and since it spoke directly to townsmen as well as to farmers it had a wider appeal than the U.F.A. doctrine. Coming from such a distance and at such a time it was received as a panacea. On this basis a Social Credit government came into power in 1935 and has since remained continuously in office.

The political unorthodoxy of both movements followed logically from the unorthodoxy of their social and economic ideas; experience had convinced their members that they could not get economic justice except by changing the system of government. The crucial political problem was to devise means to ensure that the will of the people should prevail. They wanted not only to hold government accountable for what it did, but also to tell it what to do. In this they went part of the way towards that idea of direct democracy which has had

3

a perennial attraction for pioneer communities. Yet they never ex-
perimented seriously with the "direct legislation" so often espoused by
democratic reformers in the United States.   Proposals for popular
initiative and referendum were occasionally made, but the Alberta
reformers did not regard these devices as the means to democracy.
Their ideas and practices are all the more interesting because of this.
Rather than avoiding the problem of responsible government by trying
to make the people directly responsible for legislative measures, they
accepted the necessity of being governed by representative bodies,
and addressed themselves to the real problem of making them responsive and responsible.

The devices they relied on both for enforcing accountability and
for initiating policy were applications of the principle of instructed
delegation. There was some attempt to treat elected members of the
legislature as instructed delegates. Another and more persistent device
was to treat the annual delegate conventions, in which the popular
movements were organized, as the supreme policy-making authority
for the whole movement, including the legislature and cabinet.

Whatever the means to be used, delegate democracy was incompatible with the party system and normal cabinet government. The party
system, and cabinet domination of the legislature, were attacked not
as inadequate means but as positive hindrances to the end of popular
sovereignty. The efforts of both U.F.A. and Social Credit to prevent
their own organizations from becoming political parties were not entirely successful. Each, as its tenure of office lengthened, found itself
becoming more like a regular party and adhering more to the standard
procedures of cabinet government. Yet neither of them quite settled
into the ordinary pattern. And whatever may be thought of the internal political organization of the two movements, in one respect
Alberta practice has been continuously out of the ordinary. At least
since the advent to power of the U.F.A., the alternate-party system,
which is a central feature of parliamentary government in the British
and Canadian tradition, has been conspicuous by its absence. For
the fourteen years to 1935, no party other than the U.F.A. had any
significant existence in provincial politics; from 1935, when the U.F.A.
was wiped out as a political party overnight, until the present, the
Social Credit party has held virtually the same monopoly position.

In its rejection of party and its experiments in popular control of
the government, Alberta appears unique among Canadian provinces.
In fact it is not entirely unique, for the practice of the other prairie
provinces has not been as different from Alberta's as would appear

from a merely formal examination of their electoral history. While the other provinces did not completely throw off party labels, their parties did not follow the normal pattern, and they have never operated a regular alternate-party system. But it is in Alberta that the deviations from the norm have been clearest and most fully developed, and can be most profitably studied.

What is to be analysed, then, is a series of experiments in control of representative government by popular movements, without a party system; experiments not in direct democracy (which term is better confined to a system of direct popular legislation, whether by a town meeting or by the initiative and referendum) but in delegate democracy. For some, the chief interest of the analysis will lie in the conflict between the exigencies of cabinet government and of delegate democracy. For others it will be in the extraordinary transmutation which took place in the nature of the experiments. Under the same form of delegate democracy, the substance changed from the representation of concrete group interests (by the U.F.A.) to the representation of a general will emptied of all content (by Social Credit). The movement is from pioneer democracy to plebiscitarian government.

In the following chapters the various deviant practices are examined as they arose and changed, together with the theories on which they were based and by which they were supported. What residue of unorthodoxy has remained will be apparent in the course of the analysis. We shall not try to judge whether the residue is abnormal until we have examined, in the final chapter, the rationale of the orthodox system in the light of the needs of a society with the specific economic characteristics of Alberta. It will then appear that what has emerged is a new species of government, with prospects which have some permanency and are not confined to Alberta.

This much may be said in advance. The Albertans realized, even if they did not formulate it precisely, that in a society such as theirs the ends of democracy would be less well served by the traditional apparatus of party government than by something like a one-party or no-party system. They did not always see that this was true only for unusual societies of which theirs was one, nor why this was so. When they worked out a theory, they were apt to generalize without qualification from their own rather special experience, or to adopt similarly unqualified theories from outside. U.F.A. leaders produced a theory of "group government" which they hoped would transcend party government everywhere by its intrinsic merits; the Social Credit movement took over, or paid lip service to, the Douglas theory of the plebiscitary state in which parties disappear and in which parliament and the cabinet lose their usual functions. Each of these theories has some merit, but neither can in practice be taken as far as its proponents claimed, since each rests on assumptions which are only partly valid for the Albertan and similar economies, and which are invalid for the other, and dominant, economies to which the Albertan economy is tied.

So much of the theory and practice of the Alberta movements has been consciously or unconsciously a result of the unusual nature of the Albertan economy that some account of the latter must be given. Two features of it are particularly important for their political implications: its subordination to the outside economy, and its predominantly small-propertied basis. These are described in the following two sections of this chapter; their political implications will be apparent in the theory and practice of the U.F.A. and Social Credit movements, and will be more fully discussed in the final chapter. To complete the description of the essentials of the political economy of Alberta, the last section of chapter I deals with the early non-party tradition, itself a natural outcome of the economic characteristics, and of first-rate importance to an understanding of the subsequent political developments.

§ 2. The Quasi-Colonial Economy

It has become a commonplace of Canadian economic history that the main economic policies of the central government toward the Canadian west ever since Confederation, and even before, have been designed in the interests of eastern capital; that Confederation itself was a part of a grand strategy to rescue central Canada from an economic impasse.[1] The decision to acquire the territory of the great plains was made in the hope of procuring "a region of frontier settlement capable of rapid development and capable in turn of stimulating development in other parts of the Dominion."[2] The acquisition of the prairie lands from the Hudson's Bay Company in 1870, and their administration by the federal government until 1929 "for the purposes

[1]H. A. Innis, *Problems of Staple Production in Canada* (Toronto, 1933), pp. 19, 21; V. C. Fowke, *Canadian Agricultural Policy* (Toronto, 1947), pp. 140-1, 276-7. Professor Fowke holds that "the clearest and most significant uniformity regarding Canadian agriculture for more than three hundred years has been its deliberate and consistent use as a basis for economic and political empire" (*ibid.*, p. 3).

[2]W. A. Mackintosh, *The Economic Background of Dominion-Provincial Relations*, Appendix 3 to *Report of the Royal Commission on Dominion-Provincial Relations* (Ottawa, 1939), p. 15.

of the Dominion," was initially to provide grants for the building of railways, which would stimulate settlement and thus provide new investment and trade possibilities for central Canadian enterprise, and was fundamentally to keep the land and resources of the prairies available to the central government as an instrument of development policy. The protective tariff policy, inaugurated in 1879 and never since seriously modified, was designed to promote industrial development within central Canada and to give central Canadian industry a preferred or monopoly position as supplier of the prairie region. "The decision for industrialization by means of the protective tariff was definitely related to the settlement policy; it was to be a means by which the new market which it was hoped would open up in the west would be available to the other regions."[3]

The success of these policies is indicated by the marked expansion of the Canadian economy from 1895 to 1920. "The most fundamental single characteristic of the period was the high rate of investment induced by improved expectations of profit from the exploitation of natural resources, which had been newly discovered, newly tapped by the extending railways, subjected to new productive techniques, or converted into profit possibilities by favourable shifts in costs and prices. Overwhelmingly most important were the wheat lands of the Prairie Provinces."[4]

The exploitation of new resources and techniques was a source of profit in that it was the means for the exploitation of a greatly increased supply of productive labour. "So great an investment of capital would have been soon checked by rising wages and costs, had it not been for the heavy immigration of labour and the possibility of importing much of the capital equipment from Britain and the United States."[5] In the heavy immigration of "labour" must be included the homesteaders and farmers who opened up the western prairies and whose labour was the main continuing source of profits accruing to the investors of the capital.

The dominance, in the opening up and development of the prairies, of the federal policies just described and of the interests of eastern capital, is sufficient evidence of the colonial nature of the western economy in its formative years. The prairies, peopled by producers of grain and other primary products, were developed as an area for the profitable investment of capital, as a market for manufactured goods, and as a source of merchandising and carrying profits.

It has, however, generally been assumed that as the prairie economy

[3]*Ibid.*, p. 20.   [4]*Ibid.*, p. 24.   [5]*Ibid.*, p. 25.

grew up it emerged from a colonial economic status by reason of the political strength of the organized farmers. The attainment, by western farmers' political pressure, of railway regulation, reduction of railway rates, regulation of the grain trade, and other favourable legislation, especially from 1900 to 1912 and again in the 1920's, is evidence of the farmers' political strength at least in these periods.[6] But it is not evidence of their ability to prevail against the requirements of central Canadian capital. Professor Fowke has demonstrated that the federal legislation regulating the grain trade, while it undoubtedly benefited the farmer and would not have been enacted without the political pressure of the farmer, was also required in the interests of eastern capital. Until the west was filled up, whatever legislation was needed to promote further immigration and development was needed by eastern capital as much as by the western farmers.

The successful attack made by western growers upon the monopoly position which existed in local grain markets around 1900 marks the beginning of a quarter of a century during which these growers possessed considerable political power even in the federal field. They secured and retained this power during this period because for the time being they were important to the purposes of the Dominion. . . . Settlers were pouring in and farms were being established; villages, towns, and cities were springing up; and the whole process was accompanied by investment on a scale hitherto undreamed of in Canada. Grain-trade regulation, more and more rigid, even to the point where restrictions favouring farmers were irksome to trade and transportation companies, was a small price to pay in comparison to the stakes involved.[7]

The federal government supported the western protest against monopoly in the grain trade as soon as it became convinced that such monopoly would stifle rather than promote western expansion and would thus imperil the national policy. From 1899 the federal government "used royal commissions . . . chiefly for the purpose of getting this protest on the record. . . . So sure was the Dominion government of what it wanted to be forced to do that it would entrust to no one but farmers the task of manning its early agricultural commissions."[8] By contrast, after 1920, when the farmers' protests were against the restrictive pressures of the price system, the government manned its royal commissions with those who were sure to support the price system.[9] Before 1920, when the political strength of the

[6]Fowke, *Canadian Agricultural Policy*, pp. 244–50.   [7]*Ibid.*, pp. 244–5.
[8]V. C. Fowke, "Royal Commissions and Canadian Agricultural Policy," *Canadian Journal of Economics and Political Science*, XIV, 1948, p. 169.
[9]*Ibid.*, pp. 172–3.

farmers was not yet as great as it was to be in the 1920's, the federal government gave them the grain-trade anti-monopoly legislation they wanted; afterwards, although their political strength was greater, the federal government blocked their demands which were now judged incompatible with central Canadian economic interests. Not the political strength of the farmers, but the coincidence or opposition of their interests with the interests of central Canadian capital, appears to have determined their ability to get favourable legislation.

Probably not all the successes of the western farmers in getting favourable legislation are to be explained by such coincidence of interest. Yet their other successes are of small account when compared with the consistent failure of their attacks on the tariff. The protective tariff has been the fundamental federal imposition by which they have seen themselves victimized. They have never been able to touch it.

Agrarian opposition [to the National Policy of protective tariffs] reached peaks of strength from 1907 to 1911, and again in the early nineteen-twenties. Each time agrarian political strength was insufficient to secure more than alternative satisfaction. . . . The National Policy came to an end by 1930 . . . not because of any waxing of agrarian political strength, but because the National Policy had by that time fulfilled . . . "the purposes of the Dominion"; in effect, to establish on the prairies a new agricultural frontier attached economically to the central provinces. . . . The transfer of the natural resources to the western provinces in 1930 signified that the "national" policy out of which Confederation grew in 1867, and of which Macdonald's National Policy of tariffs was but a part, had been fulfilled.[10]

After 1930 the western farmers were reduced to asking for relief instead of reform.[11]

[10]Fowke, *Canadian Agricultural Policy*, p. 270.

[11]*Ibid.*, p. 250. In this connection a comment by another student of western Canadian development is revealing. Robert England in his *The Colonization of Western Canada* (London, 1936), discussing the relief settlement schemes of the 1930's by which urban unemployed were settled as subsistence farmers, and answering the criticism that such settlement was inconsistent with the nature of the Canadian economy, wrote (p. 135): "The economic fallacy [sic] that men of frugality maintaining a local economy, consuming as much of their own produce as possible on the farm, and only selling a small surplus, are of little use because of their inability to purchase tinned meat, radios and machine-made furniture, has died hard. At last it has been recognized that even the farmer who needs no relief is a definite asset, even though his purchasing power in a period of prosperity has been limited." What Mr. England calls an economic fallacy might also be called the basis of the Canadian economy, and if this theory seemed to have died in the mid-1930's it was only because the western farmer had been temporarily reduced to such straits that, as Mr. England says, the farmer who could buy nothing, but who could stay off relief, was an asset.

The conclusion that the Canadian farmers' political power "has varied in proportion to the contribution which agriculture could make . . . to the cause of commerce, finance, and industry, rather than in proportion to farmers' numbers or their state of organization,"[12] indicates how continuously close to a colonial economic status the Canadian west has been kept.

We refer to this as quasi-colonial status, not to suggest that the prairie economy is not fully dependent, but to emphasize one significant respect in which its position differs from that of colonial areas ordinarily so called. The typical prairie producer has been from the beginning an independent operator of an individual or family enterprise; he has not been reduced to the status of a wage-earner dependent on employment. The extent to which this independence has been maintained is shown in the analysis of the class composition of the Alberta economy, which follows in section 3; its political implications are discussed in chapter VIII, section 2.

§ 3. The Class Composition

Although Alberta, with its oil and coal, has a more diversified economy than the other Canadian prairie provinces, it has been throughout the period with which we are concerned primarily a farming economy. Farming has occupied far more of the population than has any other pursuit; until quite recently, indeed, more than half the entire working force. The population, in 1946 some 800,000, grown from less than 600,000 in 1921, is spread out over about 90,000 farms (82,000 in 1921), numerous hamlets and villages, twenty-five towns with populations between 1,000 and 5,000, two cities between 10,000 and 15,000, and two large cities of about 90,000 and 100,000.[13] Until 1941 about half the population lived on farms; from 1941 to 1946 the proportion declined from 48 to 42 per cent. The number of people gainfully occupied in agriculture kept pace with the whole gainfully occupied population until the last decade. Since 1936 there has been a substantial decrease in the number of those engaged in agriculture, and since 1941 an even greater relative decrease reflecting the increasingly rapid growth of non-agricultural industries. The number of occupied farms dropped from 100,000 to 90,000 between 1936 and 1946, but the acreage of farm land in use increased by some 10 per

[12]Fowke, *Canadian Agricultural Policy*, p. 9.

[13]The 1951 census figures were only partly available when this volume was completed. For consistency, therefore, no figures later than those for 1946 are given in the text. In 1951 the population of Alberta was 940,000; that of the two large cities 129,000 (Calgary) and 160,000 (Edmonton).

cent, giving an increase in the average size of farms from 180 to 224 acres of improved land.

TABLE I

GAINFULLY OCCUPIED IN AGRICULTURE, NUMBER OF FARMS, FARM ACREAGE, AND AVERAGE SIZE OF FARM, ALBERTA, 1921-46*

		1921	1926	1931	1936	1941	1946
1	Gainfully occupied in agriculture	113,997		145,746	158,376	141,201	121,795
2	Gainfully occupied in agriculture as % of all gainfully occupied	53%		51%	53%	49%	40%
3	Number of occupied farms	82,954	77,130	97,408	100,358	99,732	89,541
4	Occupied farm land (acres, 000 omitted)		29,293	28,573	38,977	40,540	43,277	41,261
5	Improved farm land (acres, 000 omitted)		11,768	13,204	17,749	18,363	20,125	20,030
6	Average size of farms (acres of land)	352	371	400	400	434	461
7	Average size of farms (acres of improved land)	142	172	180	183	202	224

*Census of Canada, 1921, 1931, 1941; Census of the Prairie Provinces, 1926, 1936, 1946. Because of a change in the census method of computing the number of farms, the figures after 1936 are not strictly comparable with those up to 1936. The number of occupied farms in each year includes a number of "non-resident farms." Most of these, but it is not known how many, are merely parts of farms in a different census enumeration area or different municipality from the part on which the farmer lives. Up to 1936 all "non-resident farms" were counted as separate farms. In 1941 and 1946 the "non-resident farms" which were in different enumeration areas from the place the operator lived but were in the same municipality were not counted as separate farms; those which were in a different municipality from the place the operator lived were still counted as separate farms. Census data do not show either how many of the "non-resident farms" are genuine farms and how many are mere parts of other farms, or how many of the non-resident parts of farms are in different municipalities but in the same enumeration area. It is therefore impossible to calculate what decrease in the total "number of occupied farms" between 1936 and 1941 is due to the change in the method of calculating the total. The decrease attributable to this is probably slight, for the number of "non-resident farms" decreased only slightly (from 9,809 to 9,484) between 1936 and 1941.

The fairly steady increase in the average size of farms conceals a change in the size distribution. Up to 1936, while the number of farms and the average size were both increasing, the proportion of small, medium, and large farms remained about the same, about half of all the farms being under 300 acres, three-quarters of all the farms being under 480 acres, and only 15 per cent of all the farms being 640 acres or larger. Since 1936, with the number of farms declining but the average size still increasing, the proportions have shifted. The number of farms under 300 acres decreased from 1936 to 1946 both absolutely and relatively (from 49 to 41 per cent of all farms); so did the number of farms under 480 acres (from 75 to 70 per cent); while the number of farms of 640 acres and over increased both absolutely and relatively (from 15 to 19 per cent). In the same period the proportion of the total farm acreage in farms of 640 acres and over increased from 47 to 54 per cent. The variations in the concentration of farm holdings are indicated in Table II.

TABLE II

Size Distribution of Farms, Alberta, 1921–46

	1921	1926(a)	1931	1936	1941	1946
Percentage of farms under 300 acres	48		48	49	46	41
Percentage of farms under 480 acres	(a)		75	75	73	70
Percentage of farms 640 acres and over	(a)		15	15	17	19
Percentage of total farm acreage in farms 640 acres and over	(a)		47	48	51	54

(a) Not available.

Changes in the tenure of farm land may also be noticed. The proportion of farms operated by the owner is still high (64 per cent in 1946), although it has declined from 1921 when it was almost 80 per cent. More significant is the proportion of farms operated by farmers who either own all the land they farm,[14] or who own part and lease part of it; these made up in 1946 85 per cent of all farms as compared with about 90 per cent in 1921. Farms operated by tenants increased from 10 to 15 per cent from 1921 to 1946.

In spite of the steady increase in the average size of farms since 1921 and the noticeable tendency toward concentration of farming in farms of a whole section of land (640 acres) or more since 1936, the predominant type of farming has remained the "one-family farm," employing no permanent paid labour and very little part-time paid labour. The amount of hired labour, compared with the labour of the farmer and his family, has always been small in prairie farming, and it has declined with increasing mechanization. In Table III, lines 1 and 2 show the decline in the amount of employed labour per farm, lines 3 and 4 the decline per 100 acres, thus taking into account the increase in the average size of farm.[15] Neither of these averages

[14]I.e., have the title to it, with or without mortgage.
[15]Weeks worked (lines 1 and 3) is a better measure than expenditure (lines 2 and 4), but figures for the latter are given to make possible some comparison with the years before 1930, for which no figures of weeks worked are available.

shows the change in the concentration of employment on a smaller proportion of all the farms; this is indicated in lines 5 to 8.

TABLE III

Hired Labour per Farm, per 100 Acres, and per Farm Employing Hired Labour, Alberta, 1920–45

	1920	1925	1930	1935	1940	1945-6(a)
1 Weeks of hired labour per occupied farm (b)			11	12	10	7
2 Expenditure on hired labour per occupied farm (b)	$261	$211	$170	$124	$143	$193
3 Weeks of hired labour per 100 acres of occupied farm land (c)			2.7	3	2.3	1.6
4 Expenditure on hired labour per 100 acres of occupied farm land (c)	$74	$57	$43	$31	$33	$42
5 Farms employing hired labour (d)			39,454	43,370	36,329	28,146
6 Farms having hired labour as % of all farms			41%	43%	36%	31%
7 Weeks of hired labour per farm employing hired labour			26	28	28	24
8 Expenditure on hired labour per farm employing hired labour			$421	$286	$391	$617

(a) June 1/45 to May 31/46; the figures in the other columns are for the calendar year.
(b) Farms on the census date; weeks of and expenditure on hired labour on these farms during the previous year.
(c) Acres of farm land on the census date; weeks of and expenditure on hired labour during the previous year.
(d) Farms on the census date, reporting expenditure on hired labour during the previous year.

It will be noticed that the decline in the amount of hired labour per farm and per acre, and in the proportion of farmers employing any hired labour, is continuous except for 1935. The increases for that year may be assumed to reflect the unusual cheapness of labour and extent of urban unemployment. The concentration of employment on fewer farms is also continuous except for 1935. The average amount of hired labour on those farms which had hired labour increased from 1930 to 1940 and decreased in 1945.

What is relevant to our inquiry is not so much the decline in the amount of hired labour as the fact that in each of the census years throughout the twenty-five years the amount of hired labour was a small fraction of the amount of labour by the farmers and their families. Though the number of working weeks in the farmer's year may be less than 52, it is very much greater than the 7 to 12 weeks average of weeks of hired labour per farm, or than the 24 to 28 weeks average of weeks of hired labour per farm employing hired labour.

A similar picture emerges from the classification of all those whose main occupation is agriculture, according to their status as "farmers employing," "farmers not employing," "unpaid family labour on the farm," and "paid farm labourers." This is shown in Table IV.

TABLE IV

STATUS OF GAINFULLY OCCUPIED IN AGRICULTURE, ALBERTA, 1921–46

	1921	1926	1931	1936	1941	1946
Farmers (a) employing			34,689	55,929	29,928	16,196
Farmers not employing			57,767	38,428	62,254	69,147
Total farmers (b)	82,224		92,456	94,357	92,182	85,343
Unpaid family workers on farms (c)	14,720		27,056	32,169	26,012	21,414
Total farmers + unpaid family workers	96,944		119,512	126,526	118,194	106,757
Paid farm labourers (d)	16,707		25,836	31,316	22,562	14,355

(a) "Farmers," throughout, includes stockraisers (following the Census definition).
(b) It will be noticed that the number of farmers in each year differs from the number of occupied farms as shown in Table I. The discrepancy is due partly to the existence of a number of farms run by those whose principal occupation is not farming, partly to the inclusion in the number of farms of a number of parts of farms (see note to Table I), and partly to the operation of some farms by brothers or partners each of whom would be listed as a farmer by occupation. The discrepancy between the number of farmers employing and the number of farms reporting hired labour (Table III, line 5) is due to the same factors and to the year's difference in date in each case.
(c) The 1921 census figure is for "farmers' sons"; subsequent census figures are for "unpaid family workers" contributing to the income of the farmer, mainly farmers' sons.
(d) This does not include those whose principal occupation was not farm labour but who did some paid farm labour; these are included in Table III, line 5.

The farmers outnumber farm labourers by ratios ranging from 3 to 1 (in 1936) to 6 to 1 (in 1946). Farmers with their working sons outnumber farm labourers by ratios ranging from 4 to 1 (in 1936) to 7 to 1 (in 1946). The latter ratios are the more significant for our purposes. When class is defined by the individual's relation to the means of productive labour, sons working on the family farm are properly to be classified with the farmers, for they are rather partners in the enterprise than employees.

These ratios are not peculiar to Alberta, or even to the prairie provinces. In 1941, the last year for which census data for all provinces are available, the ratio of farmers with their working sons to farm labourers was 5 to 1 in Alberta, 4 to 1 in Ontario, and 5 to 1 in Canada as a whole. But the significance of these ratios for the class structure of Alberta appears when the proportion of those occupied in farming to all others gainfully occupied in Alberta is compared with the proportion in an older province and in Canada.

In 1941, farmers made up 32 per cent of all the gainfully occupied people in Alberta (36 in 1921, 32 in 1931) as compared with 11 per cent in Ontario (13 in 1931), and 16 per cent in the whole of Canada (16 in 1931). Farmers and their unpaid working sons on the farm in 1941 made up 41 per cent of all the gainfully occupied in Alberta (43 in 1921, 42 in 1931), compared with 15 percent in Ontario (18 in 1931) and 21 per cent in the whole of Canada (24 in 1931). The 1946 proportions in Alberta are lower, farmers being 28 per cent, farmers and farmers' sons 35 per cent. There are no census figures for 1946 for Ontario or Canada.

The proportion of industrial employees (i.e. wage and salary workers in every occupation except agriculture) to the whole gainfully occupied population is correspondingly low in Alberta as compared with the older provinces. Wage and salary earners outside of agriculture in 1941 made up 41 per cent of the whole gainfully occupied population in Alberta (41 in 1931) compared with 71 per cent in Ontario (60 in 1931) and 63 per cent in the whole of Canada (60 in 1931).[16] If agricultural wage-earners are added, to give the whole body of employed persons, the proportions are 49 per cent in Alberta (just under 50 in 1931), 75 in Ontario (72 in 1931) and 67 per cent in Canada (65 in 1931). The proportion of those outside the farms who work on their own account (that is, neither employing anyone nor being themselves employed) was in 1931 and 1941 about the same in Alberta as in Ontario and in Canada—from 6 to 7 per cent in each case; and the proportion of employers, outside the farms, was small in each case, being between 1 and 2 per cent in Alberta and between 2 and 3 per cent in Ontario.

The outstanding features of the class composition of Alberta, as compared with the more industrial provinces, are (1) that independent commodity producers (farmers and farmers' sons working on

[16]Comparative figures for 1921 and 1946 are not available. In Alberta in 1946 non-agricultural employees were 49.5 per cent and agricultural employees were 5 per cent of the whole gainfully occupied population.

the family farm, and those in other occupations working on their own account) have been from 1921 until 1941 about 48 per cent of the whole gainfully occupied population while in Ontario they have been from 20 to 25 per cent, and in Canada about 30 per cent; (2) in Alberta the industrial wage and salary earners (that is, other than on farms) have been 41 per cent of the whole, in Ontario about 70 per cent, in Canada about 60 per cent.

The very large proportion of independent producers in Alberta appears from these figures. It might be questioned, however, whether a significant proportion of all the farmers may not fall outside the class of independent commodity producers, some because they are subsistence farmers not producing commodities mainly for the market, and others because they rely mainly on wage labour for the production of their commodities. We cannot determine accurately the number of farmers in either of these groups, but we can establish the order of magnitude of both.

With the subsistence farms the problem is one of definition, since most subsistence farms do sell some of their produce. If we adopt the Census definition, which classifies subsistence farms as those selling less than half their produce,[17] we have a measure of the number of subsistence farms. In 1936, based on the value of 1935 produce, these numbered 20,285 out of 100,358; for 1940, 5,233 out of 99,732; for 1945, 3,028 out of 89,541. The high proportion in 1935 reflects the unusually adverse conditions in that year. If 1940 be taken as a more normal year we find about 5 per cent of the farms are subsistence farms producing not mainly for the market but for the consumption of the household.

What fraction, if any, of the farmers should be classified outside the class of independent commodity producers because they employ a substantial amount of wage labour is more difficult to determine from the available figures. How many farms in Alberta depend on the use of any considerable amount of employed labour, as much, say, as a year's work of one farmer, is not accurately known. But it appears that the number of such farms must be very small. One measure, an imperfect one because of the nature of prairie farming, is the number of farm workers hired the year round. These numbers

[17]The 1936 *Census of the Prairie Provinces* is the first to classify farms in this way. "Self-sufficing farms" are there defined as those on which the value of the products consumed by the operator's household was 50 per cent or more of the total value of the products sold or to be sold or consumed. In the 1941 census the term "subsistence farm" is used, defined as a farm on which the value of the products consumed or used by the farm household amounted to 50 per cent or more of the gross farm revenue.

were, in Alberta, 7,200 in 1930; 9,267 in 1935; 4,805 in 1940; and 3,700 in 1945-6. For one year we have also figures for the number of farms employing year-round hired men. In 1936, 7,494 farms reported having had in 1935 any such hired men. Of these, 6,447 farms had one such hired man, 751 had two, 161 had three, and decreasing numbers of farms had more than this, down to 23 farms reporting 9 or more. Thus only 7½ per cent of all farms had any year-round hired men, and only 1,047, or 1 per cent, had more than one year-round hired man.

But because Alberta farming is such that a substantial amount of hired labour may be employed by a farm without any year-round hired men, a better measure of the amount of hired labour is the number of weeks of work done by hired labour both permanent and temporary. We have already seen, in Table III, the average number of weeks of hired labour on farms employing hired labour in each of the last four census years. For 1940 we have in addition the average number of weeks of hired labour on farms of each of several size groups, together with the number of farms, and the number employing any hired labour, in each size group.

TABLE V

Weeks of Hired Labour by Size of Farm, per Farm, and per Farm
Employing Hired Labour, Alberta, 1940*

Size of farm	Number of farms(a)	% of all farms	Weeks of hired labour (b) per farm	Number of farms having hired labour(c)	% of all farms	Weeks of hired labour per farm having hired labour
1–200 acres	42,342	42	3	8,164	8	16
201–479 acres	30,398	30	8	12,327	12	21
480–639 acres	10,303	10	14	5,312	5	27
640–799 acres	6,417	6	18	3,683	4	32
800–959 acres	3,067	3	24	1,986	2	36
960–1,119 acres	2,134	2	29	1,400	1	44
1,120–1,279 acres	1,188	1	36	812	1	53
1,280 acres and over	3,883	4	49	2,645	3	72
All sizes of occupied farms ..	99,732	100	10	36,329	36	28

*Based on data in *Census of Canada, Alberta 1941*, *Census of Agriculture*, and supplementary figures supplied by the Dominion Bureau of Statistics.
(a) Number of occupied farms 1941.
(b) Weeks of hired labour in 1940 on farms reporting in 1941.
(c) Number of farms in 1941 reporting expenditure on hired labour in 1940.

From these figures no precise conclusion can be drawn as to the number of farms employing a substantial amount of hired labour. The grouping of farms by acreage does not correspond accurately with a grouping by value of product; differences in intensity of operations mean that some of the smaller farms may employ an amount of wage labour considerably greater than the average for that size of farm. However, in view of the fact that of all the farms having hired labour only those in the two largest size groups, which included only 3,457 farms or 3½ per cent of all occupied farms, employed an average of as much as 52 weeks of hired labour, it seems safe to say that only about 5 per cent of all the farms employ as much hired labour as the labour of one farmer. Accordingly, we may say that only about 5 per cent of all farms fall outside the class of independent commodity producers by virtue of their employment of a substantial amount of hired labour.

It is not part of our inquiry to establish why mechanization has not led to a still greater concentration, which in some parts of the United States has replaced the family farm by the large "farm factory" where, with a high degree of mechanization, a very large acreage is put into production under one management with much employed labour. We need only notice that this kind of concentration has not taken place in Alberta to any significant extent.

Prairie farming in Canada has indeed become considerably more mechanized in the last two decades. This has meant that the average farmer has been able to dispense with a certain amount of hired labour, notably harvest labour, on which he was formerly dependent. It has also meant that the average farmer has had to have more capital to stay in operation or to get the same returns as before, since widespread mechanization and cheapening of production tend in the long run to lower the relative price of cereals. It has further meant that the average acreage of the family farm has had to be increased. For with increasing mechanization, once the slack in the unused productive capacity of the land is taken up, it requires not only more capital but also more land to make full use of a given amount of productive labour. In other words, with mechanization each unit of labour sets to work more capital and needs more land. But the unit of labour has remained, or rather has not decreased below, a year's work of a farmer and his family. The result has been that while the scale of farming, as judged by acreage or capital per farm, has increased, the relation of the farmer to labour has not much altered. The family farm, depending on very little hired labour, is still the predominant type. The farms are more capitalist in the economic sense of requiring a larger capital for their operation, but are not more capitalist in the social sense of involving the employment of more wage labour.

Thus we find that of all the Alberta farmers a proportion of the order of 5 per cent might be excluded from the class of independent commodity producers as being subsistence farmers, and another 5 per cent as relying chiefly on the employment of wage labour. This exclusion does not significantly affect the estimate of the class composition of Alberta. At most it would bring down the proportion of independent producers from 48 to 45 per cent of the whole gainfully occupied population.[18] No similar calculation of the number of farmers in Ontario who fall outside the class of independent producers has been attempted, but it may be assumed that it is not substantially different. The comparison between the class composition of Alberta and Ontario may therefore be assumed to be substantially unaffected by any allowance to be made for such farmers.

While the foregoing analysis has placed almost all the Alberta farmers in the class of independent commodity producers, it is not intended to suggest that there are no gradations of interest within their ranks. They range from small farmers just above subsistence to substantial grain growers, ranchers, and other specialized producers. The size of the farm, in acres, is not an accurate indication of the scale of operations, nor is the amount of labour employed. Classification of farms by value of farm production, which is made for the first time in the 1946 census, is a more useful indication of the gradations in scale of operation. Table VI classifies the 89,541 occupied farms in Alberta in 1946 by the total value of farm products sold or used in 1945. This table of course affords no indication of gradations of farm income or of net returns on farm operation, for the amount of capital and current expenditure required to produce these gross values varies greatly between different types of farming. The most it affords is a rough index of the variation in the scale of operations. It suggests also that the family farm is for the most part still on a very modest scale, as some 87 per cent of all farms which reported produce showed a gross revenue of less than $4,000.

[18]The 48 per cent in 1941 is made up of 32 per cent farmers, 9 per cent farmers' sons, and 7 per cent those not in agriculture working on their own account. If 10 per cent of the farmers are taken out of the class of independent producers, the proportion of independent producer farmers in the whole gainfully occupied population drops from 32 to 29 per cent. The other proportions remain the same. The proportion of independent producers to the whole gainfully occupied population thus drops from 48 to 45 per cent.

TABLE VI

FARMS BY VALUE OF FARM PRODUCTS, ALBERTA, 1945

Value of farm products, 1945, on occupied farms, 1946	No. of occupied farms (a), 1946, reporting produce in 1945	% of occupied farms, 1946, reporting produce in 1945, in each class
Less than $1,000	29,247	34
$1,000–$3,999	45,373	53
$4,000–$5,999	6,286	7
$6,000–$9,999	3,630	4
$10,000 and over	1,809	2
All farms reporting produce	86,345	100

(a) It will be noticed that the total number of farms shown in this table is some 3,200 less than the total number of occupied farms. It cannot be inferred that there were 3,200 non-productive occupied farms, for the total "occupied farms" includes an unknown number of "farms" which were simply parts of other farms (see note to Table I). The produce of these would in most cases be listed as the produce of the other farm. Some of the 3,200 would be genuine farms which reported no produce because they were just beginning operation or were operated for pasture purposes. But the percentages in the third column would not be substantially altered if an estimated number of whole farms with no produce were added to the less-than-$1,000 class and to the total.

Thus, although technological development since the pioneer days has increased the acreage and the amount of capital needed to produce a living from a farm, or to farm profitably, the relations into which the farmer enters in the process of production have not significantly changed. The predominant mode of farming is still independent commodity production. And in the whole economy of Alberta, independent commodity producers (farmers and others) have, until 1941, outnumbered industrial employees, the former being about 45 per cent, the latter 41 per cent, of the gainfully occupied population in 1941. This is sufficiently different from the prevalent proportion in Canada as a whole, where independent producers were less than 30 per cent and industrial employees some 60 per cent, that we should not be surprised to find some difference in political behaviour.

§ 4. The Non-Party Tradition in the West

The political tradition of the Canadian west is a non-party tradition, and had been so for a long time before the U.F.A. and Social Credit administrations in Alberta. The alternate-party system was not indigenous to western Canada; it did not develop of itself in the first years of representative government there; and when it was introduced it did not take firm root or become fully operative. This may at first sight seem strange, for the other provinces have found the party system adequate to their purposes from the beginning. But the needs of the prairie provinces were different.

In them, two characteristics, not found together in any of the other provinces, combined to discourage the introduction and development of a party system. One was their relatively homogeneous class composition, the other was their quasi-colonial status. The former seemed to make a party system unnecessary, the latter led to a positive aversion to party. The absence of any serious opposition of class interests within the province meant that alternate parties were not needed either to express or to moderate a perennial conflict of interests. There was apparently, therefore, no positive basis for an alternate-party system. The quasi-colonial position of the western provinces made it a primary requirement of their provincial political systems that they should be able to stand up to the national government, that is, able to make effective demands on it and to resist national legislation which they regarded as exploitive. That they should be able to do so was all the more important as their quasi-colonial status was not only economic but also political. Unlike the provinces which had entered Confederation at the beginning, the prairie provinces were creations of the federal government; and the federal government retained control over their natural resources until 1930. They were not equal members of a federation; the federal government was to them not only a federal but an imperial government. It was therefore essential to the purposes of the provincial community that its government should be an effective offensive and defensive weapon against this imperial power. A provincial party system in which each of the alternate parties was a subordinate section of a federal party had nothing to commend it as a weapon against the central government; from this fact, a strong antipathy to the party system appeared in the west soon after the federal parties had managed to establish themselves in provincial politics. In view of all this, what needs to be explained is not why there was a non-party tradition in the west, but why the party system ever made any headway there at all. The answer is to be found in the exigencies of the federal parties.

A brief view of the development in Alberta before 1921 will show how these forces operated, and will show the stages of non-party, party, and anti-party feeling. Three stages can be seen: (1) before the creation of the province in 1905, abstention from and finally outspoken rejection of the alternate-party system; (2) from 1905 to

1910, acceptance of one party as providing a "business" government; (3) from 1910 to 1921, a sceptical experiment with an alternate-party system, leading to its complete rejection in 1921.

For seventeen years before the creation of the provinces of Alberta and Saskatchewan in 1905 the people of those territories had enjoyed a measure of representative government as the North-West Territories. During the whole of this period the Territorial legislature and cabinet were conducted on strictly non-party lines; during the last two years, when the pressure from federal parties to introduce a party system into Territorial government was strong, the Territorial legislature's abstention from such a system became an explicit rejection of it.

The reasons for this abstention are clear enough. In the first place the homogeneity of the western community and the virtual unanimity of the citizens' needs were especially marked in this period of early settlement. What the settlers wanted from governments was basic facilities for life and work: schools, roads, railways, and the like. The common need for these was urgent, and transcended any differences for which party division might be a natural or appropriate system. There was, in short, nothing in the internal requirements of the Territories to call for a party system; the choice of representatives was better based on ability or administrative record, which, at such a primary level, were not too difficult to gauge. The internal functions of the Territorial government were the business functions of a municipal government.

In the second place, the external function of the Territorial government, namely, the representation of western interests to the federal government, was thought to be better performed by a non-party than party government. Indeed the west was slow to divide along party lines even for the election of its federal members of parliament. In federal politics a party system was fairly well in operation in the rest of Canada by 1878, but was not accepted in the North-West Territories until 1896.[19] For what the Territories wanted of the federal government was, above all, railways; and because of the system of deferred elections whereby the results of the eastern voting were known before the west voted, the west generally voted for the party which it knew would be in office. This discouraged the building of party machines; western voters preferred not to give steady allegiance to either of the eastern parties. Not until the transcontinental railway

[19]The reasons for this are fully set out by Escott M. Reid, "The Rise of National Parties in Canada," *Papers and Proceedings of the Canadian Political Science Association*, IV, 1932, pp. 187–200.

had been built and the system of deferred voting abandoned were the eastern parties established in the west as the regular machinery for the election of federal representatives.

Even after the western territories had accepted the party system for purposes of their federal representation they continued to do without it for local purposes. The elected Legislative Assembly, instituted in 1888 with merely advisory powers, had by 1897 established the principle of responsible government: the Executive Council, appointed by the Lieutenant-Governor, was responsible to the Legislative Assembly, which was given control over expenditures.[20] While the manner of winning responsible government gave the Territories the framework of a cabinet system, it was never operated as a party system. Members of the assembly were open supporters of one or the other of the federal parties but they did not divide on these lines in the assembly or in their support of the council. The council itself always contained adherents of both federal parties, and each member of the council felt free to take an active part in federal party campaigns.[21] This separation of provincial from federal affairs was not challenged until the last year or two of the Territorial government. When it was challenged, in 1903, the position of the assembly was plainly stated by Premier Haultain:

From the earliest times . . . there has been a practically unanimous opinion on the part of the country that this House, in addressing itself to the business intrusted to it, should not introduce questions, names, and cries which had nothing to do with the particular business in hand. . . .

With regard to my position with the Conservative party, I am in thorough unison with it on all questions of principle. . . . But the policy of that party and those principles have nothing whatever to do with my position in this House or with the business of this House.[22]

Haultain's statement was a reply to the decision of the Conservative convention to run party candidates in the next Territorial elections, by which decision he and four other Conservative members of the assembly refused to be bound. The assembly in effect endorsed the premier's view by giving him unanimous support in the sessions of 1903 and 1904.[23]

The party system which the Territorial Conservatives had favoured in 1903 was introduced with a vengeance by the Liberals for the

[20]C. C. Lingard, *Territorial Government in Canada* (Toronto, 1946), pp. 5–7. There was not a full measure of responsible government, since the federal government retained control of the main sources of revenue.

[21]*Ibid.*, pp. 117–18.

[22]Quoted in *ibid.*, pp. 118-19.   [23]*Ibid.*, p. 119.

first provincial elections in 1905. The act constituting the new provinces of Alberta and Saskatchewan was passed in July 1905, to
come into force on September 1. The Liberals, at conventions in
August, determined to contest the provincial elections on federal party
lines; the Alberta Conservatives later in the same month followed suit,
though in Saskatchewan they accepted Haultain's lead in declaring
in favour of continuing the non-party system. It did not matter
which position the Conservatives took; the Liberals had it their
own way. The Liberal government at Ottawa appointed for both
provinces Liberal lieutenant-governors, who called on the Liberal
leaders of the respective provinces to form the first provincial administrations. Purely Liberal administrations were formed in September and were able to arrange things favourably for the first elections,
which were held in Alberta in November and in Saskatchewan in
December. In the Alberta election the Liberals won all but two seats.

The introduction of parties into provincial politics, despite their
unsuitability to western provincial needs and despite the volume
of non-party sentiment, is attributable to the inherent requirements
of Canadian federal parties. They are compelled to maintain permanent organizations in every province where they have any hope
of any federal seats; and there are obvious advantages to the national
organizers in having the same machine for both federal and provincial
elections. It is easier to keep up party enthusiasm and party loyalties
if the voters can be mobilized on party lines at both federal and provincial elections; the more frequently a party machine is actively used
the more smoothly it is able to run. There is a further reason for a
federal party's interest in provincial elections. If it can capture the
provincial government it has all the provincial patronage to dispense,
and provincial patronage has been on the whole more important, and
more directly useful in maintaining a political machine, than has
federal patronage.[24]

So, however inappropriate to purely provincial purposes a party
system may be, there is always a strong pressure from the continuing
needs of the federal parties to introduce and keep up the party system
in provincial politics.

The party system which was thus introduced into Alberta provincial politics by extraneous pressures remained somewhat extraneous. As long as the provincial administration elected by party

---

[24]Cf. Escott Reid, "The Saskatchewan Liberal Machine before 1929," *Canadian
Journal of Economics and Political Science*, II, 1936, p. 39; R. MacG. Dawson,
The Government of Canada (Toronto, 1947), p. 535.

methods devoted itself efficiently to the provision of the desired physical helps to the rapidly growing economy it served well enough. But it was supported less for its party principles than for its business efficiency. As long as a government provided honest, effective administration, the fact that it had been put into office by a party mechanism was incidental and the mechanism was not seriously questioned. However, when the Alberta Liberal government laid itself open to serious suspicion of large-scale inefficiency and corruption, in the Alberta and Great Waterways Railway scandal of 1910, the Alberta voters began to doubt whether parties were consistent with honest, efficient administration.[25] Distrust of the one party which had been the only effective one since 1905 led at first not to rejection of parties as such but to some support for the rival party; the Conservatives won 18 of the 56 seats in 1913 and maintained this position in 1917. Thus the immediate consequence of the inadequacy of one party was to start the alternate-party system to life. But its life was short and precarious. Even before it got started, western distrust of the federal parties as instruments of domination made their provincial position very insecure.

As early as the federal election of 1911 distrust of the old parties, widespread across the western provinces, had led to proposals that farmers' associations should organize farmers' parties or enter candidates in every constituency themselves. Both the Saskatchewan Grain Growers' Association and the United Farmers of Alberta rejected such proposals in 1911; but the defeat of the farmers' low-tariff policy in the 1911 federal election led to increased demands for independent political action, either by farmers' parties or non-party political movements.[26] Interrupted by the outbreak of war in 1914, the demands broke out again in 1915 and 1916.[27] The leaders of the farmers' associations, although in full cry against the corruption and eastern domination of the old parties, were nevertheless generally reluctant to risk the lives of their organizations by taking them into direct electoral action.

The party system itself, as well as the old parties, came under heavy fire after 1916 from the rapidly growing Non-Partisan League.[28] The

[25]L. G. Thomas, "The Liberal Party in Alberta, 1905-21," *Canadian Historical Review*, XXVIII, 1947, p. 420.

[26]These developments are concisely set out in Paul Sharp, *The Agrarian Revolt in Western Canada* (Minneapolis, 1948), chap. 3; cf. W. L. Morton, *The Progressive Party in Canada* (Toronto, 1950), chap. 1.

[27]Morton, *The Progressive Party in Canada*, chap. 2, pp. 41ff.

[28]On the Non-Partisan League in western Canada, see Sharp, *The Agrarian Revolt in Western Canada*, chaps. 5–6.

League spread into Canada from North Dakota in the summer of 1916, and was particularly effective in Alberta. In the provincial election of 1917 it ran four candidates and elected two, and its propaganda was increasingly successful in the next two years.[29] The League's main aim was the supersession of the party system by a "business government," in which the legislature would deal with public business on its merits and not along party lines. Constituency autonomy, and control of members of the legislature by constituency conventions made up of delegates of local units, were emphasized. This entailed rejection of the right of a government to treat a vote in the legislature on any measure as a vote of confidence. "There can be no such thing as a business administration while the defeat of a government measure means the dissolution of the House. This foolish practice in itself is sufficient to keep the party spirit alive indefinitely. . . ."[30] The life of a government was not to "depend on the defeat of any measure whatsoever."[31]

In its attack on cabinet domination, the Non-Partisan League was not alone. There was dissent even in Liberal circles; the *Calgary Morning Albertan* was critical, and its owner, W. M. Davidson, independent Liberal member of the legislature, seconded a motion of G. J. Turgeon, a Liberal member, in the Alberta legislature in 1920 calling for the discarding of the practice.[32]

The Alberta Non-Partisan League's campaign to replace the party system by a "business government" based on delegate democracy, with constituency control in place of cabinet domination, won such response that the U.F.A. leadership was forced to take over the League organization and principles and embark on direct electoral action itself. The western voters' wholesale rejection of the old parties in favour of the Progressives in the federal election of 1921, and the Alberta voters' decisive rejection of the Liberal party in favour of the U.F.A. in the provincial election of the same year, were the culmination of ten years of mounting anti-party feeling, which covered the whole period in which the alternate-party system had any semblance of existence in Alberta. It is no wonder that the provincial parties, having to contend with this feeling between 1910 and 1921, and not then having the utilitarian justification of providing a "business" administration which the Liberal party had had up to

[29]See Chap. II, note 26.
[30]*The Alberta Non-Partisan*, March 15, 1918.
[31]Statement of Principles, *ibid.*, May 22, 1919.
[32]W. L. Morton, "The Western Progressive Movement and Cabinet Domination," *Canadian Journal of Economics and Political Science*, XII, 1946, pp. 138–9.

1910, never took root. While 1921 was primarily a revolt against the party system in federal politics, it was quite logical that it should be carried over to the provincial parties in so far as they were subordinate parts of eastern-dominated federal parties and had no functional basis of their own. Of the two, the provincial party system was the more easily swept away, for it had never got a strong foothold. In short, 1921 marked a return, after a brief and partial deviation, to the non-party tradition in western provincial politics.

CHAPTER TWO

The U.F.A.: Social and Political Theory

-»>«<-

§1. The Place of Theory

For the first ten years of its existence, the U.F.A.[1] felt no need of a theory of society or government, and had none. It was not the sort of organization in which one would expect to find a central theory. The life of the U.F.A. was largely the activities of the locals, established by the initiative of the farmers and farm women in each neighbourhood to be centres of community life. In the locals, with the help of a small central organization, the farm population provided for itself the recreation and the technical and cultural education it wanted. The other purpose of the U.F.A. was to build up and consolidate the pressure of farmers' demands on governments. In this work the U.F.A. was concerned with practical matters of immediate need or desirability—freight rates, grain trade regulations, roads, and other things directly affecting their incomes and welfare.

While the members of the U.F.A. were thus united by a common desire to better themselves and sometimes by a common resentment of the treatment of western farmers, no single social, economic, or political theory emerged. For the U.F.A. brought together men of diverse backgrounds—American populists, free silver men, single-taxers, Non-Partisan League adherents, English free traders, guild socialists, Labour Party men, to mention only some. Many U.F.A. men were attracted by newer doctrines without abandoning earlier ones. Such a diverse membership could unite in the practical day to day work but did not readily develop a common theory. The intellectuals in the U.F.A. saw a need for deepening the movement's theoretical understanding, and tried to provide material, notably in the *Grain Growers' Guide* and later in *The U.F.A.*, but the intellectuals themselves were often eclectic, more concerned to provide a variety of provocative materials in the hope of stimulating some theoretical discussion than to develop a consistent social or political

[1]Formed in 1909.

theory. Free trade, monetary reform, and quasi-socialist principles were presented without any sense of inconsistency.

However, within a year or two of the U.F.A.'s entry into direct political action in 1919, a coherent political theory was worked out, under the stress of practical organization, and became the guiding theory of the leadership. Indeed, two elements of the theory, the principles of strict "class" political organization and "constituency autonomy," came to be so firmly held and so extensively acted upon, particularly in federal activities, as to earn the U.F.A. the title "doctrinaire" in contrast to the Saskatchewan and Manitoba farmers' movements with their more flexible theory and practice.[2] The whole theory of which these principles were a part was developed and expounded chiefly by Henry Wise Wood,[3] ably seconded by William Irvine.[4] It appears to have been widely enough accepted within the Alberta movement in the twenties to justify its description as the political theory of the U.F.A., and it is discussed under that title in section 3 of this chapter.

It is doubtful whether the more general and logically more fundamental analysis of society, which is described in this chapter as the social theory of the U.F.A., was ever held as widely by the whole movement as was the political theory. It was not so much the social philosophy of the U.F.A. as the personal philosophy of H. W. Wood. Yet there is no doubt that it had a wide appeal; its vista of social progress and its great moral assurance made it a sustaining force among the United Farmers. It may therefore not improperly be described as the social theory of the U.F.A. We shall deal with the social theory first, as both logically and chronologically prior to the political theory; to separate them is somewhat artificial but makes possible a clearer analysis.

§ 2. The Social Theory of the U.F.A.

Henry Wise Wood and William Irvine both developed their social theory in evolutionary terms. Relying on a belief in natural law they

[2]W. L. Morton, *The Progressive Party in Canada* (Toronto, 1950), chap. 5.

[3]Wood was the outstanding leader of the U.F.A. from 1916 to 1931. For a comprehensive account of his life and his political and economic activities, see W. K. Rolph, *Henry Wise Wood of Alberta* (Toronto, 1950).

[4]William Irvine was a noted publicist, first of the Non-Partisan League (see note 26) and then of the U.F.A. (see note 10). In 1921 he was elected to the House of Commons as Labour member for Calgary East. Defeated in 1925, he secured election in 1926 as U.F.A. member for Wetaskiwin. Active in the formation of the C.C.F. in 1932, he ran as a C.C.F. candidate in 1935 and was defeated. From 1945 to 1949 he was C.C.F. member for Cariboo.

produced optimistic gradualist doctrines of social change and progress. Wood's ideas, expressed publicly as early as 1917 and repeated at intervals throughout his career as president of the U.F.A. (1916-31) in his annual presidential addresses, election speeches, and expository articles in *The U.F.A.* and the *Grain Growers' Guide*, were the most influential. His theory of "group government" did not emerge until 1919; when it did it was readily presented as a natural extension of the broad social theory expounded in 1917 and 1918, although in the earlier years he had been opposed to farmers' organizations entering politics.

The burden of Wood's social theory was that in the prevailing competitive economic order there was a necessary and increasing opposition of interest between "the masses" and "the plutocratic classes," that this opposition was becoming more conscious and open as the mass of the people organized themselves in occupational groups, and that it would come to a head in a final conflict in which the defeat of the plutocratic forces would put an end to the competitive order and establish a harmonious co-operative society.

This forecast of the pattern of social development was placed in a long evolutionary perspective, and idealized, by being shown as the culmination of a conflict between two principles animating society from the beginning—the principle of competition and the principle of co-operation. Competition compelled co-operation for survival, but co-operation made competition fiercer. Competition, operating between increasingly large and strong groups, had now reached a point of destructiveness, in class conflict and international war, which would compel men, as rational and moral beings designed for social life, to transcend the competitive principle and follow only the co-operative principle. Moral values were assigned to the two principles: competition was the true law of animal life and the false law of human life, co-operation was the true law of human life; and nature's design required that the human law, being the higher, should triumph.

The loftiness and moral fervour of Wood's social theory can best be appreciated from his own words. His first extensive exposition of his views, published in the *Grain Growers' Guide* in December 1918 and apparently given as Chautauqua addresses,[5] deserves considerable quotation.

Wood sketched the development of man from savagery by means

[5]"Organization for Democracy," *Grain Growers' Guide*, Dec. 4 and 11, 1918. Extracts were published in the *Western Independent* of Jan. 21, 1920, as extracts from Wood's speeches at Chautauqua.

of competitive struggle which, being the law of animal life, was the only pattern the savage knew; the competitive principle was carried into the first stage of social organization which, accordingly, from the beginning took the form of autocracy rather than democracy.

So we have the development of practically all past ages based on the law of animalism, carried out by the method of animalism, developing into an animalistic form of organization, all justified by the false teaching of the divinity of the state and the divinely appointed wardens of that state.

To rebuild civilization and put into operation the true laws of life was possible, though the majority probably did not yet think so. Wood believed it possible, indeed, inevitable, on teleological grounds:

We . . . see everywhere the works of nature brought under perfect obedience to the laws of nature, until we come to man. . . . We see man in a state of unfinished development, disobedient to the true laws of life. Is the supreme effort of nature, namely, man, going to be the one supreme failure? I do not believe it. I believe this work is going onward and upward until man will be brought into perfect obedience to the true laws of life and become a perfect social being, operating a perfect civilization.

The prospect thus opened was not one of automatic betterment; it was one of continuous effort to strengthen the popular forces for a decisive conflict with the autocratic forces.

Democracy is in its infancy. . . . Nature points out to this infant democracy the only way that leads to ultimate success. This way is slow evolutionary development through years, decades, and, perhaps, centuries of continuous effort and growth, all the time increasing in strength and efficiency, and all the time accomplishing more and more till finally the work is done. What is the work to be done? To meet in deadly conflict all the autocratic forces that bar the way to human progress, and these we will find entrenched at every point where man comes in contact with his fellowman, more especially at every point where trade is involved. . . . The conflict is between animal selfishness and social unselfishness; between autocracy and democracy; between Mammon and God.

The pattern for the development of the popular forces had already emerged; it was organization by occupational or industrial groups, which Wood always referred to as classes.

The forces of democracy are just beginning to gather. They are gathering in class organizations. This kind of organization is not democratic in the fullest sense but I believe it is the only kind that is practical at the present time. Nature takes the course of least resistance. Each of these classes represents a group, the members of which have a common interest in and are affected alike by the problems of trade. Each class first studying these problems from its own viewpoint can much more easily learn the rudiments

of trade problems than they could otherwise. Thus they are taking the way
of least resistance. But as a truly democratic class comes to understand these
problems from its own standpoint it will develop an understanding of them
in a broader and more democratic way, and thus all democratic class organizations will gradually converge into a higher and more democratic
organization.

Here already is the emphasis on long gradual development of
popular organization leading to a "deadly conflict" with the autocratic forces, which was the theme, made increasingly explicit, of
his later discourses. The conflict is described both as a conflict
between groups of men, not yet more clearly defined than the democratic forces and the autocratic forces, and as a conflict between
principles. There is, too, a notable contempt for the state as a
false divinity. And, not least, there is the emphasis on trade as
the determinant of social relations. The relations engendered by
trade produce the autocratic forces, and it is by organizing in groups
with common trading problems that the democratic forces are to find
their strength.

In 1922, in a still more extensive analysis,[6] Wood traced the
economic basis of social development and of present class alignments.
Beginning, as in his earlier exposition, with the contrast between the
principles of competition and co-operation, and finding the development from savagery to the present dominated by competition, he
decisively rejected social Darwinism,[7] and summed up the development to the First World War, and the future prospect, as follows:

Thus competition, begun by individual savages, had driven co-operation up
through the various increasing units until practically all of the nations
in the world were embraced in two great co-operative units. Speaking
from a national and military standpoint, competition can drive co-operation
but one degree higher, when all of the nations will be embraced in one
co-operative unit and military competition will have been destroyed.

War itself was simply the result of commercial competition between
the huge commercial aggregates known as nations.

Germany did not wage war primarily for military supremacy. Her real
object was commercial supremacy. True, the brute call to man and to
nations has often been strong enough to cause them to fight for glory and

    [6]"The Significance of Democratic Group Organization," The U.F.A., March
1 and 15, April 1 and 15, 1922 (the first four issues of the official U.F.A. paper).
The same material, under the title "The Efficient Citizenship Group" was published in the Grain Growers' Guide, March 22 and 29, 1922.
    [7]"Science tells us that [competitive struggle for survival] is the true primary
animal law, but only the fool will tell us that it is the true ultimate social law."

power. But through the ages, greed . . . has acquired the power and arrogated the authority of a god and is enthroned as Mammon, directing the competitive activities of the nations and the peoples of the earth. Mammon, by holding dominion over commerce holds it also over war.

Wood made it plain, however, that he was not condemning commerce as such. "Commerce is not the cause of war, but the wrong use of it is. Commerce, systematically used in accordance with the true social laws of life, would be the greatest binding tie in the social system." Indeed, true to his fundamental economic liberalism, Wood saw society itself as the result of trade:

. . . we may imagine what the first actual step of social progress was. Somewhere, at some time, a primitive savage conceived the idea of trading some article he possessed beyond his immediate needs, for something he wanted that another savage had. Anyhow, this first trade was made, and my imagination can conceive of no more appropriate event to fix as the first step of social progress, and the first discovery of the great central institution of present day civilization, namely, trade and commerce.

But commerce had come to be destructive of civilization in the measure that competition had become monopolistic. The industrial revolution had widened markets, increased the size of firms, made competition between them destructive, and so led to mergers and combines and finally to all-embracing manufacturers' associations. The manufacturers destroyed competition between themselves in order to save themselves from destruction. But in so doing

they had not, as many thought, destroyed competition. On the contrary the competitive unit had been gradually raised from the individual factory to the combine, and then to greater combines, and then to the economic class. This is the most deadly unit of competitive strength that has ever been organized in the commercial world. . . . When the manufacturers had eliminated competition between themselves by organizing as an economic class unit, they began to compete against other economic classes. They found the great masses of the people unorganized and totally incapable of protecting themselves against organized competition.

Thus,

plutocracy has gradually built up a competitive strength operating between the primary producer and the ultimate consumer, that will eventually reduce the great masses of the people to abject poverty, unless the people can build up a counter strength equal to or greater than that which has already been built up by the plutocratic classes, among which the Manufacturers' Association is outstanding and perhaps the most relentless.

The obvious moral, which Wood proceeded to expound, was that the farmers and all other "democratic" classes needed, and were justified in building, an organization which could defeat the "pluto-cratic classes," destroy the competitive social order, and replace it by a producers' co-operative economy. Not only ought the democratic classes to do this, it was inevitable that they should do so. It was also inevitable that the process would be a long slow development cul-minating in a decisive conflict and a decisive victory of the forces of democracy over the forces of plutocracy.

Great natural forces, working themselves out in the development of social order, are in the process of throwing up these organized groups, and their manifest destiny is to bring order out of the present chaotic trade conditions and thereby lay the foundations for world peace and social perfection. The birth and development of this new order will necessarily be slow. Before it can be fully established a conflict of social forces, perhaps the greatest of all the ages, seems inevitable. The two contending forces in this conflict will be organized plutocracy on one side, pitted against organized democracy on the other. . . . To say that democracy will fail will be to say that the design of nature in creating a social being and bringing him into obedience to social laws has failed. It will be to say that nature has failed in her supreme effort; to say that wrong is stronger than right, error stronger than truth, Mammon stronger than God.

It will not fail. It cannot fail, because the Supreme Power . . . has this work in hand and will not let it fail.

It is apparent that this analysis gave Wood, and was intended by him to give others, a fortifying faith. It justified the organization of the U.F.A. as a body uniting farmers on the basis of their "class" interest; it showed that nature and nature's laws were on the side of class organization; it opened a long vista of effort "onward and up-ward" toward a harmonious and "true" society. At the same time it defined, sharply enough for Wood's purposes, the lines on which the struggle was to be conducted, and revealed the face of the enemy—the plutocratic classes. It promised a good fight and a victorious end, but counselled patience by placing the decisive contest far in the future and leaving the contestants vaguely defined.

The arts of the homespun orator and the ardent faith of the propagandist cannot conceal the narrowness of Wood's social analysis. It is bounded by the vision of the independent commodity producer, owner of the means of his own labour. Wood's notion of the origin and development of society, though not Darwinian, does not indeed depart far from the assumption of the liberal political economists: man is a trading animal. "When we learn to trade right we will have largely learned to live right." Wood had, what the liberal economists did not have, a strong sense of the exploitation of the mass of the people by the few, which drove him to predict and demand the decline and replacement of the competitive system. Yet he stayed within the liberal assumptions in attributing this exploitation not at all to the command of capital over the labour of the many consequent on the divorce of labour from the means of labour, but solely to the unfair competitive strength of some producers in the commodity markets.

This characteristic outlook of the independent producer is reflected in Wood's concept of economic class; class was defined not by status in the process of production but by position in the commodity market. The significant present classes were the competing commodity producer groups, notably farmers and manufacturers, with consumers sometimes added as another class. Conflict was engendered in the disposal of the products, not in the process of production, and had only become serious when the industrial revolution had transformed the market and given rise to monopolistic competition. No conflict of economic classes before then found a place in Wood's analysis. And when he envisaged the ultimate conflict to come he did not think of it as conflict between two classes defined by their relation to capital but as conflict between all the "democratic classes" on the one hand and the "plutocratic classes," never further defined than those who had succeeded in monopolistic competition, on the other.

The narrowness of Wood's social analysis is, no doubt, responsible for his reliance on natural law and hopeful moral evolution. If the only significant trend was towards monopolistic competition between producers, there was nothing for it but for the relatively unorganized producer groups in the commodity market to organize as strongly as the manufacturers and to battle them to a standstill. It is significant that the only interest groups other than manufacturers that Wood could consider of any importance in his theoretical analysis were the farmers and the consumers, although in practical politics, as we shall see, he recognized organized labour as another group. How the carrying of monopolistic organization to its ultimate stage by the organization of farmers and other producer groups would end in a harmony of interests was never clear. But why it must do so was clear in Wood's reading of moral law. The exploitation of man by man was wrong, was against nature; it must therefore disappear in the working out of nature's laws. "When the race will have been built into one co-operative unit in the interest of human welfare, there will be nothing left to exploit except the gifts of nature."[8]

[8]H. W. Wood, Presidential Address to the U.F.A. Annual Convention, 1926, (U.F.A. Minute Books; the minute books are preserved in the central office of the U.F.A. in Calgary).

The limitations of Wood's social thought were in the circumstances a strength rather than a weakness. No one else in the farmers' movement publicly challenged Wood's reading of history and society, or propounded an alternative theory. Wood's insight matched the limits of the agrarian independent producer's vision.

William Irvine, although not nearly as important a figure as Wood, nor perhaps as much of a formative force as one or two of the other leading men in the U.F.A. whose ideas are not as fully recorded, was a prominent spokesman of the movement at the time of its greatest political activity[9] and was for many years a Labour or U.F.A. member of parliament. His social ideas may not have been as representative as Wood's but they merit attention, not least for their adaptation of a labour philosophy to an agrarian situation. His writings[10] reflect a consciousness of the demands and thinking of organized labour which was lacking in Wood, yet he reached essentially the same conclusions.

Preaching a new social order for Canada, Irvine summed up its aims by quoting from a British Labour party statement of principles.[11] He was aware, as Wood was not, that "the nature of man's struggle for the means of life is the foundation of the society in which he lives, and decides, in the main, its forms,"[12] but he turned for his sociology to Herbert Spencer, whose *First Principles* he cited in support of his view that gradualism is the law of social development.[13] The natural law which Irvine expounded had a more scientific flavour than had Wood's teleological doctrine, but its substance was the same: competition between increasingly large groups becomes increasingly destructive and must be superseded by co-operation between groups, the way to which and the techniques for which are pointed by the increasingly large areas of co-operation within groups forced by the competition between groups.[14] The conflict at present involved three main classes: capital, labour, and farmers. Between these, "class war rages, not only in Canada, but in every civilized country in the world. That class war will go on until the collective mind discovers salvation in co-operation."[15] The role of organized farmers is to be to prevent "a fight to the death" between capital and labour which

---

[9]See note 26 below.

[10]William Irvine, *The Farmers in Politics*, with a foreword by the Rev. Salem G. Bland (Toronto, 1920); and *Co-operative Government*, with a foreword by H. W. Wood (Ottawa, [1929]). The latter is a collection of popular lectures "given at various times and places throughout the Dominion" (p. viii).

[11]*The Farmers in Politics*, p. 47.   [12]*Ibid.*, p. 26.   [13]*Ibid.*, p. 79.
[14]*Ibid.*, pp. 140–3.   [15]*Ibid.*, pp. 146–7.

would destroy society. These two classes "cannot be destroyed; if they could be abolished it would mean turning back the wheels of society. These groups must learn to co-operate between themselves in the same manner as individuals did in forming their several groups. This is what the laws of social progress say, and this is why we have a United Farmers' movement. But the farmers alone, of the economic groups in Canada, have discovered the higher law of co-operation."[16]

Here is a rather different approach from Wood's. Irvine took "class war" between capital and labour as given; the function of the organized farmers was in Irvine's view to hasten the inevitable transformation of class war into class co-operation. The need to transcend class conflict was given by its increasing destructiveness; the possibility of transcending it was given by the law of social development that competition compels co-operation for survival. The farmers' movement was the natural agent of the final transcending of class conflict because "the farmer, in reality, combines in his own profession the two antagonists. He is both capitalist and labourer. He knows that production is not furthered when war is going on between the two. He sees, also, the hopeless deadlock between organized capital and organized labour . . . and is thus led to the discovery of co-operation as the synthesis without which progress cannot be made."[17] And, "although fathered by oppression, the farmers' movement has escaped that bitterness of feeling against capital, and that extreme rashness both of expression and action, so characteristic of labour."[18] Thus Irvine made a virtue of the ambiguity of the farmer's position, and saw the farmer as transcending the conflict and leading the way to its resolution.

While the main contenders in the present conflict of classes were capital, labour, and farmers, the solution of this conflict would reveal that the real permanent classes were occupational groups. "The fact is that there are a great many economic classes in society. Let us suppose that capital and labour have had their final struggle, and labour has been victorious. What then? There will still be farmers, miners, transportation workers, and a great number of other skilled and unskilled classes in competition with each other over the spoils of capitalism." Each would want as much as possible of the others' products in exchange for his product. "The fight, therefore, after the overthrow of capitalist exploitation, would go merrily on even as before. . . . The real classes are the industrial groups, and of these there are as many as there are industries."[19]

[16]*Ibid.*, pp. 147–8.   [17]*Ibid.*, pp. 101–2.   [18]*Ibid.*, p. 101.   [19]*Ibid.*, pp. 230–2.

This analysis shows the same preoccupation as Wood's with conflict between groups of producers over the terms of trade for their products; these are the "real classes," and the real class conflict arises in the exchange of their commodities in the market. Indeed, in his insistence that the conflict of interests between producer classes would continue even after the end of the exploitive order, Irvine set a more difficult problem than did Wood with his faith in the growth of rational co-operation. Irvine's solution, however, was not basically different from Wood's: the "new system must recognize the many existing classes and provide self-determination for each. A government on the basis of no class would be as false as a government on the basis of two classes. All classes must be recognized."[20] Rational co-operation is assumed. Irvine's socialism was readily assimilated and subordinated to the independent commodity producers' outlook which is found unalloyed in Wood.

§ 3. The Political Theory of the U.F.A.

(i) Emergence of a political theory

By the political theory of the U.F.A. is meant those ideas which, developing with the entry of the U.F.A. into direct political action in 1919, justified and gave coherence to its political work in the subsequent years. It is well known that the pressure to take the U.F.A. into politics came from the rank and file rather than the leadership.[21] Wood, as president of the U.F.A., was opposed to its taking independent political action; in 1917 in a message to U.F.A. locals and members issued on election day (June 7) he urged them to think over the calibre of candidates and to prepare to get better ones in the next election not by making independent nominations but by working within the old party of their choice. "Go to your party caucus and help send delegates to your party convention, who will nominate the right candidate. If you fail here you will fail everywhere. If you succeed here you make good everywhere. Right here is where the machine starts. . . . The machine is all right if it is run right, and it will be easier to run it right than it will be to build another one—another party."[22] Later in the same year in an

---

[20]Ibid., p. 232.

[21]Paul F. Sharp, The Agrarian Revolt in Western Canada (Minneapolis, 1948), p. 147; W. L. Morton, "The Social Philosophy of Henry Wise Wood," Agricultural History, XXII, 1948, pp. 120–1.

[22]H. W. Wood, "The Price of Democracy," Grain Growers' Guide, June 20, 1917.

address to a conference of U.F.A. social leaders, he expressed his view of the proper function of the U.F.A.: "Instead of building up a new political party we are promulgating safe and sane political ideals. We will be piling up political force, and through that force piling up useful legislation. We do not want to mix with any organization, but we do want to influence the men who do make the laws so that our mobilized voters will have an equal influence with the superior organization and money of the special interests."[23] Even after Wood had gone along with the U.F.A. convention of January 1919, which passed the resolution authorizing independent political action, he was lukewarm. Commenting on the sentence in the resolution which called for "purely democratic and independent political action" he wrote:

I would put by far the greatest emphasis on the word "democratic". . . . . If political action is going to be an element in the democratic force we are trying to build, it must be democratic in its construction and in its operations. There has been considerable speculation as to whether or not the political force we are trying to develop will be a political party. I do not believe it makes any difference whether it is called a party or not, or whether or not it really becomes a party.[24]

It is apparent from this indifference in May 1919 to the form to be taken by the political activities of the U.F.A., that Wood had not yet carried to its conclusion in political organization the principle of occupational group organization which he had begun to expound some months earlier.[25] But by the time of the by-election campaign in the Cochrane provincial constituency in October and November 1919, he appeared as an outspoken critic of the party system and began his long advocacy of "group government." The theory of group government soon became the official political theory of the U.F.A. For exposition of the theory we may turn both to Wood and to Irvine, for Irvine, as editor of the official organ of the Alberta Non-Partisan League which became the official organ of the U.F.A. Political Association, was recognized as an authoritative expositor.[26]

[23]Wood, "The Organized Farmer and Politics," *ibid.*, Sept. 19, 1917.
[24]Wood, *Political Action in Alberta*, leaflet "reprinted from the *Grain Growers' Guide*, May 7, 1919."
[25]Wood, "Organization for Democracy," *Grain Growers' Guide*, Dec. 4 and 11, 1918, as quoted in sect. 2, above.
[26]The 1920 U.F.A. Convention passed the following resolution: "That this Convention endorses the principle of Economic Group Organization for political purposes, as explained by the President of the U.F.A. and by the Editor of the *Western Independent*" (U.F.A., *Annual Report*, 1919, with minutes of 1920 Convention). Irvine was editor of the *Western Independent*. Irvine's influence, and

The gist of the U.F.A. political theory, over and above the general theory of occupational group organization which has already been discussed, was (1) an analysis and denunciation of the party system as an autocratic mechanism through which the moneyed interests divided and ruled the mass of the people, and which was inherently unsuited to a democratic movement; and (2) the advocacy of political representation by democratically organized occupational groups each nominating and instructing its delegates to the legislature.

(ii) The U.F.A. critique of the party system

A decade or more of western discussion, in the *Grain Growers' Guide* and elsewhere, had made the case against the party system as an instrument of plutocracy so familiar on the prairies by 1919 that little elaboration of this aspect of the case was deemed necessary. Wood, in the longest and most systematic presentation of his views,[27] could take it for granted that the parties were controlled by the money of "the highly organized economic classes," with only a brief reference to the history of tariff lobbying and to the inability of either of the old parties to protect "the masses of the people" from economic oppression. The point of departure of the U.F.A. political theory was indeed the denunciation of plutocracy or the rule of the special interests. The attack on the party system arose out of the attack on "the interests"; it was the sense of their own and "the consumers'" exploitation that led the United Farmers to find in the party system the political mechanism which upheld it.

Today we have . . . the most efficient system of manufacturing, transporting and distributing that the world has ever seen. . . . [It] should have brought the primary producer and the ultimate consumer much closer together . . . and put the necessities and comforts, and even the

---

the relation between the work of the Non-Partisan League and the U.F.A.'s entry into independent political action, are indicated by the sequence of newspapers. *The Nutcracker*, edited by Irvine, was the first proponent of the Alberta Non-Partisan League. It ran from November 1916 to September 14, 1917, when it was succeeded by *The Alberta Non-Partisan* (Sept. 29, 1917, to Sept. 11, 1919) as the organ of the Alberta Non-Partisan League, with Irvine continuing as editor. In October 1919 the title was changed to *The Western Independent* and, still under Irvine's editorship, it became the official organ of the U.F.A. Political Association. The Alberta Non-Partisan League dissolved when the U.F.A. Political Association was established. The *Western Independent* continued as the organ of the U.F.A. Political Association until that Association was dissolved and its functions assumed by the U.F.A.; with the issue of February 4, 1920, the paper became the organ of the U.F.A. and continued as such until June 1920 when the U.F.A. Board of Directors discontinued the U.F.A. financial assistance to it.

[27]"The Significance of Democratic Group Organization," *The U.F.A.*, April 1, 1922.

luxuries of life in reach of more people than . . . ever . . . before. Today [they] are farther apart than they have ever been before. . . . The first cause is that the plutocratic classes have organized as economic classes, . . . operating between the primary producer and the ultimate consumer, and getting as much out of each as possible. The second cause [is that] this great economic force has also developed into a dominant political power operating through the political party system. . . . The political party is a structure ideally adapted to plutocratic control.[28]

But the U.F.A. analysis of the party system went further than the observation that the old parties were dependent on campaign funds from industrial and financial interests and so were subservient to them, though this was spelled out by Irvine particularly.[29] Nor did the U.F.A. analysis stop with the conclusion that the party system was an instrument to divide and rule the people, though this too was stated forcibly. "The autocratic strength of the old party system lies in its adaptability in dividing democratic forces and ruling them. . . . Continued domination by the autocratic classes depends entirely on the continual division and consequent inefficiency of the masses."[30]

Deeper than this, Wood's fundamental criticism, which applied not merely to the old party system but to any party system, was that parties were inherently conglomerate, therefore unstable, therefore incapable of transmitting the democratic force of reform-minded citizens.

At the last election in Canada there were over three million votes cast. Dividing the entire citizenship into three million units not only reduces the unit of strength to the vanishing point but creates the greatest possible amount of confusion and discord. It is true these individual units have been divided up into two or more political parties, but the political party system does not raise the citizenship unit. Each party is composed of a conglomerate mass of individuals, and the individual is still the unit.

It is true that the parties are divided against each other on one or more questions. Sometimes this division is real and well defined, but hardly ever so on more than one question, and that a temporary one. On all other questions there are all sorts of differences of interests and opinions among the individuals in each party, consequently all sorts of confusion and instability. Few questions are ever settled permanently by political parties, and none that deal with primary social problems.

The political party is an unstable structure. . . . On account of its instability the great effort of politicians is to hold the unorganized elements of their unstable group together, and at the same time make every possible

---

[28]Wood, "Neither Farmers Nor Labor Can Break into the Plutocratic Classes," an address delivered at the convention of East and West Calgary U.F.A. District Associations, Oct. 7, 1921. Leaflet issued by U.F.A., October 1921.

[29]Irvine, *The Farmers in Politics*, e.g., Part II, chap. 2, sect. 5.

[30]Wood, Presidential Address to the U.F.A. Annual Convention, 1924 (U.F.A. Minute Books).

appeal for reinforcements to the dissatisfied individuals in the other party.
. . . On this false basis has grown not only helpless confusion but lament-
able insincerity. . . . Patriotism is prostituted to the service of the most
selfish interest and designs. Few questions are seriously discussed on their
merits. Truth is frequently not sought after, but systematically concealed in
a mass of confusion. All of this is made possible because the individual
unit of citizenship is so low that the masses of the people have no citizenship strength. They have been like the sands of the desert, blown back
and forth by the changing winds of false propaganda. The unit of citizenship strength must be raised to an infinitely higher degree. This can never
be done through the political party system.[31]

Here is the core of Wood's political analysis. Party is a search
for power. It must appeal to everybody. It can have no unifying principles. It cannot therefore be an effective organization for attaining
the ends desired by the mass of the people. Party is unstable, which
is what makes it so useful a tool of plutocracy. Party becomes
hypocrisy.

Wood saw what has become the commonplace of Canadian his-
torians, that the conglomerate nature of Canadian parties makes them
unstable and lacking in principle. But what others have seen as a
virtue of the party system, enabling it to hold together in some sort
of equilibrium the many conflicting class, group, and geographic
sectional interests, Wood saw as a basic defect, rendering the system
fundamentally undemocratic. The difference in judgment is not surprising. To Wood, forms of political organization had to be judged
by their probable efficacy as instruments for sweeping social reform.
The party system was rejected because it could never be an instrument
for defeating plutocracy, which was his grand aim. When he spoke
of "citizenship strength" he meant the strength of the demand for
the abolition of exploitation. Citizenship was equated with destruction
of the competitive order. If political organization is seen as a means,
not of adjusting many divergent interests within a given social order,
but of changing the social order, all his criticisms of the party system
are immediately understandable.

Wood left no doubt that the goal was the destruction of the competitive social order, "the overthrow of class domination by the
masses."[32] To this end the strategy in the field of political action was
to line up the masses against the classes, to organize the "democratic

[31]Wood, "The Significance of Democratic Group Organization," *The U.F.A.*,
April 1 and 15, 1922.
[32]Wood, Presidential Address to the U.F.A. Annual Convention, 1924 (U.F.A.
Minute Books). Subsequent quotations in this and the next paragraph are also
from this address.

forces" as effectively against the "autocratic forces" as the latter were already organized against the former. The alignment must be clear-cut, and it was just this that was impossible under the party system. "Will any one claim that the old party system is a better way than ours to mobilize democratic forces? In its entire existence all those whose interests are democratic have never been drawn into one party, and those whose interests are autocratic drawn into another. There is no reason for believing that this alignment of forces will ever be accomplished under that system, even should the effort be continued for a thousand years." The task was to do away with the party system and so "remove one of the greatest barriers to real social progress, and bring the autocratic and democratic forces into more direct contact with each other, and each force into the open. The conflict between these two forces is irreconcilable, and the sooner the division between them is clearly defined, the better it will be." "The primary and irreconcilable division between social elements is that between autocracy and democracy, and all democratic elements must be mobilized into one working force."

The very opposition by press and politicians to the U.F.A.'s political organization and theory was cited by Wood as evidence of the validity of this analysis. "The reactionary forces of partyism" have avoided "frank and fair discussion of the underlying principles of the two systems."

. . . In fact they give no logical reasons, and viewed in the light of their history we should not expect it. In the fight between autocracy and the people, autocracy has never deemed it necessary to give reasons. In the people's long struggle for the right of the franchise there were only spurious reasons given for the opposition to their efforts. Why should we expect anything except spurious reasons for the present opposition to the people's efforts to use their franchise more intelligently and more efficiently? It has always been purely a matter of force and perhaps will be to the end.

Wood's well-known opposition to the U.F.A. sponsoring or par-ticipating in a political party, as distinct from its entering politics as a strictly class organization, follows from his fundamental principles. To build a party would be to enter the competition for votes from all classes, groups, and sections; in this competition the farmers' movement would lose its firm basis of economic group interest, would become amorphous, and would be beaten again, as so many farmers' and popular parties had been beaten before, by the superior political machines which served and were served by the moneyed interests. A

farmer party might stay uncorrupt but it would have to have a centralized organization; success in manoeuvring within a party-divided
legislature demanded that any party be dominated by its legislative
members and leaders. In the old parties this was the mechanism of
domination by the interests, and even a new reform party must, in
allowing control from the centre, become undemocratic. Irvine went
further, holding that even a farmers' party would necessarily become
corrupt. "The fact that a party is a *farmers'* party will not prevent
it bearing fruit according to its kind. Power has a wonderful fascination. Once enjoyed by a farmers' party it would be sought after to
the exclusion of all else. In order to hold on to it, the party would have
to cater to certain influences, and by and by would become as corrupt
as its rivals."[33] Thus in either view, to become a party was to have
the worst of both worlds. In creating a political machine the movement would lose its democratic control from below but would not,
so long as it stayed uncorrupt, gain a machine as efficient as those of
the old parties. It would lose its stable base in identity of occupational
class without gaining the power, conferred on the other conglomerate
parties by money, to gather the votes of all classes and sections.

The U.F.A. critique of the party system may be summarized as
follows: the worth of any method of political organization is to be
tested by its efficiency as an instrument for hastening the destruction
of the competitive social order; the old party system is a method of
maintaining that order by dividing, confusing, and ruling the masses,
the old parties being subservient to the moneyed interests; no new
party, however democratically begun, can be an adequate instrument
for social change, since a party as such is conglomerate, unstable,
lacking in principle, and undemocratic. The farmers as an organized
democratic force seeking a new social order must therefore reject
party organization.

(iii) *The theory of group government*

The positive proposal that the party system be replaced by the
political organization of occupational or industrial groups, or economic
classes as Wood preferred to call them, each uniting the stable
interests of the members of the group and each nominating and electing its representatives to the legislature, was implicit in the analysis
we have already examined. The social theory found occupational
grouping to be the natural and inevitable power grouping, and the
only one which, intelligently used by the farmers and other "demo-

[33]*The Farmers in Politics*, p. 228.

cratic" forces, could lead to the supersession of the competitive social order. The critique of the party system demonstrated that merely economic organization by occupational groups was not enough, because the legitimate economic demands of the farmers and others were blocked by a party system which was now in the hands of the exploiters and which could not be made over to suit the needs of the masses. The obvious alternative to the party system was the political mobilization of the people along occupational group lines; each unit, with its own solid basis of common interest, nominating and electing legislative representatives. It was the obvious alternative not only because it lay ready to hand in the existing occupational organization of the United Farmers but also because occupational interests appeared to the farmers to be the most stable and permanent interests distinguishing and uniting individuals. The new system would be an instrument of democratic advance; each unit would be democratic within itself, being free of any need for machine control; and all units which were democratic in aim, that is, which sought the establishment of a new social order, would together be able through their more effective organization to overthrow the power of the vested interests and inaugurate the new social order. The party-divided legislature would become an industrial group legislature, artificial opposition and party discipline would disappear, issues would be decided on their merits as judged by the various groups, the cabinet would be made up of representatives of the groups in proportion to their numbers in the legislature, each group would thus bear a share of the responsibility of government, and the conventions of party government such as the resignation of a government on the defeat of a government measure would be discarded.[34]

In spite of its name the essence of the theory of group government was not an examination of the problems of government by occupational groups and the possible relations between them, nor an analysis of the electoral or legislative arrangements entailed by group representation. How little was said on these matters is shown below.

The essence of the U.F.A. theory of group government was its concept of democracy. Enough has been said already to show that this concept was not parliamentary government with universal franchise, nor the "responsible government" of Canadian tradition; parliamentary or responsible government was party government and was therefore the opposite of democracy. Democracy, in the U.F.A. theory, had two meanings, not always carefully distinguished but regarded as

[34]*Ibid.*, pp. 238ff.

complementary. Both were developed in the critique of the party system.

In its most fundamental sense, democracy was a social order in which there was no exploitation of man by man or class by class. Democracy was the ending of the exploitation of "the masses," a term Wood used surprisingly often, and which of course included the farmers. It is apparent that democracy in this sense was a moral concept, and it involved a moral problem which the opponents of the U.F.A. made the most of, and to which the U.F.A. leaders found an answer novel in Canadian political thinking, though with obvious antecedents in European socialist thought. The morality of democracy derived from its end, the destruction of class exploitation. This end could be achieved only by the organization of "the masses" along industrial group lines, each group clearly based on its selfish interest, for this was the only stable and effective basis of popular organization. The task, then, was "to develop a class opinion, make our class articulate. We must mobilize class opinion, and then mobilize votes behind it. Every industrial class in Canada has got to do the same thing."[35] But selfish class organization did not appear to be highly moral. This objection, pressed by the opposition, was a matter of great concern to the U.F.A. It was not sufficient for the U.F.A. spokesmen to say that "Canada never had anything but class government,"[36] that it was those who were "exploiting and impoverishing the people" who were raising the cry of class selfishness against the farmers,[37] or that the farmers "would naturally object less to their own class ruling them than to the rule of the class at present in power";[38] none of these answers established the morality of the U.F.A. scheme. It was necessary to show that the farmers' selfishness would lead to a new higher morality.

Wood's first attempt at this demonstration did not produce a very positive moral prospect:

We are human, the same as everyone else, and I do not deny that if we were the only class organized we would make unjust demands; but other classes will organize and resist unjust demands, and out of this reaction they will find a common ground of settlement.[39]

A somewhat more positive morality was propounded in 1922 as an outcome of the mutual resistance of economic groups.

[35]Wood, speech at Crossfield, Oct. 20, 1919, as reported in the *Manitoba Free Press*, Nov. 1, 1919.   [36]*Western Independent*, editorial, Oct. 22, 1919.
[37]H. W. Wood, "The Significance of Democratic Group Organization," *The U.F.A.*, April 15, 1922. [38]*The U.F.A.*, Nov. 1, 1926, article by William Irvine.
[39]Wood, speech at Crossfield, Oct. 20, 1919, as reported in the *Manitoba Free Press*, Nov. 1, 1919.

It is true that selfishness has been rampant in the economic classes that are already organized, but unresisted power has always been selfish. Resistance to that selfish power is the present necessity of democratic organization. Resistance creates stability, power treats with power on equal terms, in the hope of equitable adjustment. . . . The economic class . . . is the only basis on which groups can be organized with reasonable hope of solving social problems on the basis of justice and unselfishness.[40]

This doctrine of resistance, however, envisaged no more than a temporary morality of lessened injustice: while all the presently exploited groups were organizing along group lines their resistance to the dominant class would lessen the present injustice, and their resistance of each other's demands would prevent any one of them from becoming too selfish. But the real morality of class organization was not this temporary morality; it was the immanent morality of its goal. "Class organization" was the way to strengthen the popular forces to the point where they could inflict a final defeat on the forces of "organized plutocracy." With the destruction of the competitive social order, a harmonious, moral, co-operative social order would follow. "When the race will have been built into one co-operative unit in the interests of human welfare, there will be nothing left to exploit except the gifts of nature. But, by that time, humanity will have developed sufficient intelligence regarding human welfare to understand that by co-operating with nature her gifts will be multiplied."[41]

The U.F.A. concept of democracy was thus based on the assumption of a natural harmony of group interests, to emerge when the exploitive order was destroyed. The whole position is summed up in a few sentences:

It is because the U.F.A. desires to prevent class rule that it urges all classes to organize. . . . When all classes are organized and in a position to take an intelligent part in the duties of citizenship, then the conflict of groups will give place to co-operation. . . . The self-interest of each group will be seen to be inseparably connected with the interests of the whole; organization will reveal this connection, and each group will seek co-operation for its own self-protection, if for no higher reason.[42]

This was the full answer of the U.F.A. leaders to the charge of class selfishness. They preached a temporary class morality to oppose the class morality of the existing ruling class, but its purpose was to destroy the basis of all class morality by destroying the exploitive

[40]Wood, "The Significance of Democratic Group Organization," *The U.F.A.*, April 15, 1922.

[41]H. W. Wood, Presidential Address to the U.F.A. Annual Convention, 1926 (U.F.A. Minute Books).

[42]William Irvine, in *The U.F.A.*, Nov. 1, 1926.

order. The farmers' class morality was redeemed by its instrumentality in transcending class-divided society.

One other aspect of the U.F.A.'s moral concept of democracy should be noticed. It mistrusted power, and felt that power was somehow incompatible with democracy.

The most undemocratic phase of partyism is its aim at complete power. The full control of the state is the ambition of all parties. . . . Democratically speaking, no party has the right to govern. In a democracy there can only be a partnership in power. The right of a party to form a government is the right of might, might of propaganda, of manipulation, or of numbers. The party that has one vote more than another assumes the right to rule, as though justice resided in a majority. The industrial group in politics does not seek to become all-powerful in the state. It seeks representation, or a share in the administration.[43]

This moral concept of democracy as a goal, a non-exploitive, just, co-operative social and political order in which no organization would have to exercise power, and would therefore not misuse it, was probably the strength of the U.F.A.'s doctrinal appeal.

Closely related to it was the concept of democracy as a means, a method or type of political organization and responsibility, by which the end was to be attained. This second meaning of the term democracy in U.F.A. thinking was more specific: democracy was the control and instruction of elected representatives by the groups which nominated and elected them. This involved more than the general notion of the responsibility of elected representatives to their constituents. It meant that the elected members were regarded as delegates,[44] subject to specific instruction by the group. It meant that the group must finance itself and operate its nominations and its election campaigning, in order that the member when elected should owe nothing to anyone but the group. It meant that the elected members of any one organization should not "assume the prerogative of organizing political machinery. . .; [this] would be a violation of the fundamental principle of political democracy, which is that the organization of all political machinery must originate with the citizenship."[45] And it meant that the groups must be formed on a specific and stable basis of one overriding interest common to

[43]Irvine, *The Farmers in Politics*, pp. 225–6.

[44]In the classic sense of that term as established by Burke. In Social Credit usage, as will be seen, the terms delegate and representative bear meanings precisely the opposite of the general usage.

[45]Wood, Presidential Address to the U.F.A. Annual Convention, 1923 (U.F.A. Minute Books).

all members of the group, in order that clear decisions on policy for the guidance of the elected member could always be reached. This basis, of course, was the occupational group. In all these respects democracy was the opposite of the party system; revulsion from the party system is the fixed point of reference. "When we get all classes thoroughly organized and with proper representation . . . each class will send its representatives to the legislatures and parliaments according to its numerical strength, and these representatives will go as our lobbyists, not hired, but belonging to us body and soul, and go there to settle class differences."[46]

By substituting occupational group units for conglomerate party constituency organizations the U.F.A. exponents of group government believed they had solved the problem of the accountability of the elected member to his constituents, which was in their view the essence of democratic machinery. But they solved the problem of the democratic relation between member and constituents only by shifting the real problem to a more remote level. If the members of the legislature are the accountable delegates of occupational groups, how can they in the legislature agree on policy and legislation? There is no obvious basis for agreement. To this the U.F.A. theorists had no adequate answer. They gave little thought to the way in which group government was to operate. In effect they held that the solution would work itself out when legislatures took on their new character of group legislatures, and that no solution could be or need be propounded in advance. They did not feel called upon to examine the implications of a system which could not begin to operate effectively until several industrial groups were organized and sending representatives to legislatures. "Given the group organization in the constituencies the form of government will look after itself. . . . The new form of government cannot be constructed beforehand by any individual. Suffice it to say that the group government which will result from the new forms of political organization must be molded to fit the new conditions. It will be a natural outgrowth of group representation. . . ."[47] They were confident that it would work out, because in their view all political problems were fundamentally economic problems, all economic problems reduced themselves to the interests of occupational groups, and, once the exploitive order was overthrown, all group interests would be funda-

[46]Wood, speech at Crossfield, Oct. 20, 1919, as reported in the *Manitoba Free Press*, Nov. 1, 1919.
[47]Irvine, *The Farmers in Politics*, pp. 235–6.

mentally harmonious and all differences soluble by intelligent co-operation.

Even the form which group representation in the constituencies was to take was not very fully examined. The logical implication of the demand that legislatures be made up of industrial group representatives is the abolition of territorial and the substitution of industrial or occupational constituencies. But this was not proposed by the U.F.A. leaders, and on the few occasions when such a proposal was introduced at a U.F.A. annual convention by an individual member or a district association it was defeated.[48] Wood, speaking against the proposal at the 1928 U.F.A. convention, revealed the limitations of the group representation system:

President Wood believed that the possibility of different classes voting their own ticket already existed. "We put our representatives in Edmonton to represent and speak for agriculture, and labour is doing the same thing. Another primary element of our people in Alberta is the urban element, and we've been pleading with them to do the same thing and they won't do it. There is nothing to hinder them from doing it. Of course they have one representative from Edmonton. I don't see that you can facilitate voting by industrial classes in Alberta much more. . . . Some of the small towns might group and put in representatives, but I think you have let theory run away with you. You are theorizing about something that is already in practice."[49]

This statement in effect abandons the possibility of group representation in the provincial legislature on the scale that had been anticipated in the earlier advocacy of group government. In fact, Wood had always had difficulty in seeing what industrial groups other than farmers and organized labour could give substance to his concept of group government; he dealt with the problem only a few times in his recorded speeches, and each time his ideas were inadequate to his concept of group government. In a campaign speech during the Medicine Hat by-election in 1921 he touched on the question of the fate of small groups which would be unable to elect legislative members by themselves.[50] "Such groups can select a larger group that comes nearer representing their group interest than any other and attach themselves co-operatively with that group." This was only a temporary expedient: "when a just system of Proportional Representation is inaugurated, these groups through that system can get what

---

[48]Minutes of U.F.A. Annual Convention, 1924, pp. 102-3; *The U.F.A.*, Feb. 23, 1928, report of the 1928 Convention proceedings.

[49]*The U.F.A.*, Feb. 23, 1928, report of the 1928 Convention proceedings.

[50]Wood, speech at Medicine Hat, June 25, 1921. Text in U.F.A. leaflet *Co-operation between Organized Democratic Groups.*

representatives they are entitled to." Wood was apparently still thinking in terms of territorial constituencies, with or without proportional representation, but there was no mention of what smaller groups he had in mind.

The presidential address to the 1925 U.F.A. convention attempted some definition of groups for purposes of political representation: beginning with a division of interests into rural and urban, the natural groupings suggested were labour, "the general urban citizenship," farmers, and "small town interests," which, being intimately connected with agriculture, should have an "accordingly close" working relationship with it.[51] There was no suggestion how the "urban citizenship" could be expected to have a specific common economic interest to render it a stable group. In view of this vagueness it is not surprising that Wood appealed repeatedly and in vain to all other "economic classes" to organize on the same basis as the farmers and co-operate in the responsibility of administering the business of Alberta.[52] With the exception of a few pockets of organized labour there was in fact no basis for a system of industrial group organization in the province, at least while territorial constituencies were kept, since there were no other industrial groups of sufficient size in any area to elect members to the legislature and of sufficient common economic interest to have that stability which was, in Wood's view, the essential virtue of the organized industrial group.

Irvine later produced a remarkable variant of this theory, advocating a completely occupational basis of parliamentary representation with no periodical general elections at all. There is no evidence that this view was taken up within the U.F.A. but it is worth recording here if only to show that denigration of popular elections is to be found in Alberta radicalism long before the Social Credit Board created a sensation in 1947 by advocating the abolition of elections by secret ballot.[53]

Popular election [Irvine wrote] is one of the most inadequate and outworn parts of the party machine. The only function it performs is to decide which party shall take office. . . . Every other feature is harmful in the extreme to the body politic. As a means of deciding an issue, popular elections are ridiculous.[54]

Popular elections will not be required when people are organized, and

[51]H. W. Wood, Presidential Address to the U.F.A. Annual Convention, 1925 (U.F.A. Minute Books).

[52]Presidential Address to the U.F.A. Annual Convention, 1930 (U.F.A. Minute Books). Cf. presidential addresses of 1925, 1926, 1928.

[53]See below, Chap. VII, p. 210.

[54]Co-operative Government (Ottawa, 1929), p. 258.

democracy is capable of minding its own business. When that time comes, each organized group will elect its own quota of representatives to Parliament. When one of the elected members dies, another will be sent; when one, for any reason, becomes incompetent, he or she will be recalled and replaced by another. All the fuss and uproar of general elections will slip into the past where they belong. . . . While the group representative must still put up with the folly of popular elections, he expresses the economic and social needs of his group and takes his chance.[55]

An additional advantage urged for a system of purely functional representation was that it would permit a substantial reduction in the size of parliament: "a dozen or two of the best informed men and women from the various functional groups of the country . . . would do many times more business than is now done by the two hundred and forty-five members, and would do it more efficiently, more quickly, and less expensively."[56] These ideas, however, cannot be considered part of the U.F.A. doctrine. H. W. Wood's brief foreword to Irvine's book pointedly refrains from endorsing its content: "William Irvine has written this book . . . I haven't as yet had an opportunity to read it. . . ."[57]

On only two points did the U.F.A. leaders develop definite views regarding details of the working of group representation or group government. Each of these points was raised in the practice of co-operation of the farmers' group with other bodies. Under Wood's leadership the U.F.A. took a strong position on the method of electoral co-operation with other bodies, particularly with organized labour. In those constituencies where only the combined strength of farmer and labour votes could capture a seat or seats, some form of electoral co-operation was obviously advantageous. The U.F.A. leaders, however, rejected all proposals for an amalgamation of platforms. Instead they insisted that the interests of farmers and labour, being different, could not be amalgamated even in a joint electoral platform, let alone in a merger of organizations, and that each group must retain its distinct identity as an economic class. Electoral co-operation would take the form of one group endorsing and mobilizing votes for the candidate of the other group, but on the understanding that when elected the representative would be responsible only to his own group. "We are not asked to adopt any part of Labor's Platform. We do not ask Labor to adopt any part of our platform. The co-operation that is proposed here is entirely a co-operation of voting strength. We propose to assist them with our voting strength in electing a candidate that we have no part in selecting, and will have no claim on

[55]*Ibid.*, pp. 242–3.   [56]*Ibid.*, p. 221.   [57]*Ibid.*, p. v.

after elected, while they in return give their voting strength to help us elect a candidate that they will have no claim on after elected."[58] This kind of electoral co-operation was successful in the Medicine Hat federal by-election of June 1921, in Medicine Hat and Calgary in the provincial election of July 1921, and in East and West Calgary in the federal election of December 1921. It was a nice embodiment of Wood's doctrine of the purity of economic group political organizations and co-operation between groups with distinct interests. Wood held that only this kind of electoral co-operation was consistent with the democratic control of the elected member by the organization which elected him; an elected member could be democratically controlled only by an economic class organization with a clear and distinct basis of common interest. Amalgamation, even though undertaken to strengthen the democratic forces against the plutocratic forces, would be undemocratic in confusing and weakening the clear and stable basis of economic class organization. The same reasoning justified Wood's stand, which became the U.F.A. stand, against "broadening out," this is, admitting to the U.F.A. political organization any non-farmers who shared the general reform zeal of the U.F.A. This was more of an issue in the federal progressive movement than in Alberta provincial politics.[59]

The second point on which the U.F.A. developed any definite theory of the working of group government was the question of the relation of U.F.A. members of the legislature to other legislative groups. This also was of real importance only in the federal parliament, where the problems of the relations of the U.F.A. members with the members from the other provincial farmer movements and with the Progressive party were acute. The U.F.A. group, true to Wood's ideas, refused not only to take part in any coalition government but to become part of a Progressive party. The position of the U.F.A. in federal politics has been held responsible for the failure of the Progressive party.[60] The principle on which the U.F.A. took its stand was the principle, sometimes called "constituency autonomy," by which elected legislative members were held to be responsible to the U.F.A.

[58]Wood, "Neither Farmers Nor Labor Can Break into the Plutocratic Classes," address at the convention of East and West Calgary U.F.A. District Associations, Oct. 7, 1921. Leaflet issued by U.F.A., October 1921.

[59]See Sharp, *The Agrarian Revolt in Western Canada*, pp. 140ff., 161ff.; Morton, *The Progressive Party in Canada*, pp. 89–90, and chap. 5 *passim*.

[60]See Morton, *The Progressive Party in Canada*, where a full description and analysis of the U.F.A. attitude and actions in federal politics in the 1920's is given.

locals which nominated and elected them, and to be in effect delegates of their local organizations rather than representatives of their constituents or of a party. This principle was held to rule out the formation of a central executive committee by the federal farmer members of Parliament. "As this proposed central political machine functioned downward, or outward, it would inevitably come in conflict with citizenship authority. These opposing authorities would be irreconcilable, and one or the other would have to give way. An institution half autocratic and half democratic can no more continue to exist than a nation can continue to exist 'half slave and half free.' "[61]

§ 4. Implications of the Social and Political Theory of the U.F.A.

The theory of the U.F.A. consisted essentially of a concept of democracy as a non-exploitive social order and a concept of democratic government as a scheme of popular control of elected representatives. Both concepts were critical; the first was developed from opposition to the economic exploitation to which the farmers felt themselves subject, the second from opposition to the party system and "responsible government," which their experience suggested were essentially a part of the machinery of exploitation. The merit of the theory is to be judged by its critical effectiveness and by the effectiveness of the critical practice based on it. The proposal of occupational group representation, which gave the U.F.A. political theory its name and its distinction, was an integral, though secondary, part of the theory; secondary in that it was presented only as a means to popular control of elected representatives, integral in that it was presented as the only means to popular control and to the transformation of the social order. The whole case for occupational group representation was that it was the only stable basis, first, for the democratic control of elected representatives, and second for developing the sweeping power of popular forces in their struggle against the existing order.

Both parts of this case must be examined, but neither is to be judged by the usual criteria of Canadian political theory. The fact that the U.F.A. theory collided with all the requirements of a political system which could adjust the existing variety of political interests of the Canadian people and maintain some equilibrium between them is not necessarily a criticism of the U.F.A. theory, for it was based on the assumption that the existing variety of interests was a con-

[61]Wood, Presidential Address to the U.F.A. Annual Convention, 1923 (U.F.A. Minute Books).

comitant of the exploitive society which had to be ended. What needs to be examined is this assumption. Again, the fact that U.F.A. theory paid little attention to the problems of group representation in a parliament organized on traditional party lines, or of making group representation fit in to the cabinet system, is not necessarily a criticism of that theory, for the U.F.A. had no intention of making group representation fit in to the cabinet system. It had announced its irreconcilable opposition to the party system and cabinet responsibility, and until sufficient other occupational groups were organized in the constituencies to send an array of occupational group representatives to parliament there was nothing the U.F.A. could do except use parliament as a platform for advocating the abolition of all the conventions of cabinet government. The U.F.A.'s rejection of the party system, more consistent than that of the farmers' movements in the other provinces because based on a more penetrating analysis of the system, carried with it the rejection of parliamentary government. In the circumstances the U.F.A. in federal politics retreated into its concept of democratic organization without attempting to adjust it to the despised realities of the parliamentary struggle for office.

That the U.F.A. found some difficulty in applying its theory in the provincial legislature after 1921, as will be seen more fully in the next chapter, it not surprising. In effect there was no place there for group government, partly because the U.F.A. had such a preponderance of seats, but ultimately because there was, as has been said, no basis in the economy of Alberta for a variegated group representation in the legislature, and no possibility of changing the existing economic order by purely provincial legislation.

Fundamental criticism of the U.F.A. theory must start from its concept of the exploitive nature of the Canadian economy. The limitations of this concept have already been indicated. Shaped by the farmers' experience as independent commodity producers, it was a narrow concept not applicable to the whole Canadian economy. Their own weak competitive position in a monopolistic market economy was to them the pattern of all exploitation. They knew, of course, that manufacturing and other industries were carried on in relations which admitted of exploitation of wage labour, but such a conception was not borne in upon them by daily experience. They understood very well the exploitation of one kind of commodity producer by another, but had little thought for the relations which existed between owners and wage-earners in the industrial sector in which ownership and productive labour were separated, nor did they appreciate the numerical preponderance of that sector in the Canadian economy. Because their concept of the competitive social order was defective in this respect, their concept of democracy as the supersession of the competitive order by a co-operative order was inadequate.

The co-operative order which was to be the essence of democracy was envisaged as a harmony of producers, of groups of citizens in their capacity as producers. To expect such a harmony, it must be assumed that the sole or main conflict of interest in competitive society is that between commodity producers. This was the assumption of the U.F.A. theory. The assumption was invalid, for it left out of account the conflict of interests between employed labour and capital.

Another assumption, mentioned already, was implicit in the U.F.A. concept of democracy as a harmonious co-operative social order, namely, that the existing variety of interest groups was a concomitant of the competitive economic order, and that all the marked differences of religion, culture, and language would lose their political weight when the economic order was changed. This assumption the U.F.A. theorists did not examine, but their position is clear enough. The exacerbation of national and religious differences was the work of party politicians intent on finding issues to divide and confuse. The differences were real, but it was the party system which brought them into politics. Hence the differences could be expected to cease to be contentious politically as soon as the party system was discarded, that is, as soon as the reason for the party system disappeared with the disappearance of the competitive economy. The adequacy of this assumption can neither be proven nor disproven by theoretical analysis, but it had some basis in the farmers' experience: the one co-operative economic order they knew, namely, the local co-operative elevator groups, did cut across religious and cultural differences most effectively.

The weakness of the U.F.A. concept of democracy as a social order was reflected in their idea of the way in which the change to the new order was to be brought about; there was, that is to say, a corresponding weakness in their theory that group organization was the only means by which the strength to overthrow the existing order could be built. Even in the one pattern of action on which they were clearly determined, namely the organization of the people into industrial or occupational groups, they found it impossible, as we have seen, to say what groups, other than the farmers and labour who were already organized, could participate. They did not realize how narrow a qualification their concept of economic class imposed on their prescription for democratic organization. To be a stable and effective democratic group it was, they held, necessary for the members to be united by a clear common economic interest, the only basis of which was gainful occupation, whether as employer, employee, or self-employed, in the production of a specific commodity or group of commodities. Thus the united farmers and the trade unions qualified. Manufacturers, financiers, and all other "plutocratic classes" were of course ruled out as anti-democratic groups. In effect then the only other possible democratic groups would be groups of producers whose position in the economy was similar to the farmers', that is, other groups of independent commodity producers. But there were, apart from the farmers themselves, no such groups of any significance in the economy either of Alberta or of Canada. The failure of the U.F.A. method of political organization was not arbitrary; it was a natural outcome of the U.F.A. leaders' idea of the economy as a congeries of commodity producers, and of their failure to investigate the relations which held in the production of non-agricultural commodities.

The U.F.A. case for political representation by occupational groups as the only basis for developing the sweeping power of the popular forces against the exploitive order was therefore inadequate. It might of course be argued that the two substantial groups—trade unions and organized farmers—were enough to constitute a system of occupational group government, but this was never the U.F.A. idea. The United Farmers were sufficiently conscious of a difference of interest between themselves and organized labour, to have no confidence in a system which contained only the two.

The second part of the case for group government shows similar weaknesses. The argument was that the industrial or occupational group was the only stable basis of democratic control of the elected representatives who made up the legislature of the modern state. The premise was that when grouped on this basis, and only when so grouped, the mass of the people could escape from being confused, divided, and done out of the control of their own representatives. A man's interests as a producer, it was argued, are his clearest interests; he cannot easily be fooled on matters he knows so well. There is obviously something in this contention, but it is not so applicable to any other popular groups as it is to the farmers. Legislation which affects prices—the tariff and other fiscal legislation, the regulation of banks and other credit institutions, of railways and of middlemen—affects farmers more directly and clearly than other groups, even than industrial wage-earners, for the farmers are direct producers for the market and each farmer plans and carries through his whole productive operation. But in industries which, unlike farming, are carried on mainly by employed labour, the clearest interest of the producers is not their interest as producers of a certain commodity but their interest as wage-earners. The two interests are not mutually exclusive, but they are not identical, as the farmers seemed to assume. The wage-earner has a more direct and immediate knowledge of wages, hours, and relations with his employer, than he has of the position of his industry's product in the market. So the assumption that the individual's dominating interest in legislation is his interest as a producer, though not self-evident even of farmers, is much less evident of any other substantial industrial or occupational group. Accordingly it is not apparent that industrial or occupational grouping could be expected to save the people generally from confusion and domination or to facilitate control of representatives based on direct knowledge of issues.

The serious weaknesses that have been indicated in each part of the U.F.A. political theory appear even more formidable when the parts are considered together. The two concepts of democracy were, in the circumstances, contradictory. The democracy the United Farmers willed as an end involved a decisive attack on the established economic order, yet in the name of democracy they rejected the necessary means. If they had been able to set aside for a moment their preoccupation with the faults of party, they could scarcely have failed to see that nothing less than party organization would serve. A political force sufficient to subvert an economic order which was, on their own recognition, strongly entrenched politically, can only be built within that order and within the limits of parliamentary action (that is, without extra-constitutional means) by an organization prepared to take and use parliamentary power. It must be prepared, so long as it eschews revolutionary action, to impose its will through the conventions of cabinet government. Thus, whether it be called a party or not, it must act like a party and must develop the characteristics which the U.F.A. most distrusted, namely, central leadership, coherence in the legislature, and a considerable measure of control of the whole organization by those elected to the legislature. Certainly it must, wherever there is a strong opposed party, abandon the constituency autonomy of which the U.F.A. made such a point. The price not only of office but of political effectiveness where there are strong opposed interests is a degree of central organization and control inconsistent with the U.F.A. concept of democratic organization.

At times, indeed, the U.F.A. leaders did recognize that a movement which seeks power must be built as a party capable of taking office; and, consistently, they rejected not only the taking of office as a party but also the exercise of power. What they did not recognize was that this rejection made it impossible for them to alter the existing order; they would not admit that they would need such power as only a party in office can command. Instead they contented themselves with the vague notion that co-operation would replace conflict of interests in the new political arrangements.

The contradiction in the U.F.A. theory was partly but not entirely of their own making. It was partly so, because it was their own assumptions, convincing them that group government was the answer, that emboldened them to dispense with party. These assumptions— that the essential class relations were the relations of groups of commodity producers, that each such group had a distinct interest in legislation, and that only such groups could be stable democratic units—were, we have argued, inadequate; and while they were natural they were not inescapable assumptions for farmers to make, as witness the different position taken by the Saskatchewan and Manitoba farmers' movements.

But the contradiction was not entirely of their own making; it was ultimately in the facts with which the theory had to deal and which the U.F.A. leaders assessed astutely. While their rejection of party defeated their end, the reason they rejected party was a compelling one. The reason, it will be remembered, was not only that party was held to be inconsistent with strict democratic control of elected members but also, and more fundamentally, because party was necessarily conglomerate and unstable. In having to appeal to all kinds of people a party necessarily became unprincipled (that is, ceased to be guided by principle) and so could not serve as the instrument for fundamental social change. Now it is apparent that in countries where there is one economic class large enough to sustain singly a party able to take office there is no necessary tendency for a reform party to become unprincipled. In such a country a labour party, for instance, does not need to appeal much beyond its own class and hence need not lose that singleness of aim and that stable basis in identity of class interest which Wood rightly saw must be kept by any democratic reforming organization. But to the extent that this basis is lacking, a party becomes unprincipled, for much the reasons Wood gave.

In Canada this basis has so far been lacking, mainly because of the unusually large proportion of independent farm producers in the whole gainfully occupied population. What the U.F.A. theorists asserted of party in general was therefore true enough of party in Canada. But their assertion was too sweeping because, seeing the problem through the eyes of the independent producer class, they assumed that that class was the preponderant one in any society. However, if it be allowed that their analysis of party was valid for Canada, it must be concluded that they had set themselves an insoluble problem. The problem may prove to be insoluble for a long time yet in Canada, because power sufficient for sweeping reform requires party, and party tends to become unprincipled, not in all cases (as the U.F.A. thought) but in cases where there is no single class large enough to be the sole support of a party. As long as the farmers are, and see themselves as, a separate class, which yet is not large enough to give them a party capable of being the government, this condition may be expected to prevail in Canada.

The factors here adduced to explain the failure of the U.F.A. in federal politics, in spite of the partial validity of its analysis of federal party, were absent in provincial politics. Their absence invalidated any provincial application of the U.F.A. theory of party but permitted the U.F.A. to succeed in provincial politics. It could act as a party in Alberta without entirely losing that democratic control of the elected member, or that singleness of purpose and stable identity of class interest, which its leaders considered to be the essentials of democratic organization and had declared to be incompatible with party. This was possible because in Alberta the independent commodity producers formed so large an economic class that the U.F.A. did not need to appeal outside its own class; it could be a party without being conglomerate and unprincipled.

Further, there were within Alberta no strongly opposed interests, that is, no interests strongly opposed to the limited purposes which the U.F.A. could set itself within the restricted jurisdiction of a provincial legislature. As a provincial political organization the U.F.A. could only seek to ameliorate, not to replace, the existing economic order. Hence it did not need that concentration of authority within the organization which is needed where opposition is strong. Finally, the size of the class on which the U.F.A. was based gave it such a predominance in the provincial legislature that it could afford to allow an unusual degree of constituency autonomy. The United Farmers did in fact become a party in Alberta although, enchanted by their theory, they continued to speak of themselves as something different. Their theory of party, put forward as universally valid, was, paradoxically, invalid for Alberta, where they were most successful, and valid for Canada as a whole where their insistence on it made them impotent.

CHAPTER THREE

The U.F.A.: Democracy in Practice

→»«←

§ 1. Four Problems of Authority

We have now to examine what happened to the U.F.A. theory of democracy when the U.F.A. entered the provincial political field. In its first provincial general election, in 1921, the U.F.A. won some two-thirds of all the seats in the legislature, and it held approximately that position through two more general elections, keeping a government in office until 1935. If this success may be attributed in part to the U.F.A. theory, which canalized all kinds of resentment into a determination to get away and keep away from the party system, yet it raised unforeseen problems and led to the quiet abandonment of much of the theory.

The problems, which we shall consider in turn, may be stated as follows: (1) the maintenance of the strict delegate democracy of the annual convention; (2) the claims of the constituency organization versus the claims of the cabinet on the elected member of the legislature; (3) constituency autonomy versus provincial convention control of policy; (4) provincial convention supremacy versus cabinet supremacy. Consideration of these problems requires some description of the delegate democracy of the convention and of the methods and principles of U.F.A. constituency organization.

§ 2. The Delegate Democracy of the U.F.A. Convention

The democratic organization of the U.F.A., before its complication by the addition of electoral units, functioned well and appeared entirely explicable in terms of the idea of delegate democracy. The lines of authority and responsibility were simple. Each local elected annually both its own executive and its delegates to the annual provincial convention, which was the governing body of the U.F.A. Each local was entitled to one delegate for each ten members. The convention, meeting for four days every year in January, elected the president, four vice-presidents, and the secretary of the U.F.A. In 1919 the four vice-presidents were replaced by four executive committeemen, elected by the convention, two elected each year for a two-year term.

This change was made in order to assure some continuity of membership in the executive, but it was provided in the amended constitution that the annual convention could recall any member of the executive by a resolution supported by three-fifths of those voting thereon. This provision was used by the 1922 convention, which recalled Mr. Rice Sheppard from the executive in the middle of his two-year term because after failing to win the U.F.A. nomination in the federal constituency of Strathcona in 1921 he had run as a Labour candidate in opposition to the U.F.A. candidate and had emphasized in his campaign that he was still an executive officer of the U.F.A.

The president, the executive committee-men (one of whom was vice-president), and *ex officio* the president of the U.F.W.A. (the United Farm Women of Alberta, the women's section of the U.F.A.), made up the executive of the U.F.A. The board of directors, or central board of the U.F.A., consisted of the executive, plus ten or fifteen directors (their number increased with the number of federal constituencies in the province), and the executive of the U.F.W.A. One director was elected, at the convention, by the delegates from each of the federal constituency areas of the province, nominations being made at separate meetings of the delegates from each area. The central board was the governing body of the association except when the convention was in session, but since the board had fifteen or twenty members scattered over the whole province it generally met only four or five times a year, and delegated much of its work to the executive which met as often as ten or twelve times a year. The executive had full powers to act in the name of the U.F.A. when neither convention nor board was in session, subject to the disallowance of any action by the board within thirty days. Thus, except for the representation of the U.F.W.A., all members of the governing bodies of the U.F.A. were directly elected by the delegates at the annual convention. The delegate relationship existing between the convention and the locals was extended to the governing bodies as far as possible. The officers were regarded as delegates of the convention, and many resolutions passed by the convention were instructions to the board or executive, just as the delegates to the convention had in many cases been instructed by their locals on specific issues.

The handling of local resolutions by the convention provides some indication of the extent of the delegate relations. The locals sent resolutions direct to the convention, and as long as the number of delegates and of resolutions was not too great, most of these resolutions were separately discussed by the convention, although there was no guarantee that every resolution would get to the convention floor. The central board customarily met a day or two before the convention to look over the resolutions that had been sent in, and it was free both to bring in a resolution combining the sense of several local resolutions, and to decide on the order of priority in which the resolutions should be put to the convention.

The executive and the board could of course exercise considerable influence at the convention because of the wider knowledge that closer and more constant contact with the problems gave them, but their prestige and influence depended pretty directly on the opinion of their work and their policies formed by the local delegates and even by the primary membership. The directors, between conventions, spent a good deal of time reporting to and getting the feeling of the locals which they represented; and since each director was responsible for the growth and strength of the movement in his district he was likely to know it well and be well known in it.

The striking increase in U.F.A. membership after January 1919, when the decision to become an electoral organization was taken, put some strain on the simple delegate democracy of the convention. Membership, which had grown fairly steadily from 2,000 in 1909 to 18,000 at the end of 1918, increased during 1919 to nearly 29,000, during 1920 to nearly 31,000, and during 1921 to nearly 38,000. After the excitement of the election year it dropped sharply; at the end of 1922 it stood just below 19,000, and for the next four years varied between 12,000 and 15,000.[1] The annual conventions in the crucial first few years of electoral organization, during which the new patterns of relationship were largely set, were so large that delegate initiative tended to yield to executive direction. There were 1,389 accredited delegates at the 1920 convention and 1,465 at the 1921 convention. Physical limits induced the 1921 convention to alter the basis of representation for future conventions from one delegate per ten members of a local to one delegate per twenty members, a thing

[1]Presidential Address to U.F.A. Annual Convention, 1928 (U.F.A. Minute Books) and U.F.A. *Annual Reports*. The figures, here given to the nearest thousand, include the membership of the U.F.W.A. and of the Junior U.F.A.; the latter two together generally accounted for about a quarter of the total.

which the convention had refused to do a year earlier; even so, the 1922 convention had 1,042 accredited delegates. After the decline in membership during 1922, conventions generally had about 500 delegates in each of the next several years.

The increase in membership and in the number of locals meant an increase in the number of resolutions sent from locals for the consideration of the convention. Even before the big increase in membership there had been growing concern about the convention's inability to discuss all the resolutions; the 1919 convention at its closing session had to table some of the 139 resolutions on the order paper and refer several score more to the executive. It did this "after a general discussion in which expression was repeatedly and forcibly given to the desirability of devising, if possible, some method for dealing at the convention with all the resolutions sent up by the locals, those of minor importance as well as those of outstanding importance which claim first attention."[2] No such method was devised. In 1920, 248 resolutions were sent in, of which only about half were dealt with in the four days of the convention. The task of the committee on resolutions was lessened, as was direct access of the resolutions of locals to the convention, by the decision put into effect in 1921 that locals should be asked to send their resolutions first to a district convention, which should send on only the ones it thought important, and that resolutions approved by the district conventions should have precedence over resolutions received direct from locals. In 1922 the number of resolutions submitted was still greater, and direct access of local resolutions to the conventions was formally discontinued by a requirement that all resolutions to be considered by the convention should first be passed either by a constituency or district association or by the board of directors. The 1923 convention, however, was still able to deal with less than half of the resolutions submitted; the remainder being dealt with, as before, by the board of directors after the convention session, or referred untouched to some outside body. Thus, on the recommendation of the order of business committee, the 1923 convention agreed that all resolutions on municipal questions be referred to the Rural Municipal Association, those on hail insurance to the Hail Insurance Board, those on dairies and dairying to the Dairymen's Association, and those on railways to the provincial minister of railways.[3] The number of resolutions submitted to subsequent conventions ran from about one hundred to more than two hundred, and almost always a con-

[2]*Grain Growers' Guide*, Jan. 29, 1919.   [3]*Ibid.*, Jan. 24, 1923.

siderable number had to be left over for the board's decision and action.

Neither the increased size of the convention nor the changes in the procedure of dealing with resolutions seriously weakened the democratic character of the U.F.A. The convention, though large, never degenerated into a merely inspirational or convivial gathering; issues were debated concretely, resolutions of any substance and backing among the locals were sure of a hearing, and serious differences of view on policy continued to appear and to be fought out vigorously. Nevertheless the board and executive became increasingly important. H. W. Wood, elected annually as president from 1916 to 1930, developed a tactical ability in handling the convention which is still remembered with admiration by those who were in a position to appreciate his operations.

The convention remained jealous of its control over all the officers, to the extent of removing the election of the vice-president from the board to itself in 1923, and refusing in the same year to give the election of the executive to the board.[4] But at the 1926 convention Wood's view prevailed, after an initial defeat two days earlier and a further heated debate, and the constitution was amended to provide that the executive officers hitherto elected by the convention were thereafter to be chosen by the board from its own membership.[5] As the executive officers had previously been elected by the whole convention by a system of proportional representation, the effect of this change was to reduce the possibility of a substantial minority group opposed to board policy getting a representative on the executive. No doubt this made it easier for the executive and the board to work together, but by removing the executive from its direct relation to the convention the change weakened the delegate democracy which had prevailed in the U.F.A. structure.

These strains on the delegate democracy of the convention would probably not in themselves have altered the character of U.F.A. democracy. The decisive changes were rather a result of the new problems raised by the creation of new units of organization—the constituency associations—and by the emergence of a U.F.A. cabinet in control of the province. Of the new problems, some concerned the relation of responsibility within the new part of the structure, that is, between the elected legislative group and the constituency associations, and some arose from the new ambiguity of the lines of responsibility now that the locals were the base of two parallel struc-

[4]*The U.F.A.*, Feb. 1, 1923.   [5]*Ibid.*, Feb. 1, 1926.

tures, the one culminating in convention and board and executive, the other in the members of the legislature and the cabinet.

§ 3. Constituency Control versus Cabinet Control of the U.F.A. Members of the Legislature

The entry of the U.F.A. into independent electoral activity required organization at the levels of the federal and provincial constituencies. The resolution of the 1919 convention which authorized independent political action extended the pattern of the delegate convention to cover the new activity, and left the initiative entirely up to the locals. It urged the locals in each federal constituency—organization for federal elections seemed more urgent than for provincial—to organize a district unit for the purpose of holding at least one convention each year in each district (i.e. federal constituency). "The primary purpose of such convention shall be to discuss ways and means of taking independent action and selecting an independent candidate. The convention may, however, discuss and deal with any other district U.F.A. matters." The central office was to give assistance in calling and arranging for such a convention on request of 10 per cent of the locals in any constituency. Not only the initiative but the responsibility of each district convention was emphasized. "Each Convention shall be responsible for its action in putting a candidate in the field, in financing and electing such a candidate. . . ."[6] Official explanatory articles issued by the U.F.A. emphasized that the responsibility of the district organization meant district autonomy. "This places the responsibility on each district organization, of carrying on the political activities of the district. Democratically speaking, responsibility and freedom of action must go hand in hand, so each district has complete autonomy."[7] Another statement emphasized the ultimate responsibility of each local:

Each Federal Riding has had full autonomy and following the principle practiced throughout the Organization of forcing responsibility on the locals themselves every local, of which we now have upwards of 1,500 active, is a self-governing, self-functioning unit of the whole Organization. . . . This system has lent itself less to the manipulations of the old line politicians than any other yet devised. All responsibility has begun and ended in the locals, and that is the place where the scheming politicians usually have the least chance of making any successful headway. . . . Both in the Provincial election and in the Federal election there were many aspirants for

[6]U.F.A., *Annual Report*, 1918, with minutes of 1919 Convention.

[7]H. W. Wood, *Re the U.F.A.–How Organized and Purposes* (?1921), mimeo., 3 pp.

seats, who imagined they could get some assistance through the officers of the Central Organization. All such people, of course, were referred politely to the District Organizations and the District Organizations referred them to the locals, and the District Convention. Some politicians were very much disappointed when they found that no influence could avail them in getting them a seat in the Province.[8]

District conventions were held and district associations set up in every federal constituency during May and June 1919. The district associations usually named themselves U.F.A. District Political Associations to emphasize their primary function of political action, although they were authorized to deal with all U.F.A. district matters. In July 1919 the executives and directors of the district associations met in convention and formed themselves into the U.F.A. Provincial Political Association, under the general authorization of clause 6 of the 1919 resolution on political action which had provided that the district conventions might call a provincial political convention separate from the regular U.F.A. provincial convention. This provision for keeping the political activities separate from the regular U.F.A. provincial convention appears to have been inserted in the resolution because of Wood's fear that political action might not be successful. But by the beginning of 1920 it was apparent that the enthusiasm and energy being put into it made it unnecessary to regard political action as suspect, and at the regular 1920 U.F.A. provincial convention a resolution was passed bringing all U.F.A. work, political and otherwise, under the U.F.A. board and executive, "recognizing no other authority than this convention."[9] The U.F.A. Political Association then dissolved itself. Any uncertainty as to the position of the district associations, which of course remained in existence, was settled by a resolution of the 1921 U.F.A. convention instructing "the Central Board to submit to the next Annual Convention, Constitutional Amendments providing for a U.F.A. District Association in each Federal Constituency, such Association to be an integral part of the U.F.A. and to be composed of all Locals in the Constituency."[10]

Organization of units for the provincial constituencies came after the organization of the federal constituencies. The provincial constituency of Cochrane was organized, by the same method of locals asking the central office to call a convention, in July 1919, and the organization was successful in electing its candidate in the by-election

8Method of Organization for Political Purposes in the United Farmers of Alberta [1921], mimeo., 3 pp.
9U.F.A., Annual Report, 1919, with minutes of 1920 Convention.
10Ibid., 1920, with minutes of 1921 Convention.

on November 3. A resolution submitted for the 1920 convention by one of the locals, providing that the central office call a convention in any provincial constituency on request of 25 per cent of the locals in the constituency, was not thought sufficiently urgent to be brought before the convention, but the board in dealing with unfinished business after the convention, passed the resolution, with 25 per cent amended to 20 per cent. One other provincial constituency was organized under this authorization in March 1920. The 1921 convention passed a resolution recommending that every provincial constituency be organized. When in June 1921 a provincial general election was called only 12 constituencies had been organized, but within ten days the total was brought up to 44, by the locals petitioning the central office to call conventions, and 44 candidates were run in the election. Of these, 38 were elected. The revised constitution adopted at the 1923 U.F.A. provincial convention provided for federal and provincial constituency organizations each to be composed of all the locals in the constituency, but true to the principle of autonomy, the U.F.A. constitution said nothing about the constitution of a constituency association.

The very insistence on the autonomy of the locals in respect of the new political function, however, put the constituency associations in a weaker position than they would otherwise have been in. For it was left to each local to decide how the constituency association would be financed. Although the U.F.A. constitution said that a constituency association consisted of all the locals in the constituency, a member of a local was not necessarily a member of either of the constituency associations. The fees for membership in the constituency associations were separate from the local and central fees. Some locals required every member to subscribe to one or both constituency associations, some did not. At U.F.A. provincial conventions through the 1920's pressure was exerted by various constituency associations to have the collection of constituency fees made compulsory on each local,[11] but this was never done. The nearest a provincial convention came to adopting even the principle was in 1924 when a resolution was carried "by a rather close vote" asking the central executive to give "serious consideration" to having all the fees "collected in full with a system of rebate of a certain sum back to the district associations for their maintenance. . . ."[12] But

[11]A resolution to this effect was discussed but tabled by the 1922 convention, and was voted down by a large majority at the 1923 convention. *Grain Growers' Guide*, Feb. 1, 1922, and Jan. 24, 1923.

[12]Minutes of U.F.A. Annual Convention, 1924, p. 55.

at the 1925 convention the resolutions for the consolidation of all
the types of fee failed to pass, even when amended to allow an
individual to contract out.[13] Compulsory consolidation was not undertaken, as the constituency association dues were considered by some
to be primarily for political action and some members did not
support political action. A partial solution to the financial difficulties
of the constituency association was found in 1929 when the convention passed a resolution submitted by the board (replacing eight
other resolutions) making possible the collection of U.F.A. fees
"through any of our Pools."[14] A member might sign authorization
slips enabling a pool to deduct from his receipts and remit to the
U.F.A. the amount of all his U.F.A. fees, but "any member not
desiring to have one or both of these Constituency dues collected in
this manner may so indicate by cancelling such space on the authorization form."[15] All members were to be encouraged to have their fees
collected in this way, but there was no compulsion.

Thus with the entry of the U.F.A. into electoral action, its organization was expanded to include two new levels of association, the provincial and the federal constituency associations, each with its delegate
convention and its executive. The constituency convention, like the
annual provincial convention of the whole U.F.A., was made up of
delegates sent by the locals; it was responsible to and derived its
authority directly from the locals. Its mandate was therefore not
inferior to the mandate of the provincial convention except in the
comprehensiveness of its local base. This was to lead to a conflict
between constituency autonomy and central convention control, discussed in section 4 below. And since the constituency association's
primary function was the nomination and election of U.F.A. candidates to the legislature and the subsequent control of elected members of the legislature, the problem of constituency control versus
cabinet control of the U.F.A. members of the legislature emerged
with the first U.F.A. cabinet's assumption of office. To this we now
turn.

The direct and complete responsibility of each elected legislative

[13]Minutes of U.F.A. Annual Convention, 1925, pp. 111–12, 183–4. Cf. *The
U.F.A.*, Feb. 2, 1925, and *Grain Growers' Guide*, Jan. 28, 1925.

[14]That is, the wheat pool, and other marketing pools.

[15]Minutes of U.F.A. Annual Convention, 1929, pp. 6–7. A resolution to have
membership fees collected through the wheat pool had been decisively rejected
by the 1924 convention (*Grain Growers' Guide*, Jan. 23, 1924) and by the 1925
convention (*ibid.*, Jan. 28, 1925). The 1926 convention passed a resolution "suggesting" that members be allowed to authorize payment through any of the
pools (Minutes of U.F.A. Annual Convention, 1926).

member to his constituency association was emphasized from the outset both in U.F.A theory and in campaign literature, as we have seen. It was written into the 1921 provincial election platform of the U.F.A.: "Each elected representative is answerable directly to the organization in the constituency that elected him."[16] It was held to be a fundamental working principle of political organization; reflection on the opposite practice of the old parties was enough to give the principle continuous meaning and importance. A practical sanction was provided in the separate financial responsibility of each constituency association, which got the necessary funds from the political fees of the locals and small contributions from individual members. Autonomous constituency financing was intended to ensure that no legislative party should grow up to weaken each constituency association's control of the member it had elected. "There is very little necessary expense in carrying on the campaign, but that expense is borne by the voters, and not by the candidates. The candidate is no more responsible for carrying on the campaign than other voters. After he is elected he has nothing to do with operating political machinery, but is expected to give all his time and attention to the duties of his office."[17]

Further, it was emphasized that the elected member's responsibility to the constituency organization was to be so direct as to rule out cabinet domination of the legislature. Specifically, the U.F.A. demanded, before the 1921 election, the abandonment of the practice by which a premier compelled his supporters in the legislature to vote for any government bill or proposal by treating the vote as a vote of confidence in the government, in other words, by threatening dissolution of the legislature or resignation of the government if the bill were not carried. The U.F.A. convention had gone on record against this practice in January 1921,[18] and the demand for the abandonment of the practice found a place in the 1921 Provincial Platform: "4. *Freedom of Members and Stability in Government*: That no government be considered defeated except by a direct vote of want of confidence." In addition, clause 2 of the platform endorsed "the principle of the initiative, referendum and recall."

[16]United Farmers of Alberta Provincial Platform, 1921. The text of the platform is reproduced in the account of the provincial election in the *Grain Growers' Guide*, Aug. 17, 1921.

[17]Wood, *Re the U.F.A.—How Organized and Purposes.*

[18]U.F.A., *Annual Report*, 1920, with minutes of 1921 Convention, p. 35. The resolution expressed approval of the Turgeon-Davidson resolution which had been introduced in the 1920 session of the legislature and ruled out of order by the Speaker.

Since in the 1921 provincial election, as in the Cochrane by-election of 1919, the U.F.A. campaign was fought mainly around these reform principles rather than on specific demands for legislation, it is no wonder that the members who were elected thought of themselves as delegates of their constituency conventions, and were not prepared for party discipline in the legislature. The constituency associations, in their turn, generally considered the member to be a delegate subject to their instructions. The pattern was not invariable; some members, and some constituency associations, were less enamoured of the group government theory and its corollaries than others; and where the member was less so than the association, the relation depended largely on the relative personal strengths of the member and the leading men in the constituency association. But generally, in the first few years, the delegate relationship was the accepted one on both sides. The member was expected to appear annually before the constituency convention—this appearance was in addition to his customary annual tour of the constituency when he would hold meetings in every locality—to explain his actions in the last legislative session. Here the delegate democracy of the U.F.A. was at work; the convention itself consisted of delegates from the locals, and there were many speakers to urge various courses of action or protest the member's lack of action in the legislature. The member was, of course, able to urge his view on the convention, often successfully, but when he was unable to argue it out of a resolution to which he was opposed he was expected to accept its instruction or to resign his seat. On one such occasion the member was able to maintain his position and his seat by insisting that the convention was unrepresentative and that a special meeting be called on the particular issue. Since that convention had in fact been unrepresentative the special meeting was never called.

It did not need recall arrangements to give the elected members a strong feeling of independence of the cabinet. In fact, recall arrangements played a minor part in the relation of members to constituents. The U.F.A. candidate in the 1919 Cochrane by-election had submitted to an informal recall proviso, that is, had at the beginning of the campaign put his written resignation in the hands of the executive of the constituency organization, to be handed to the speaker of the legislature whenever the organization was dissatisfied with his course in the legislature. In the 1921 elections, some candidates were asked to give the same advance resignation but most were not. No uniform policy on this type of recall was laid down by the provincial convention or even recommended. Wood thought that "while the probabilities of its doing much real good may not be very great, there is even less probability of its doing any real harm."[19] There is no record of this type of recall ever having been put into operation. Enthusiasm for the recall principle declined after 1923. The 1923 U.F.A. convention asked for provincial legislation making recall legally enforceable,[20] but the 1924 convention defeated a resolution from one of the provincial constituency associations asking that recall provisions be written into the provincial statutes.[21]

The first and perhaps the decisive step away from the U.F.A. principle of group government and constituency control of the legislative member was taken immediately after the 1921 elections. Strict application of the principle of group government would have required that the new premier and cabinet be chosen by the whole legislature at its first meeting. This was not done, nor apparently was it even contemplated. It was Wood himself, chief advocate of group government, who announced shortly before the election that the U.F.A. would accept the responsibility of forming a government if its candidates were returned in a majority. It did not appear to occur to him, or to anyone in the U.F.A., that to take this responsibility was to accept the conventions of the cabinet system. Once the responsibility had been accepted, the only remaining question, after the U.F.A. had won two-thirds of the seats, was how it should choose a legislative leader who could be called to the premiership. Until a leader was chosen the U.F.A. could not form a government. And this was all that stood between it and office; the Liberal premier, Mr. Stewart, following the conventions of the cabinet system, had announced his readiness to hand over the reins of office as soon as there was a recognized U.F.A. legislative leader.

To the question how and by whom the legislative leader should be chosen, U.F.A. principles gave a clear answer: the successful U.F.A. candidates, the members-elect, should choose their own leader. There was no question of the U.F.A. executive or board or provincial convention choosing the political leader. It was understood that not the central U.F.A. organization but the separate constituency organizations had won the seats. The principle of the direct responsibility of elected legislative members to their constituency organizations was assumed to rule out the choice of the legislative leader by anyone

19Wood, *Re the U.F.A.—How Organized and Purposes.*
20*The U.F.A.*, Feb. 15, 1923.
21Minutes of U.F.A. Annual Convention, 1924, p. 95.

but themselves and to give them all the necessary authority. What was not seen was that to give them the choice of the legislative leader who would then accept the premiership with all its usual powers and responsibilities, was to inaugurate a legislative party with distinct interests and responsibilites separating it from the outside movement.

In the event, then, the first action of the successful U.F.A. candidates after the election, was to meet to choose a premier-designate. At this meeting the premiership was offered to H. W. Wood, as the outstanding leader and president of the U.F.A. He declined it and favoured Mr. Brownlee. The members-elect demonstrated their independence of presidential suggestion by passing over Mr. Brownlee because he was not a farmer, but it is significant of the relative strengths of the president and the legislative group at the time that the latter could not persuade the man of their next choice, Mr. Greenfield, to take the position until they had got Wood to support their request.

More important than the fact that the choice of premier was left to the elected members, was that the members from the beginning followed the conventions of the cabinet system in leaving it to the premier to choose his cabinet. This course was unavoidable in 1921, for the members had some difficulty in persuading Mr. Greenfield to accept the position, and he finally consented only on condition that he should have an absolutely free hand in choosing his cabinet, including the right to go outside the elected group for cabinet material. Mr. Greenfield also made it a condition that he could run things as he ran his own business. These stipulations suggest that it was the legislative inexperience of all the members-elect, as well as of their nominee for the premiership, which led to their unwitting acceptance of this much of the principles of party government. In any case there does not seem to have been any attempt to have the whole cabinet chosen by the legislative members.

The premiership changed hands only twice in the subsequent fourteen years of the U.F.A. administration, and in each case the choice was made by the U.F.A. members of the legislature. In the first case the members were also responsible for the resignation of the premier. In November 1925 a group of members told the premier that the general feeling of the members was that he should make way for a different leader. On being satisfied that this feeling was general and on being told who was their choice for a new leader, Mr. Greenfield agreed to resign. The members' choice for premier, Mr. J. E. Brownlee, then the provincial attorney-general, was induced to accept the position, rather than resign with Mr. Greenfield, only when the persuasion of H. W. Wood was added to that of the members.

Although the legislative members did not seek formal endorsement of their action by the U.F.A. convention, the next convention did pass, along with a motion of appreciation of Mr. Greenfield's work as premier, a motion declaring their "full confidence" in Mr. Brownlee as premier and pledging him their "earnest support."[22] The same convention effectively disposed of a resolution from a district association condemning the existing method of forming the provincial government as undemocratic, and calling for the nomination and election of the premier and members of the cabinet by the legislature at its first meeting after each provincial election, by referring it back for consolidation with resolutions dealing with group organization.[23] This was the last flicker of the principle of group government in the convention.

Thus within the pattern established with the attainment of a majority in the 1921 elections and the formation of the first U.F.A. government, two contradictory forces were at work: on the one hand, in the members of the legislature, a lively sense of independence of party discipline and cabinet control, flowing from the emphasis, in convention and platform and campaign, on the direct responsibility of the member to his constituency and the freedom of members from the threat of dissolution; on the other hand, the predominance given the premier by allowing him to choose his own cabinet and to assume full responsibility for the work of the government.

It was the independence of the members that was uppermost during the first session of the new legislature in 1922. One leading member of the cabinet has privately described the government's position in the first few months of the session as a nightmare, so strong was the independence of the members. Although frequent caucuses were held —it was said that in the first session the U.F.A. members spent more time in caucus than in the legislature—with a view to getting agreement on policies before bringing them into the legislature, frequently the members who had agreed in caucus would disagree in the house. During the first month or two the government never knew, when it went into the house, what would happen before it came out. Less serious, though somewhat disruptive of a government programme, was the practice of members bringing up issues from the locals without discussing them with the government or in the caucus. Some

[22]Minutes of the U.F.A. Annual Convention, 1926, p. 18.   [23]*Ibid.*, pp. 22–3.

private members made a point of their independence by refraining from mentioning in caucus their intention of taking an independent line in the house. A striking example of this was provided at the very opening of the 1922 session. The caucus, before the opening of the session, had accepted the government's nomination of O. L. McPherson for speaker. At the opening of the session, after the premier had put forward the nomination, Alex Moore, a U.F.A. private member, nominated J. S. Stewart, a Conservative member. Mr. Moore, who said he had six or more U.F.A. members ready to support this nomination, explained that he had no antagonism to Mr. McPherson but was making the other nomination as a matter of principle, to protest against the new government following in the footsteps of the old. "I object to the machine of the government selecting a speaker and asking the private members merely to act as its rubber stamp."[24] The problem on this occasion was settled by Mr. Stewart withdrawing his name.

Speaking and voting against the government came to a head in the second month of the first session on the occasion of the Dairymen's Bill. The bill had in fact gone through all its stages in the house without much interest being taken in it, but just after the third reading was carried a U.F.A. member got up and said he hoped that wasn't the end of it as he had some things to say. Two others said the same. The premier then suggested to the speaker that in view of the apparent misunderstanding by some members the speaker might consider that the question had not been put. The speaker did this, whereupon several U.F.A. members criticized the bill, and the opposition, which had not objected to the bill before, now spoke against it. In the end all the opposition voted against the bill and so many U.F.A. members voted against it that it was only saved by the votes of the labour members.

After this the government reached an understanding with the U.F.A. members. In regard to any issue the members were to let the cabinet know whenever there was anything to which they objected or which they wished altered, and if the cabinet did not make changes which satisfied them they were free to speak and vote against the measure. The objection might be taken in caucus or, in the case of measures which were not brought into caucus, at an early stage in the house. From then on the government knew in advance what support it had for each measure and was not troubled by unpredictable actions of private members.

[24]*Edmonton Journal*, Feb. 3, 1922.

This understanding, however, still left private members free to oppose government measures and they frequently did so. And, as was to be expected, some of the private members, to establish their freedom of voting on government measures, sought the legislature's endorsement of the reform proposal of which so much had been made during the election, that no government should be considered defeated except by a direct vote of want of confidence. A motion to this effect was introduced at the 1922 session of the legislature by two U.F.A. members, Alex Moore and J. R. Love. The motion, "that the premier ought not to consider the defeat of any government measure or motion a sufficient reason for tendering the resignation of his government unless such defeat be followed by a vote of non-confidence in the government," was drained of its content by an amendment substituting the principle that the government should not "*be bound* to accept the defeat of any government bill or measure as an occasion for resignation unless followed by a vote of non-confidence."[25] The motion carried as amended; the government had won the day. The premier showed himself fully aware of and content with the implications of cabinet government; he intended, he said, to follow the unwritten rule of British parliamentary procedure, that the ministry should resign if it lost the confidence of the house, and he reserved the government's right to decide on what measures it would consider that a defeat required its resignation. In effect, notice was served on the members that no matter what resolutions they liked to pass about votes of confidence the government retained the threat of resignation or dissolution.

The premier's insistence on cabinet control and his understanding of its implications were demonstrated again in the 1925 session when W. M. Davidson, an Independent member, moved for the establishment of a select standing committee on the estimates, to which the annual estimates would be referred for criticism before they were presented to the house. The premier, Mr. Greenfield, objected that the committee would have to call in experts, which would mean duplication of the work of the government's experts, and that the resolution aimed at the root of responsible government. Another minister, Mr. Hoadley, took the resolution as a request that the government should move further away from the party system, as it was pledged to do, but said that in view of the partisan attitude of the Liberals little useful work could be expected from such a committee.

[25]Alberta, Legislative Assembly, *Journals*, 1922, pp. 60-5 (my italics); cf. *The U.F.A.*, March 15, 1922.

The premier made it clear that the government intended to retain responsibility for the estimates.[26] The government was even chary of inducting the U.F.A. private members into the mysteries of the government departments. A proposal made by the members and apparently accepted by the premier in 1922,[27] that the members be formed into groups, each group to take up the study of one department and to hold meetings with the minister, was dropped, and in reply to a question in the 1923 session the attorney-general, Mr. Brownlee, denied that the government had announced the intention of setting up such groups.[28]

The private members' knowledge, after the premier's statement on the occasion of the Moore-Love resolution, that the government was determined to proceed by the normal method of cabinet government, was generally sufficient to give the premier the support he needed thereafter. Mr. Brownlee during his premiership (1925-34) made it equally clear that he intended to follow the same procedure. It is not to be inferred that only the members' knowledge of this procured the premier his support. Serious disagreement between the premier and any substantial number of private members was rare, between the premier and any substantial fraction of the cabinet rarer still. The premier's policy, where members in caucus disagreed with points in his proposed measures, was to give way on minor matters or matters on which he did not feel strongly; in such cases the resulting measures therefore had the general support of the members. Further, on government measures which the premier thought of relatively little importance, members who disagreed with the measure as brought into the house, whether or not it had been through the caucus, were given unusual latitude in speaking and voting freely. The party whip was taken off more frequently than was usual in modern parliamentary practice, not from weakness but from indifference.

But on the few occasions when there was a serious disagreement in caucus with proposals on which the premier was determined, he used the threat of dissolution to get the necessary support. The pressure from the farmers in the early 1930's for a moratorium or adjustment of farmers' debts more radical than the government was prepared to undertake, led to a series of debt adjustment acts each year from 1931 to 1934, and on at least one occasion the feeling ran

[26]*The U.F.A.*, April 15, 1925.

[27]*Ibid.*, May 1, 1922: "Departmental Notes from the Capitol, by the Publicity Commissioner, Government Building, Edmonton."

[28]*Edmonton Bulletin*, March 5 and 7, 1923.

so high in the legislature, and the U.F.A. members were so divided, that even after the premier had told the caucus that he would resign if his bill were defeated, the bill just got through the house. In the 1932 session the threat came out into the open: a week or two after the U.F.A. convention had come dangerously near to passing a resolution demanding a moratorium instead of the government's less radical debt adjustment legislation, the premier in his opening speech in the legislature took the unusual course of denouncing the moratorium proposals as the worst possible thing for the province and announcing that he would oppose them with all his strength.[29]

There is no doubt that the premier's power of dissolution was an effective, though rarely invoked, instrument of cabinet supremacy and party discipline in the house. The U.F.A. as a whole apparently acquiesced in the abandonment of its crucial reform principle; defeat of the reform resolution in the house in 1922 created scarcely a ripple at subsequent U.F.A. conventions. After the 1926 federal constitutional crisis over the power of dissolution[30] a U.F.A. Federal Constituency Associations' Conference, held in Calgary (July 23) to define policy and methods for the U.F.A. federal members, asserted, as one of its three unanimous recommendations, that the prime minister should not have the power to advise a dissolution without obtaining the sanction of the majority of the House of Commons. The recommendations of the Calgary Conference were endorsed by the 1927 annual convention of the U.F.A., and the convention made this recommendation "applicable also to the Province."[31] This action of the convention was, however, regarded as merely an afterthought, put in to give the appearance of consistency, and the provincial cabinet paid no attention to it. A similar resolution was proposed at the 1930 convention and was passed, in perhaps an intentionally careless form, with as little effect.[32]

The establishment of cabinet control at the expense of the cherished principle of the freedom of members within the first year or two of

[29]*The U.F.A.*, Feb. 15, 1932.
[30]On the part played by the U.F.A. federal members, see W.L. Morton, *The Progressive Party in Canada*, chap. 8.
[31]Minutes of U.F.A. Annual Convention, 1927, p. 91.
[32]The resolution, as amended and passed, read: "Whereas at present the date of our Provincial and Federal elections may be set by the authority of one man, the Premier, who may select any date, not taking into consideration the benefits of the public at large; Be it resolved that we urge that Parliament be responsible for the calling of elections instead of the Prime Minister." The orginal motion was that the dates of elections be fixed as in the United States. Minutes of U.F.A. Annual Convention, 1930, p. 72.

the U.F.A. administration, and its maintenance throughout the rest of the fourteen years of U.F.A. government, is evident from the foregoing account. Yet the initial force of opinion in favour of independence of members and against cabinet control was strong, as we have seen, and it had a practical basis in the constituency control of nominations and of campaign finances. The premier did not have all the sanctions which normally support the threat of dissolution and cabinet control of members. He had neither the disposal of nominations nor the usual patronage, because as part of its reform principles the U.F.A. had set its face strongly against patronage.

What other forces prevailed against these factors making for freedom from cabinet control? To see it merely as a problem of what other sanctions the premier had for making a threat of dissolution effective is to pose the question too narrowly. There were, of course, other sanctions; at first the difficulty there would have been in replacing the cabinet from among the inexperienced legislative group, and later, as the members got experience and settled into their positions, a corresponding reluctance to go unnecessarily to the polls.

But fundamentally what compelled the members to give up their freedom was the need of the U.F.A. to prove its ability to govern and to finance the province. The farmers' government was under persistent attack by the city newspapers, the old parties, and "the interests"; the whole prestige of "the farmers in politics," and the whole proof of the ability of the farmers' movement to take independent political action, depended on the U.F.A. members supporting the government in whatever course the government chose to follow or was compelled to follow by reason of its dependence on the outside bond market.[33] Elected to replace party government by group government, the U.F.A. members found themselves in an absolute majority and able to support a government by themselves.[34] In order to make a success of independent political action they had to support their government; in order to support the government they had to dispense with those principles of group government which conflicted with the cabinet system. Specifically, the primary responsibility of the member to his constituency association had to give way to his responsibility for maintaining the government, that is, to his responsibility to the cabinet.

[33]See below, p. 88.

[34]The first U.F.A. cabinet included one Labour member, but this was as far as the U.F.A. could go in putting group government into effect. After the 1926 election, in which this member was defeated, the cabinet consisted entirely of U.F.A. members.

The pattern of direct responsibility of elected delegate to those who elected him could not be carried over intact from the old internal democracy of the U.F.A. convention. For the member of the legislative assembly was not, like the delegate of the convention, chosen *ad hoc* for one convention of four days' duration; he was elected for the whole term of the legislature. His voting on particular measures in accordance with the wishes of his constituency became less important than his maintaining the farmers' government in office. That the constituency associations by and large recognized this is indicated by their lack of insistence on the position they had initially taken about the members' independence of the cabinet and responsibility to them.

Their willingness or inability to insist on their initial position led to further weakening of the constituency associations. Having lost much of their power, many of them declined in activity. As early as the election of 1926 and more extensively by the election of 1930 many provincial constituency associations had become so atrophied that it was necessary for candidates to set up their own machinery and pay the expenses of canvassing out of their own pockets. In such circumstances the successful candidate could afford to take an aggressive line towards his constituency association and was likely to feel that his primary responsibility was to the government rather than the constituency.

Thus the original victory of cabinet government over members' independence weakened the constituency associations still further. Little was left but a semblance of the original U.F.A. principle of constituency control of the elected member of the legislature.

§ 4. Constituency Autonomy versus Provincial Convention Control of Policy

We have already seen that within the political structure of the U.F.A., constituency control of the legislative member gave way to cabinet control. We have now to notice that constituency control of the elected member gave way also to provincial convention control. It will then remain to examine (in section 5 below) the changing relations of the cabinet to the provincial convention.

Whether the elected member of the provincial legislature was responsible only to his constituency or whether, in case of difference between the policy of the constituency association and the policy of the provincial convention, he was bound to follow the latter, never became as serious an issue in provincial politics as in federal, perhaps because the provincial members had already lost their independence in the legislature, but it was a matter of recurrent concern. The difficulty was inherent in the fact that the constituency conventions had just as direct a mandate from the locals as had the U.F.A. provincial convention.

Concern with this problem was apparent at the 1924 provincial convention, in the following resolution from the Coronation Provincial Constituency Association: "Whereas it is the opinion of some of our Provincial members that they are responsible only to their own constituency conventions, and Whereas, if this idea is carried out it will prevent unity of action; Therefore be it resolved that our member be in duty bound to support any resolution passed by the Coronation Convention and also passed by the Provincial Convention." The motion was lost, the opinion being "that this matter was not properly under the jurisdiction of the Convention."[35] It was apparently still a problem at the end of 1924, when the Stettler Provincial Constituency Association passed the following resolution for presentation at the 1925 provincial convention:

Whereas, our U.F.A. representatives in the Provincial Legislature have taken the stand that they receive their instructions only from the Provincial Constituency Associations and not from the Annual Convention of the organization as a whole, and
Whereas, our Annual Provincial Convention is and must remain the central and supreme authority in the organization,
Therefore be it resolved, that this Convention affirm its adherence to the principle that our U.F.A. members be instructed to regard the decisions of the Annual Provincial Convention as the voice of the organization acting as a whole, and that they take their final instructions from that Convention.[36]

Concern over convention control of provincial constituency associations was merged with the more urgent problem of control over federal constituency organizations during 1924 and 1925. When the problem in respect of the U.F.A. federal members of parliament became serious during 1924 it was necessary to redefine the relation of the member of parliament to the U.F.A. convention and to the constituency, and the new definition was made to apply to the members of the provincial legislature also. An article in *The U.F.A.* in the summer of 1924, prepared by Wood at the request of the central board, showed which way the wind was blowing.

[35]Minutes of the U.F.A. Annual Convention, 1924, p. 68.
[36]*The U.F.A.*, Dec. 1, 1924.

While I think there is no disposition on the part of any one to limit the fullest degree of district or local autonomy, I do believe that a false impression has developed from an exaggerated use of the word "autonomy" in relation to the district organizations. To take the proposition that any sub-unit, no matter how autonomous, is independent of the whole body would be disastrous. It is true that an elected member is answerable directly to his own district, but it is just as true that a district is just as answerable to the whole, not autocratically but democratically controlled.[37]

The same position was laid down by the provincial convention of 1925, which adopted unanimously a "Declaration of Principles of Political Action" on January 23, 1925. Clause 1 declared that "each U.F.A. member is responsible directly to his own U.F.A. constituency organization and that organization is responsible to the U.F.A. organization as a whole."[38] Wood, in speaking to this, took the position that the authority of the constituencies to put candidates in the field came from the provincial convention. All authority orginated in the locals, whose will was expressed in the provincial convention and passed from the convention to the constituencies.

The primary responsibility of the elected members to the central U.F.A. bodies rather than to their constituency associations was further emphasized by a resolution of the 1927 provincial convention: "This convention recommends to the Federal and Provincial Constituency Associations that the members of the Federal and Provincial U.F.A. groups, who may be elected, recognizing the supreme authority in the Association, the Annual Convention, and their delegated officials, the U.F.A. Central Board and Executive, report as group units to these bodies."[39] Like the 1925 Declaration of Principles this resolution was intended primarily for the federal constituency associations and members; as first moved at the convention it referred only to them (being taken verbatim from the resolutions of the 1926 conference of federal constituency associations), but it was referred back to a drafting committee so that it would apply uniformly to all political activities, most of the discussion having been directed towards amending the resolution to include provincial members as well.[40]

That there still remained some disposition on the part of constituency associations to go against the policies of the provincial convention is apparent from the action of the 1931 provincial convention in amending the 1925 Declaration of Principles by the addition of a new clause: "7. Resolutions passed by constituency associations which involve any departure from the policies laid down by the Annual

37*Ibid.*, Aug. 15, 1924. 38*Ibid.*, Feb. 2, 1925. 39*Ibid.*, Feb. 1, 1927.
40*Grain Growers' Guide*, Feb. 1, 1927.

Convention of the United Farmers of Alberta, shall not in any way be applied to the guidance of candidates or elected members unless and until such time as they have been submitted to and adopted by the Annual Convention of the United Farmers of Alberta."[41]

The right of the provincial as well as of the federal constituency association to instruct the elected member gave way, wherever there was disagreement, to the right of the central convention to lay down policies binding on all elected members. Thus at the same time that the member of the provincial legislature was being subordinated to the cabinet, his popular base, the constituency association, was being subordinated to the central convention which was increasingly under the influence of the board and executive. In the contest between constituency autonomy and convention control the convention had the victory, for what it was worth; it was not worth much in provincial politics because neither the constituency association nor the convention had much control over the elected member of the legislature once the exigencies of cabinet government had made themselves felt.

§ 5. Provincial Convention Supremacy versus Cabinet Supremacy

Although both the independence of members in the legislature and constituency autonomy were effectively submerged, there was still one major problem of democratic practice: the relation of the cabinet to the annual convention and the board and executive. The convention was able to assert and maintain its authority to control the actions of the U.F.A. federal members of parliament, but its attempts to control the members of the provincial legislature were less successful, for the latter, including the cabinet, were responsible for the administration of the province.

The first convention after the 1921 provincial elections amended the constitution of the U.F.A. to provide that "no member of parliament, provincial or federal, shall be allowed to hold office on the Executive or Board of Directors of the Provincial U.F.A."[42] This provision automatically removed several officers from the board and executive. The prohibition was maintained until 1931 when it was removed to allow Robert Gardiner, M.P., to replace Wood as president of the U.F.A.

Throughout this period the relation between the government and the leading organs of the movement as a whole was a relation between separate bodies, having no overlapping membership and having

[41]Minutes of the U.F.A. Annual Convention, 1931, pp. 161–2.
[42]The U.F.A., March 1, 1922.

co-ordinate authority from the primary units of the U.F.A. The cabinet and members of the legislature derived their authority, within the U.F.A., from the constituency conventions which in turn derived their authority from the locals; the president, executive, and central board of the U.F.A. derived their authority from the provincial convention, or sections thereof, which in turn derived its authority directly from the locals.

The formal relationship was straightforward. The president made it a point never to interfere with or try to impose policy on the cabinet. The convention did not claim the right to impose policy on the cabinet. The staple of successive annual conventions was resolutions requesting the government to do things, but the resolutions were framed as requests, such as might be made by any outside association, not as demands. The cabinet, without acknowledging that the U.F.A. had any special status, gave methodical attention to all the resolutions of the convention and the board. Every year, after the convention, the cabinet received a deputation bringing resolutions from the U.F.A., but it also received deputations from the teachers' association, the school trustees' association, the local councils of women, municipal associations, labour and other bodies. Some members of the cabinet regularly attended the annual U.F.A. convention, but they also attended other conventions: the minister of labour was always at labour conventions, the minister of education and sometimes the minister of health attended teachers' and trustees' conventions, the ministers of municipal affairs, of highways, and of health generally attended the municipal conventions; and in any case it had been customary in the Liberal administration prior to 1921 for some cabinet members to attend the U.F.A. convention to explain and defend government policy, and to receive U.F.A. deputations. In Alberta the farmers' convention was an important body for any government to reckon with.

The formal relations between cabinet and convention tell us little, but their content is more revealing. The cabinet treated the annual set of resolutions brought to it from the convention with considerable freedom. Not only did the cabinet not consider itself bound to carry out the requests of the resolutions; it did not even feel bound to explain its refusal to act on many of them; and its reception of the committee presenting the resolutions was even sometimes noticeably cool.

The cabinet's independent position is illustrated both in the replies given by ministers when the resolutions were presented, and in the formal memoranda which the government later sent to the U.F.A.

On February 15, 1924, for instance, a U.F.A. committee presented the following resolutions to the cabinet, which reacted as indicated: that writs for by-elections should be issued within 30 days of a vacancy (the government will consider); that mortgage legislation be revised (rejected by the premier and attorney-general as ultra vires, arbitrary, etc.); that municipal taxes have priority over all other claims (the government will consider); that owners of farm land should be free of mineral tax (virtually rejected); that the new liquor control act be made stringent to prevent bootlegging (the cabinet merely smiled); that child welfare work be consolidated (probably too costly); that the province assume the whole cost of mothers' allowances (refused on budget grounds).[43] The formal memoranda which the cabinet sent to the U.F.A. central office before the convention, stating the government's action on or attitude to each of the resolutions of the previous year's convention, showed even more independence. On some resolutions the requested action had been taken, on some the government stated why action had not yet been taken, on others the government simply stated that it did not think it desirable to introduce such legislation. Thus in the memorandum covering the 42 resolutions of the 1926 convention we find such replies as the following:

31. *Municipal Schools.* [Resolution] asking that one or more be established to test feasibility. Reply—The principle of this resolution has been considered by the Government on several occasions, but on account of very serious objections in this Province, it has not been thought advisable to introduce such legislation.

36. *V. D. Medical Examination.* [Resolution] that all parties seeking marriage shall submit health certificate. Reply—The Department of Health is administering certain sanitary regulations, but it has not been thought advisable by the Government to take the action suggested by these resolutions.[44]

But though the cabinet treated the resolutions with some freedom it went out of its way to treat the actual meetings of the convention very seriously. The convention, meeting as it did every January, before the opening of the legislature, sometimes got from the premier a fuller statement of government policy than the legislature got. The Liberal leader in the legislature, alert to the possibility of exploiting the situation, attacked the premier at the opening of the session in 1923 for not having mentioned in the speech from the throne government policies which had been outlined to the convention the week before. He complained specifically that it was to the convention

[43]*Edmonton Bulletin*, Feb. 16, 1924.   [44]*The U.F.A.*, Jan. 15, 1927.

rather than to the house that the premier had given his explanation why the wheat board, provided for by legislation passed at a special session of the house in July 1922, had not functioned, and had outlined the government's future policy on that issue.[45]

More significant than the announcement of government policy to the convention, as an indication of the importance which the cabinet attached to the convention, were the strenuous efforts made on occasion by leading ministers to persuade the convention not to pass certain radical resolutions. In these efforts they came up against the convention's strong jealousy of its own rights, especially in the early years. At the 1922 convention, the first since the elections, but held before the first U.F.A. cabinet had met the first U.F.A. legislature, most of the members of the cabinet and many members of the legislature were present, and those who were not delegates from their locals were given the privileges of the convention. The 1923 convention, however, although as usual it heard an address from the premier on opening day, did not permit ministers to take part in the discussions[46]—on one resolution asking a statement of government policy it was the deputy minister who informed the convention that the government had not decided on a policy in the matter[47]—and it was only when a radical financial resolution was on the point of being passed that the attorney-general obtained the floor by special permission.[48] Later conventions generally granted the privileges of the floor to legislative members but a proposal at the 1928 convention to amend the constitution to confer these powers at all times was rejected; the convention kept the right to decide each year what privileges it would extend.[49]

Although after 1923 the convention became noticeably less sensitive to ministerial efforts to influence its debates, it was not always persuaded to the cabinet's view. For instance the 1926 convention passed a resolution favouring an increase in the liquor licence fee to provide funds for the relief of families left destitute as a result of the liquor traffic, after the reading of a government memorandum opposing such action on the ground that it was unnecessary. It also passed a resolution asking that every lawyer who handled trust funds be required to take out a substantial bond with a trust or guarantee company, after a memorandum from the government had been read

[45]*Edmonton Bulletin,* Jan. 26, 1923.
[46]*British Columbia United Farmer,* April 1, 1923.
[47]*Grain Growers' Guide,* Jan. 24, 1923.
[48]See below, p. 88.   [49]*The U.F.A.,* Feb. 1 and 16, 1928.

discouraging the passage of this resolution on the grounds that the requirement would be invidious and was unnecessary.[50] On such matters the logic of the experts and men of affairs could not offset the impression of experience or imagination on the working farmers who made up the convention.

By 1928 a regular procedure had been worked out by which, as resolutions came up for discussion, the U.F.A. directors, the cabinet minister concerned, or one of the federal members of parliament, would be interrogated and asked to give an opinion. A long-standing officer of the U.F.A. recorded with satisfaction that "a great deal of fruitless discussion and waste of time was thereby avoided."[51] The convention had apparently been tamed, as much by its own leaders as by the cabinet, though when the problem of farm debt became urgent serious differences between the cabinet and the convention again developed. At the 1932 convention a resolution for a moratorium of debts was defeated narrowly after the premier had spoken strongly against it, and his intervention is credited with changing the course the convention would have taken.[52]

But even when the convention was most strongly imbued with its own independence the cabinet was able to make its view prevail, ultimately by something very like the threat of dissolution. The 1923 convention was dissuaded from passing a resolution that the government should issue bonds to liquidate the debts of all the farmers in the province by a strong speech by the attorney-general, Mr. Brownlee, warning that the passage of such resolutions would probably prevent his obtaining a refunding loan of thirteen million dollars which was absolutely necessary for carrying on the business of the province, and that in such an event the government would probably fall. "He expressed a fear that, owing to the close relationship between the U.F.A. and the government, it might seriously injure the credit of the province if unsound financial resolutions were published abroad as coming from the convention. . . . The government was doing the best possible and he warned the convention that some of the resolutions it was passing might make it impossible for the government to carry on."[53]

A similar warning was effective in 1924. The convention debated for two days a resolution "that the members of the Provincial Legislature should use whatever means within their power to urge the

[50]*Grain Growers' Guide*, Jan. 27, 1926.
[51]Norman Priestly, "An Estimate of the Calgary U.F.A. Convention," *The U.F.A.*, Feb. 16, 1928.   [52]*The U.F.A.*, Feb. 1, 1932.
[53]*Grain Growers' Guide*, Jan. 24, 1923. Cf. *The U.F.A.*, Feb. 5, 1923.

present Provincial Government" to set up a provincial bank. The
resolution was defeated after (*a*) a report from the government
rejecting last year's similar resolution on the grounds of its inade-
quacies and the legal difficulties; (*b*) a speech by William Irvine,
M.P., on the proposal of President Wood, against the resolution on
the ground that it was superficial, concluding "You have a government
honestly trying to give you what you want. For this reason you should
be more careful what you ask of them"; and (*c*) a speech by Wood,
in which he held that in view of the situation outlined by the government, "the passage of the resolution would be equivalent to a vote of
want of confidence."[54]

It is significant that Wood, who was skilled in sensing the feeling
of a convention, thought it necessary to make this case at the end of the
debate. It was not argued, as it had been in 1923, that the passage
of the offending resolution might make it impossible for the government to carry on. It was simply announced, and by the president
of the association, that the government had a right to consider
this, and presumably any vote by the convention, a vote of no
confidence in the government; the memorandum to the association
stating the government's opposition to the resolution was taken to
be sufficient notice that the vote would be treated as a confidence
vote. This was not a fanciful pronouncement; these consequences
were implicit in the wording of the resolution which, without pre-
suming to instruct the government, did instruct the private members
to use "whatever means within their power" to get the government
to act. But the only means within their power, if the government
would not budge, would be to defeat the government in the house
and split the party. That the president was driven to intervene
suggests that there was some fear that the issue might be carried
to these lengths. It was, at any rate, not merely the fact that the
president was in closer sympathy with the government than with
the radical wing (in this instance the probable majority) of the
convention that led to this interpretation of the government's rights.
For as long as the convention considered that it had the right to
instruct the members of the legislature, the convention was placed in
much the same relation to the cabinet as were the private members
of the legislature. The convention's first duty became the duty to
support, or at least not to embarrass, the cabinet. The principle
announced by President Wood simply made clear what had been
implicit in the relation of the convention to the government.

[54]*The U.F.A.*, Feb. 1, 1924. Cf. *Grain Growers' Guide*, Jan. 23, 1924.

Thus while the convention never renounced its claim to lay down broad policies binding on U.F.A. members of the legislature, the exigencies of cabinet government overcame the supremacy of the convention. The threat of defeat for the government and the warning that the passage of a resolution opposed by the cabinet would be considered a vote of want of confidence, were used to bring not only the legislature but also the convention around to the cabinet's policy. The delegates to the convention, like the U.F.A. members of the legislature, were compelled to abandon the position of instructed delegates of their constituents, and to become supporters of a government. The demands of cabinet government prevailed over the theory of delegate democracy.

§ 6. Conclusion: The Success and Failure of U.F.A. Delegate Democracy

We have seen (section 3) that the direct and primary responsibility of the U.F.A. member of the legislature to the constituency association gave way to cabinet control as the cabinet and premier assumed and exercised all the powers and responsibilities usual in the cabinet system. We have seen (section 4) that the constituency associations incidentally lost out not only to the cabinet but also to the U.F.A. provincial convention in the formulation of policies. Constituency autonomy was thus subordinated to two kinds of central supremacy. Moreover, we have seen that the delegate democracy of the provincial convention, somewhat impaired (section 2) by the increased size and amount of business that came with the U.F.A.'s entry into political action, was soon definitely subordinated to the requirements of the government (section 5); the convention delegates were forced into a position similar to that of the private members of the legislature as the convention, like the legislative caucus, became subject to the demands of the cabinet on issues the cabinet thought vital. Thus both constituency autonomy and delegate democracy were overridden by cabinet government.

What, if anything, was left of the U.F.A. principles of government? At first reckoning very little appears to have been left. The decisive principle of group government, that the cabinet should be formed by and from all the groups in the legislature, was abandoned even before the U.F.A. took office, by the announced decision that the U.F.A. would take the responsibility of forming a government; the inclusion of one Labour member in the first cabinet was in these circumstances not a recognition of the group government principle.

The principle that the member of the legislature should be a delegate primarily responsible to his constituency association was abandoned. The principle of the elected members' independence of cabinet control, to be guaranteed by renunciation of the cabinet privilege of treating any vote as a vote of confidence, was abandoned. The principle that the elected members should not have anything to do with operating the political (i.e. electoral) machinery, their exclusion from this function to be guaranteed by the nominations and campaign financing being kept in the hands of the constituency associations and locals, fared rather better than the other principles. Although many of the constituency associations became atrophied and by failing to finance a campaign left it to the sitting member to establish his own local machine, no central machine controlling nominations and finances did develop.

But although none of these specific reforms required by U.F.A. political theory were effected, the underlying purpose which the particular changes were designed to serve was in some measure realized. The channels for exerting pressure and making wants felt from below were more open, more actively used, and more effective than those of the usual Canadian party. The constituency associations, which had been intended to be the main channel between the locals and the legislature, turned out to be less effective in this function than the annual provincial convention, for the latter was in a somewhat stronger position to influence the cabinet than were the private members of the legislature. Neither the constituency associations nor the provincial convention were in a position to control the cabinet, but they had some influence, and of the two the provincial convention had more because of its long-standing prestige, the publicity it commanded, and the fact that as new problems arose and the gravity of old problems changed the convention had a fresh public mandate each year.

From another point of view, too, it may be said that the U.F.A. political theory was carried into effect in greater degree than has appeared so far. Although on the record analysed in this chapter the U.F.A. did not succeed in moving very far towards its goals of group government and delegate democracy, although indeed from the moment of its success in the provincial elections of 1921 it retreated rapidly from its reform principles to an acceptance of the usual practices of cabinet government, this is not to say that its practice became indistinguishable from the party practice against which it had rebelled. If the democratic practice of the U.F.A. be measured not against its reform principles but against the prevailing characteristics of party, its difference from party is at once apparent. For it did not develop any of the characteristics of party which it had denounced. It did not become conglomerate. It did not become unstable or unprincipled in an attempt to hold together a conglomeration of interests. It did not develop a centrally controlled machine, nor put itself at the disposal of any outside interests.

In all these respects the U.F.A. in provincial politics did implement its principles. This was no mean achievement. Yet it was not enough. The subordination of the cherished principle of delegate democracy to cabinet supremacy left the U.F.A. not resilient enough to serve as the political instrument of the Alberta farmers under the shattering blows of the depression in the early 1930's. Their interests demanded policies bolder than any they could induce the U.F.A. government to entertain. Finally they transferred their hopes to a new movement which appeared to be a new embodiment of that radical delegate democracy they had lost; and they did so in such numbers that in the provincial election of 1935 the U.F.A. lost every seat, to be replaced by a large Social Credit majority in the legislature and a Social Credit government. As it developed, the new movement after its first year or two became something very different from a delegate democracy; the voters had exchanged the remnant of delegate democracy for a plebiscitarian democracy.

CHAPTER FOUR

English Social Credit: The Social and Economic Theory

-»)«‹-

§ 1. The Scope and Appeal of English Social Credit

At about the same time that Henry Wise Wood in Alberta was beginning to develop what became the leading ideas of the U.F.A., an English mechanical engineer, Major C. H. Douglas, hit on a notion which became the doctrine of social credit. Compared with the indigenous agrarian thinking of the U.F.A., English social credit theory was from the beginning urban and cosmopolitan. It was the product of a few men whose talents were not accommodated by their society and who rebelled against it. It had no roots in any stable section of English society but appealed to shifting urban groups. It was at once more radical in its criticism of society and more utopian in its proposals than the agrarian philosophy of the U.F.A., for it set out to solve all the world's problems without having an anchor in the experience of any homogeneous class.

For these and other reasons the English doctrine came to have, by the late 1930's, an extravagant flavour quite foreign to the thinking of western Canadian farmers; and when this emerged it led to a split in the Canadian movement. But in the beginning the very extent and depth of its revolt made the social credit doctrine attractive to western Canadian farmers whose own society appeared to be uprooted. The urban outlook of social credit was secondary; its primary appeal was to those insecure sections of society, whether independent prairie farm producers or middle class English city dwellers, whose economic position may be defined as *petit-bourgeois*. The social philosophy of Douglas's basic writings had much in common with the U.F.A. ideas, although his social and economic analysis went further and in a different direction. Douglas focused attention not, as Wood did, on the weak competitive position of one section of producers and their inadequate share in the whole national product,

93

but on the artificial limitation of the whole product and the unnecessary privation of the whole community.

The gist of the social credit theory was that modern technology
had made possible an era of great plenty and leisure both of which
could and should be distributed throughout the community as
unearned income, and that this could be done by some comparatively
simple monetary devices which would not interfere with the structure
of ownership and private enterprise. Social credit could thus be
regarded either as a supplement to the U.F.A. policies or as an
alternative to them. In fact it played each part in turn. In the 1920's
social credit was taken up by several prominent U.F.A. men, notably
Henry Spencer (member of parliament for Battle River, 1921-35)
and William Irvine, who added the Douglas system of credit reform
to the armoury of weapons in the western agrarian campaign against
the domination of eastern capital. As the depression deepened in
the first years of the 1930's and the traditional U.F.A. policies proved
inadequate, more and more U.F.A. men were attracted by social
credit policies. When, by a mixture of conservatism and honesty,
the U.F.A. leadership refused to commit itself to a wholly social
credit programme, social credit emerged as an alternative to the
U.F.A. policies and the way was clear for Aberhart to recruit a rival
movement. This chapter and the next give some account of the
English social credit doctrine as it was received in Alberta up to and
including the first year or two of the Aberhart movement; the later
extravagances of the Douglas doctrine and their impact in Alberta
will be discussed in chapter VII.

It will be useful before analysing the various parts of the theory
to show them briefly in perspective, for it is not generally realized
outside the ranks of social crediters that social credit was more than
a theory of monetary reform. The frustration of the engineer by the
business control of industry may be seen as the starting point of
Douglas's social thinking.

If the public of this or any other country is really desirous of once and
for ever freeing itself from the power of the economic machine, and using
the immense heritage which science and industry have placed at its disposal, it has to throw up and place in positions of executive authority
men who are technicians in so broad a sense that they understand that
the very essence of perfect technology is to devise mechanism to meet the
requirements, the policy of those who appointed them. There are thousands
of such men in every country disgusted, in their varying degree, with the
policy to which their abilities have been prostituted; but so long as the
super-producer appoints and supports the man who delivers the goods—

i.e., profits—while the public elects and supports the man who only talks, whether in Parliament or in the Trade Union, just so long will the tail of production wag the consuming dog. There is no hope whatever in the hustings; but a modified credit-system could transform the world in five years.[1]

Deeply impressed by the waste of industrial capacity and potential, Douglas developed a sweeping critique of industrial civilization. From the beginning he was concerned with the frustration not only of technologists but of humanity at large. He saw that whatever held back the progress of science in industry made it impossible for the technologist to serve the people and give them the benefit of their heritage. He saw also that the increasing concentration of power in the control of industrial production was only a part of a trend toward increasing concentration of power in government, in trade unions, and in every institution which affected the life and opportunity of every individual both as worker and as consumer.

In his early writings Douglas's main concern was to expose this trend toward the submergence of the individual, to establish its pervasive nature, and to warn that it must be defeated if the human quality of civilization was not to be destroyed. His case was presented with restraint and with telling effect. His recommendation of certain monetary devices as the way to release men from the tyranny of concentrated power was subordinated to the main analysis. His point was that men could not be free in any other way until they had got a freedom of choice both as producers and as consumers, and a level of material well-being, which the existing system of production and distribution denied them. The economic system must therefore first be reformed. Socialism was not the answer, since it would mean still further centralization of economic and political power. Monetary reform was the answer because it could destroy the mechanism by which economic power was being increased and by which the material well-being and the freedom of the individual were being diminished. Monetary reform was merely a means toward the end of establishing a new society in which human beings would be free to develop their individuality in a way that had never been possible before; men would be free of the compulsions to which they had been subjected in the industrial revolution, yet would retain the advantages of the new mastery of the environment.

[1]C. H. Douglas, *Credit-Power and Democracy, with a Draft Scheme for the Mining Industry,* with a commentary on the included scheme by A. R. Orage (London, 1921), pp. 85–6.

What gave the Douglas movement its persistent strength, even after the complete fallacy of the social credit monetary theory had been repeatedly demonstrated, was its cutting denunciation of existing society and its epochal vision of a new society. In a decade in which orthodox economists continued to believe, in the face of mass unemployment, that the economic system could not suffer from a general shortage of purchasing power, in which politicians and the press made a fetish of work and urged more production as a remedy for economic problems, it was the merit of Major Douglas to see through such claims and such policies and to proclaim that the end of man is not labour but self-development and enjoyment, that the end of production is not employment but consumption, and that the unfettered application of modern technology and modern sources of energy is capable of producing the material basis of a better life for the mass of people while leaving them much more leisure for enjoyment and self-development.

This was an attractive doctrine. It told men that they were unfree, that their resentment was just. It told them that their civilization had perverted all human values and was driving toward still greater unfreedom. It drew attention to the growing centralization of power in the state, in trade unions, and in business enterprise, and pointed to the suppression of individuality which this must entail. It argued that parliamentary democracy had become unreal, since successive governments, empowered by popular franchise, had given the people the opposite of what the people wanted.

These charges against a business civilization and its political institutions were attractive to many who felt or saw the current frustration of humanity in any of its forms, and who had found no way to fight it or who had misgivings as to the adequacy of the way they had found. Those who saw the appalling results of mass unemployment, those who felt the helplessness of the individual as a unit in the mass manipulated by the press and politicians and high finance, and especially those who were experiencing the deterioration of the position of the independent small and medium producer and of the professional class in the face of the concentration of economic power: all these were attracted by the direction of Douglas's critique. Even some socialists and some sections of the trade union movement were attracted for a time; the nucleus of the Douglas following was a group of intellectuals won over from the guild socialist position. Both Marxian and Fabian socialists rejected the Douglas doctrine, not unnaturally, since their own critiques of existing society were at least as sweeping, and since Douglas from the outset attacked their analyses.

The voice that pressed these charges offered a diagnosis and a remedy of singular attractiveness to the same strata of society to which the critique appealed. The root cause of the malaise was an error in the accounting system of industry, an error which had become entrenched in the pricing mechanism and had made it impossible for people as consumers to buy back the goods they had created as producers. On this foundation finance had built its control, first of industry and then of governments. From the policies of finance flowed all the evils of restricted production, unemployment, the suppression of freedom and individuality, the perversion of labour values, and war. None of these was inherent in capitalism; they were results of the perversion of capitalist enterprise by finance; indeed, capitalism had died seventy-five years ago and had been replaced by "creditism." The enemy was not capitalism, it was finance, that is, the control of credit by an irresponsible oligarchy. From this it followed capitalist enterprise, profits, and private ownership could all be retained. All that was needed was to restore the control of credit to the people made really sovereign, and thus enable the simple monetary devices of social credit to be put into practice. The main devices, either or both of which might be used, were the issuance of a national dividend to consumers and the issuance of subsidies to producers in aid of lower prices. Such action would remove the deficiency of consumers' purchasing power which was the root of the trouble, would liberate the productive system, and would make possible the restoration of freedom and the recognition of the human values which had been perverted.

If we now look more closely at the Douglas doctrine we shall see how much it had in common with U.F.A. theory, and how, where it diverged, it seemed not incompatible with, and in some respects more acceptable than, the U.F.A. ideas. Not until we see the later development of social credit doctrine, particularly of its political theory, will the real incompatibility of the two be apparent.

§ 2. Social Development and Moral Purpose

The social philosophy of the early Douglas writings is fragmentary and eclectic but its direction is clear. It takes the free development of individuality to be the highest social good. It denounces any exercise of power which frustrates that development. It sees human history as a purposeful evolution towards increasingly free self-development and self-expression of the individual: ". . . the history of human development . . . is one long, and, on the whole, continuously successful struggle to subdue environment, to the end that individuality may have the utmost freedom."[2] The growth of individuality, in this sense, is thus not only the ultimate good but is also the purpose which consciously or unconsciously governs humanity "in its ceaseless struggle with the environment."[3] The driving force of this evolution is the human will, which seeks freer expression by increasing control of the material environment. "The plain trend of evolution . . . is to subordinate material to mental and psychological necessity."[4] The eventual outcome is certain: the achievement of full individuality is ultimately assured because it is in the nature of things; "self-expression of the individual is . . . the certain eventual outcome of these present discontents."[5]

Douglas dissociated his view sharply from the "mangled and misapplied Darwinism" which "has been one of the most potent factors in the social development of the past sixty years,"[6] and also from "what is commonly called individualism, which generally resolves itself into a claim to force the individuality of others to subordinate itself to the will-to-power of the self-styled individualist."[7] The "individualism" of industrial capitalism is seen as antagonistic to individuality, for it is a manifestation of that will to power on the part of a few which has throughout history tried to thwart the development of individuality.

The evolution towards the fullest individual freedom, although its eventual outcome is assured, never proceeds without opposition; the will to freedom of the many is perennially opposed by the will to power of the few, and at no time has the conflict been more critical than at the present.

The real antagonism which is at the root of the Universal upheaval with which we are faced is one which appears under different forms in every aspect of human life. It is the age-long struggle between freedom and authority, between external compulsion and internal initiative, in which all the command of resource, information, religious dogma, educational system, political opportunity, and even apparently economic necessity, is at the disposal of the will-to-power, and only history offers grounds for expectation of any measure of success on the side of freedom. This antagonism does, however, appear at the present time to have reached a stage in which a definite victory for one side or the other is inevitable. It

[2]C. H. Douglas, "The Pyramid of Power," *English Review*, XXVIII, February 1919, p. 107.

[3]C. H. Douglas, *Economic Democracy* (London, 1928), p. 4.

[4]*Ibid.*, p. 68.   [5]Douglas, *Credit-Power and Democracy*, p. 144.

[6]Douglas, *Economic Democracy* (1928), p. 8.   [7]*Ibid.*, p. 5.

seems perfectly certain that either a pyramidal organization, having at its apex supreme power and at its base virtual subjection (however disguised by Garden Cities and Ministries of Health) will crystallize out of the centralising process which is evident in the inter-related realms of finance, industry, and politics; or else a more complete decentralisation of initiative than this civilisation has ever known will be substituted for external authority.

The issue transcends in importance all others; the development of the human race will be radically different as it is decided one way or another.[8]

The similarities between this and H. W. Wood's view are apparent. In both, social development is seen as purposive evolution, the outcome of rational individual action in pursuit of a fuller and freer life. In both, the advance toward the goal is assured by the nature of things. In both, the advance is hindered perennially by the selfish actions of a few who seek control over the whole society. In both, the present ills of society are due to the perversion of a rational purposive economic system: Wood blamed it on the perversion of commerce, Douglas on the perversion of production by finance. Neither saw any obstacle to individual freedom inherent in the relation of labour to capital in the process of production. Although Douglas regarded "the separation of the workman from the ownership of his tools and the control of his business policy" as an essential aspect of the industrial revolution,[9] the importance of the separation was that it had permitted the financier to intervene in the productive process. The rise of the financier, who got his power by issuing credit, was evident as early as the Crusades[10] but it was the industrial revolution, increasing the size of the productive unit and lengthening the productive process, which allowed the financiers to gain control of the whole economy. Before then, men had associated in productive communities in order to get, as consumers, the benefit of the greater productivity of associated effort. The economic system had been rational; men had produced in order to consume. Now the purpose had been inverted: the people were forced to labour in order that they might be kept in subjection.

The idea that economic society had been consciously developed for a common purpose and had only been perverted by the intervention of financiers was based on the same sort of assumption as was Wood's theory, and led to a similar conclusion. The assumption was that

[8]Douglas, "The Pyramid of Power," *English Review*, XXVIII, January 1919, p. 57; reprinted in *Economic Democracy* (London, 1921), pp. 80–1, with changes.
[9]Douglas, *Economic Democracy* (1921), p. 42.
[10]C. H. Douglas, *Warning Democracy* (London, 1931); quoted in Philip Mairet, ed., *The Douglas Manual* (London, 1934), p. 42.

there was a natural harmony of economic interests among all except the small group which had perverted the system to its own uses; the conclusion was that when the power of this group was broken no problem of individual freedom would remain. "The possibility of an increase in the real liberty of the subject depends not (as is so unceasingly proclaimed by the upholders of things as they are) in a continual compromise between individual rights, but in a continual attempt to remove limitations which are non-automatic, that is to say, do not proceed from what we call the laws of nature."[11] These limitations were those imposed by the system dominated by finance.

The similarity of the assumptions made about the nature of society by Wood and Douglas is not as remarkable as it might appear at first sight. The farmer and the engineer experience the productive process in the same way to this extent: both are engaged in direct purposive transformation of the physical environment. To them that is the essence of economic activity; they are not separated from it as are, in different ways, both wage-earners and business men. The engineer and the farmer, reading into the nature of society their own relation to economic society, are apt to think of society as naturally purposive, the product of intelligent human wills. They are apt not to recognize that in a society dominated by the market, the relations between individuals are necessarily somewhat anarchical and not the direct outcome of purposive wills. So, when confronted with a society which plainly and notoriously does not conform to any pattern desired by normal human wills, they see it as a conscious disruption of the natural order by some other wills thwarting theirs. On these assumptions it is easy to trace the ills of society to some small group (such as monopolists or financiers), and to defects in one particular part of the whole economic system (such as unequal terms of trade in the producers' markets, or the banking system) which allow that group to reach a dominant position.

This sort of reasoning was characteristic of both the U.F.A. and social credit thinking. There were differences of emphasis. Douglas, with a wider experience of the world and of the business control of the productive system, brought out more clearly than Wood the pervasiveness of the trend to submergence of individual freedom.

[11]C. H. Douglas, *Social Credit* (London, 1935), pp. 39–40. Cf. *Economic Democracy* (1921), pp. 153–4: The aim is the achievement of "a society based on the unfettered freedom of the individual to co-operate in a state of affairs in which community of interest and individual interest are merely different aspects of the same thing."

He was also more ready to see this as a deliberate design of a small number of power-seekers in every country than as a by-product of the search for profit. Although in his early writings Douglas did not emphasize the world-plot thesis which later dominated his mind, he introduced it as early as 1920 when he wrote "whether, as some would have us believe, there is an active, conscious conspiracy to enslave the world, or whether, as is arguable, only blind forces are at work to the same end, is a question immaterial to the patent fact that the danger of such a tyranny is real and instant."[12] By 1922 he had concluded that "the International Financial groups who precipitate these struggles [world wars] do not really care how frequent they are—the cost of them is simply passed on to the public in prices, and the real authors of them not merely go completely untouched by the repeated tragedies, but from villas on the Riviera or elsewhere 'glut' their love of power by contemplating the writhings of the world they have enslaved."[13]

At times in his early writings Douglas appeared to attribute the problems of society to the prevalence of outmoded "habits of thought and speech"[14] which prevent a true understanding and lead to misdirected effort. Thus he attributed the wastes of industrial society to "the obsession of wealth defined in terms of money . . . an obsession which obscures the whole object and meaning of scientific progress and places the worker and the honest man in a permanently disadvantageous position in comparison with the financier and the rogue."[15] The moral theory that mankind is not entitled to material plenty except as a reward for onerous work is so widely held that men have not yet been emboldened to demand the realization of potential plenty with less work.[16] The orthodox and popular concept of value as dependent upon scarcity has led to a society which logically proceeds to create values by creating scarcity.[17]

There is however no inconsistency between his assertion that mankind is being enslaved by a conscious plot of those who hold power

[12]Douglas, *Credit-Power and Democracy*, p. 145. Cf. his reference to "the hidden hands of finance and politics," *ibid.*, pp. 7–8; to "the ostensible Government as tools in the hands of the *real* Government," and to "the Hidden Governments of the world" (*The Control of Distribution and Production*, London, 1922, pp. 106, 108); and to the control of economic policy by "a hidden government" (*Social Credit*, London, 1924, p. 28).

[13]C. H. Douglas, *These Present Discontents and the Labour Party and Social Credit* (London, 1922), p. 164.

[14]Douglas, *Economic Democracy* (1928), p. 2.   [15]*Ibid.*, p. 77.

[16]Douglas, *Social Credit* (1924), chaps. 1 and 2. Cf. *Credit-Power and Democracy*, p. 11.   [17]Douglas, *Social Credit* (1924), chap. 5.

and his belief that mankind's failure to reach its goal of freedom is due to the prevalence of false or outmoded theories and concepts. His view is that the false concepts are deliberately fostered by the holders of power in order to maintain and increase their power. The argument is simple and is seen at its best in his analysis of the accepted doctrine of rewards and punishments and the related worship of work. The present social system, he holds, is based on and upheld by the dogma that men's actions are all deserving of either reward or punishment, and by the related dogma that the enjoyment of life should only be the reward of toil. These dogmas are so unnecessary to humanity in an age of potential plenty that their continued sway must have some explanation other than a correspondence with the real needs of society. The obvious explanation is that these dogmas are needed to keep the people in servitude to the holders of power.

The "high-priests of industry" have preached, and labour has believed

that it is only by the strenuous efforts of the orthodox worker, straining every nerve and muscle, that the world is maintained at its present standard of living; whereas it is, on the contrary, only by the most gigantic and organised sabotage on the part of the capitalistic system and Labour itself, not only positive but negative—by the refusal to use modern tools and processes, as well as by the misuse of them—that the standard of living is prevented from rising higher, with the expenditure of less human effort, than the most exacting would require at this time.[18]

The prevalent restriction of output, which is enforced by those who control finance, is a means of keeping people subservient.

A system of Society which depends for its structure on the theory of material rewards and punishments, seems to involve, fundamentally, a general condition of scarcity and discontent. You cannot reward an individual with something of which he has already sufficient for his needs and desires, nor can you easily find a punishment which will be effective in a world in which there is no incentive to crime. We might legitimately expect, in such a society, a mechanism which would ensure a continual, and if rendered necessary by the advancement of science, an artificial disparity between demand and supply of material goods and services, together with an organization which would prevent any infringement of the rules by which this disparity is maintained.

We do, in fact, find exactly such a state of affairs in the world today . . . the financial organization produces, at any rate, the illusion of scarcity . . .; the organization by which these arrangements are enforced is, of course, familiar in the form of the Common Law.[19]

18Douglas, Credit-Power and Democracy, p. 12.
19Douglas, Social Credit (1924), pp. 90-1.

The present productive system thus has as its primary object not production for enjoyment, but the moral discipline, that is, subservience, which "can only be achieved through the agency of the system and its prime constituent—employment."[20] The same position was stated even more pointedly in a speech in 1924,[21] and was summed up in the following words in 1931:

Unrestrained by the financial system, the resources of modern production would be sufficient to provide for the material desires of the whole population of the world at the expense of a small and decreasing amount of human labour. But the release of humanity from the necessity for toil would also mean their release from industrial government, a result so undesired that production for the sake of consumption is becoming the least important objective of industry. The misdirection of an economic mechanism to purposes for which, from its inherent nature, it does not lend itself, is the direct, and, it would appear, fundamental explanation of the phenomena from which the world is now suffering.[22]

One other difference between the broad Douglas social theory and the theory expounded by Wood should be noticed. We have seen that both emphasized the struggle between the people and the power-seekers, and both found that the critical hour had arrived. But while Wood preached a slow and steady but indefinitely long period of building up the political strength of the people as the only way to win, Douglas held that "a modified credit-system could transform the world in five years."[23] The Douglas doctrine took hold in Alberta after fifteen years of the slow and steady U.F.A. method had left Albertans farther from the promised land than ever.

§ 3. Technology and the Cultural Heritage

It will be seen that all of this—the critique of dominant moral values and the view of social development as a perversion of the natural purposes of the economic system—rests on the postulate of potential plenty. An imposing though elusive case was made for this postulate. The positive evidence was the emergence in the nineteenth and twentieth centuries of non-human sources of immense and adaptable energy in the form of coal, oil, steam, and electricity.

[20]*Ibid.*, p. 20.

[21]C. H. Douglas, "Social Credit Principles," an address delivered at Swanwick, November 1924; see *Social Credit*, Sept. 28, 1934. (References to *Social Credit* followed by a complete date, as here, are to the weekly journal which was the chief Douglas organ from August 1934 until September 1938. See below, Chap. VII, sect. 2, pp. 180–1.

[22]C. H. Douglas, *The Monopoly of Credit* (London, 1931), pp. 10–11.

[23]Douglas, *Credit-Power and Democracy*, p. 86.

Because of this, it was asserted, one unit of human labour could now on the average produce at least forty times as much as at the beginning of the nineteenth century.[24] Since this estimate was not accompanied by an estimate of the actual increase in products per unit of labour since 1800, no estimate of the still unrealized potential could be deduced from it. However, some numerical estimates of the potential increase in production and lightening of human labour were presented; none of them were or could be very precise, though sometimes a parade of figures of recent increases in productivity per man-hour in various lines of production was given to suggest how much more could still be achieved.[25] On the basis of a statement of an American industrial engineer it was estimated that the present product could be produced by one-fifteenth of the present amount of labour, that is, half an hour's work a day of the present labour force;[26] in another place the estimate was a few minutes' work per day to produce all subsistence requirements and "something over three hours' work per head per day" to provide "all the factors of modern life."[27] The most striking assertion was that "we can produce, at this moment, goods and services at a rate very considerably greater than the possible rate of consumption of the world, and this production and delivery of goods and services can, under favourable circumstances, be achieved by the employment of certainly not more than 25 per cent of the available labour, working let us say seven hours a day."[28] The only basis offered for this assertion was the statement that "the amount of mechanical energy available for productive purposes is only a small fraction of what it could be."[29]

There is some variety as well as imprecision in the estimates of the potential increase of productivity or leisure; they range as high as, in the last statement quoted, infinity. But the claims, though not proven, were not easily disproven. There was at least a strong presumption that technology could do much more than was now being done, and if the claims seemed high they could be heavily discounted and still establish an expectation that a substantial increase in wealth and leisure was readily available.

[24]Douglas, *The Monopoly of Credit*, p. 26.
[25]E.g. *The Monopoly of Credit*, pp. 26–7; evidence of Major Douglas to the Macmillan Committee on Finance and Industry (1930) reprinted as appendix to *The Monopoly of Credit*, p. 95.
[26]Douglas, *Credit-Power and Democracy*, p. 17.
[27]Douglas, *Economic Democracy* (1921), pp. 104–5. Cf. p. 87.
[28]Douglas, *Social Credit* (1924), pp. 18–19.
[29]*Ibid.*, p. 19.

The negative evidence for the existence of potential plenty was a catalogue of the waste and sabotage pervading the present economic system.[30] There was, first, the colossal waste of effort involved in the process of "making work" by rules designed to ensure the maximum quantity and minimum efficiency of human effort. Of this the best-known examples were the trade union make-work practices. Secondly, there was the creation of artificial demand by advertisement, which diverted production from filling real wants and so wasted effort in the production of unnecessary new models and of tawdry and unwholesome articles. Finally there were great ranges of useless work: the stupendous effort involved in the intricacies of finance and book-keeping which are "useless in increasing the amenities of life," the whole of the labour spent in the production of armaments, the work of the bureaucracy elaborating safeguards for a radically defective social system, and the cumulative export of the product of labour.

Merely to list these categories of waste, most of which appealed directly to common observation or experience, was to cut through much of the apologetics of the existing system and to reinforce the expectations set up by the estimates of the technological potential. What was even more attractive was the claim, embodied in the theory of "the cultural heritage," that every member of the community was the rightful beneficiary of this vast and obtainable increase in goods and leisure.

The cultural, or technological, heritage was of course that increment in goods and leisure made possible by the discovery of new sources of solar energy and techniques for utilizing them. The essential point was that the increment, from the point of view of the whole society, was an unearned increment. Society did not have to earn it by the expenditure of any human energy. The increment did not have to be paid for in human labour; fundamentally it cost nothing. It was due to the inventive genius and labour of "countless numbers of men and women, many of whose names are forgotten and the majority of whom are dead."[31] The industrial machine was a "cultural legacy"[32] or "common heritage."[33] Viewed in another way, the increment was an "increment of association," since it was due not only to technology but also to the social division of labour possible only when production

[30]Douglas, *Economic Democracy* (1921), pp. 76–9; *Social Credit* (1924), pp. 52–3. For a more penetrating catalogue, cf. Fourier, *Théorie de l'unité universelle*; *Œuvres complètes* (Paris, 1841), tome IV, pp. 171–9.

[31]Douglas, *Social Credit* (1924), p. 57.   [32]*Ibid.*

[33]Douglas, *Credit-Power and Democracy*, p. 18.

is carried on by the whole community working together.[34] Viewed in either way, the increment was rightfully the property of all members of the community, not by virtue of their present contribution to production but simply by virtue of their membership in the community: the "rightful beneficiaries of the modern productive system" are "the individuals composing the community, as such."[35]

Douglas presented this claim on behalf of the community both as a simple matter of equity and as a dictate of natural law. The right of the community to the increment is "founded in the nature of things because, if it is denied, the [industrial] machine begins to develop abnormal friction, with a consequent loss to every constituent member of society."[36] As a matter of equity the whole of the present capital belonged to the community, since it was all the result of the increment of association and technology in the past. Douglas even went so far as to say that "natural resources are common property, and the means for their exploitation should also be common property." "It may be said . . . that [this] involves a confiscation of plant, which is clearly an injustice to the present owners. But is it? A reference to the accounting process already described will make it clear that the community has already bought and paid for many times over the whole of the plant used for manufacturing processes. . . . If the community can use the plant it is clearly entitled to it. . . ."[37]

But fortunately, existing ownership rights in plant need not be disturbed: "under proper conditions there is no reason why every reasonable requirement of its present owners should not be met under the changed conditions."[38] Existing plant could be left in the hands of its present owners because the future technological increment, which was to be realized by the introduction of social credit, would be of far greater magnitude than the whole of the increment up to the present time, and would provide all the social credit dividends that could be desired. The future, not the past, increment was to be the source of the new abundance.

It was this concept of a vast unrealized and costless social increment that was summed up in the phrase *social credit*. Credit is belief. Social credit is belief in the capacity of the community to deliver the goods and services. In any society which uses money as a means of social distribution of the whole product, social credit, so defined, is ineffective unless financial credit keeps pace with it; the full social

---

[34]Douglas, *These Present Discontents*, p. 13.
[35]Douglas, *Social Credit* (1924), p. 57.
[36]Douglas, *Credit-Power and Democracy*, p. 18.
[37]Douglas, *Economic Democracy* (1921), pp. 112, 114.   [38]*Ibid.*, p. 114.

product cannot be realized unless financial credit corresponds in amount to the real social credit, that is, the full productive capacity of the community. It was Douglas's conviction that it was only a chronic deficiency of financial credit that was preventing the full productive capacity being attained. The existing system of financing, and thus controlling, production was, he held, such that the necessary amount of credit could never be issued. The Douglas answer of course was to issue new social credit dividends; the dividends would be unearned income for individuals, and would be at once a means of realizing the potential increment by removing the one restriction, the deficiency of financial credit, and a means of distributing the increment among the individual members of the community.

The case for these proposals was argued at two levels. At the technical level there was the theory of money, credit, and prices, devoted to demonstrating that the present system of financing and pricing production necessarily created a chronic deficiency of purchasing power, such that even the production of which the existing plant and technique were capable, let alone the presumed vastly greater technological potential production, could never be bought and therefore could not be produced.

At a broader level of generalization was what might be called the case against the financiers. It was different in two respects from the technical case. First, it emphasized not the impersonal mechanism of the pricing system but the direct responsibility of the financiers for the limitation of production. Secondly, it emphasized not the unused existing productive capacity but the frustration of the potential productive capacity, the presumed magnitude of which was much greater. This case could if necessary be argued without reliance on the technical case, for it was not necessary to prove that the system blocked the full use of existing capacity in order to maintain that it blocked the full realization of potential capacity.

We shall examine the social credit case at both these levels.

§ 4. The A plus B Theorem

The whole of Douglas's analysis of money, credit, and prices need not be examined here.[39] But the much-discussed A plus B theorem, which was the core of that analysis, does require some attention. For

[39]The Douglas economic theory and proposals have been analysed in considerable detail by several writers, e.g., H. T. N. Gaitskell, "Four Monetary Heretics," in G. D. H. Cole, ed., *What Everybody Wants to Know about Money* (London, 1936), chap. 8; W. R. Hiskett, *Social Credits or Socialism* (London, 1935); W. R. Hiskett and J. A. Franklin, *Searchlight on Social Credit* (London, 1939); John Lewis, *Douglas Fallacies* (London, 1935).

its characteristic quality—the false clarity which made it impossible either to understand it or refute it in simple terms—had much to do with the reception of social credit in Alberta and with the nature of the political movement built on it there.

The theory got off to a good start with the assertion that the purchasing power available to buy the product of industry consists of the money incomes distributed in the course of production. If the total money incomes were the same amount as the total prices, everything that could be produced could be bought. But, it was argued, the total money incomes must, under the present system, always be less than the total prices, for while prices are fixed so as to cover all costs of production, only a part of the costs appear as income paid out to persons. Therefore the purchasing power distributed in the course of production can never buy, at their prices, all the goods produced.

The crucial proposition is that a part of the costs does not correspond to any income paid out to persons and available as purchasing power. Douglas set this forth in the A plus B theorem. The payments made by a factory or other productive unit in the course of producing goods may be divided into (A) "all payments made to individuals (wages, salaries and dividends)" and (B) "all payments made to other organizations (raw materials, bank charges, and other external costs)." Of these, only the A payments create purchasing power available to buy the product. "The rate of flow of purchasing-power to individuals is represented by A, but since all payments go into prices, the rate of flow of prices cannot be less than A plus B." But "A will not purchase A plus B." Hence, in order to make it possible for all the product to be purchased, "a proportion of the product at least equivalent to B must be distributed by a form of purchasing-power which is not comprised in the descriptions grouped under A."[40] This can be done by the creation of new money, distributed as social credit dividends to consumers or as subsidies to producers to enable them to price the product below cost.

Here is a theorem, in apparently simple and compelling algebraic terms, which seems to show with complete logic that there is never enough money distributed in the course of producing things to enable them all to be bought. The fallacies of the theorem would have been readily apparent had it not been presented with such lack of definition and such variety of interpretation. Douglas was able to maintain it for some years by a nimble imprecision; the terms used could

[40]Douglas, *Credit-Power and Democracy*, pp. 21-2.

mean so many things that when the fallacy of the theorem on one interpretation of the terms was demonstrated, recourse could be had to another interpretation equally impressive. But on no interpretation could the theorem be sustained.

The politically significant point about the theorem is that it was always so loosely stated that it needed extensive definition before it could be examined, understood, or refuted. To see through it was one thing, but to explain to a believer what was wrong with it required an elaborate and tedious preliminary clarification which the believer was apt (not without justification from his experience) to dismiss as an attempt to involve and mislead him.

There is no other way to demonstrate this quality of the A plus B theorem than to indicate the kind of analysis that is required to show its fallacies. The reader who does not need this demonstration may safely omit the following five paragraphs.

The theorem begins by considering the product of one factory or firm, and appears to say that, to enable the product to be purchased, the wages, salaries, and dividends (A) paid out by that firm should be, and never can be, equal to the collective price (A plus B) of the firm's product. Granting that the collective price of the firm's product is equal to the A plus the B payments of that firm, as Douglas assumes, it is plain on his definitions that the A cannot be equal to A plus B. But since all firms must be considered together it is non-sensical to say that for the whole product of this firm to be bought, this A should be equal to this A plus B. Some other meaning, then, must be attributed to the theorem. It can be thought to mean that the wages, salaries, and dividends paid out by all firms in a given period of time, say a year (the "rate of flow of purchasing-power") must, for the whole product of all firms to be bought, be equal to, but never can be equal to, the collective price of the whole product during that year. Now on one definition of collective price of the whole product Douglas could show that the A payments could not be equal to the collective price, and on a different definition of collective price of the whole product he could show that the A payments must, for the whole product to be bought, be equal to the collective price. But on no single definition of collective price could he demonstrate both these propositions.

Thus, if the collective price of the whole product is defined as the sum of the prices of all goods (both consumers' goods, which are to be taken off the market by individual final consumers, and producers' goods, e.g., plant, machinery, raw materials, semi-manufactured goods) produced in the year, the A payments will not be equal to but will be only a small fraction of this collective price. For this collective price is got by adding together all the payments made by all the firms to each other and all the payments made by all the firms to individuals. But the A payments need not equal the collective price for equilibrium, because the final consumer does not need to purchase all the producers' goods; what is required for equilibrium, is that the A payments of all firms should equal the sum of the prices of the consumers' goods, that is, that the payments to individuals, who are assumed to be the final consumers, should equal the sum of the prices of consumers' goods.

If on the other hand the collective price of the whole product is defined as the sum of the prices of the consumers' goods produced in that year, then equilibrium does indeed require that the payments made to individuals during the year should equal the collective price, provided that we leave aside the complication of changes in saving and investment. But what is required is that A payments made to individuals this year by *all* firms, that is, the wages, salaries, and dividends paid to individuals by the firms making producers' goods as well as those making consumers' goods, should equal the collective price of the year's consumers' goods only. Major Douglas gave no reason why these sums could not be equal.

Yet on his definitions and at his level of abstraction (disregarding changes in savings and investment, and all other factors affecting output) the two are automatically equal. For on his definition the collective price of the consumers' goods coming on the market this year equals the A plus B payments of the consumers' goods firms this year. And, although he would never admit it, on his definitions and assumptions the B payments of consumers' goods firms this year equal the A payments of producers' goods firms this year. He did admit[41] that the B payments of consumers' goods firms in one period equalled the A payments of producers' goods firms in the previous period, but he held that this was irrelevant because those A payments would have been spent for consumers' goods in the earlier period and would not be available to buy consumers' goods in this period. In spite of his talk about rates of flow, he did not see, or would not recognize, that production of both kinds of goods is a continuous process, that A payments were being made this year by producers' goods firms and that these were available to purchase this year's consumers' goods. If, as Douglas assumed, the economy is neither

[41]*Ibid.*, pp. 24–5.

expanding nor contracting for some other reasons, the A payment of producers' goods firms will be the same amount this year as last year. So on his definitions and assumptions the A payments of producers' goods firms this year must equal the A payments of these firms last year, which were admitted to equal the B payments of consumers' goods firms this year. Thus the A plus B payments of consumers' goods firms this year equal the A payments of consumers' goods firms this year plus the A payments of producers' goods firms this year; in other words, the collective price of this year's consumers' goods equals the sum of this year's A payments by all firms.

This kind of demonstration of the fallacies of the theorem is as unreal as the theorem itself; what it shows is not that the economy is always in equilibrium but that Douglas's assumptions were inadequate and his conclusions unproven. However it is interpreted, the A plus B theorem does not demonstrate a necessary chronic shortage of purchasing power. Hence the main case for the continual injection of new money by way of social credit dividends or subsidies to producers appears to collapse.

We need not follow the Douglas analysis through all its additional twists and turns. The reader of the last few pages will appreciate the fascination and the exasperation which the A plus B theorem provoked. Monetary analysis depends on careful distinctions, which Douglas and his adherents did not make and in controversy showed themselves incapable of making; yet when the distinctions are not made and their necessity is not seen, the theorem has all the appearance of an irrefutable demonstration. The use of symbols and of such undefined concepts as a "rate of flow of prices" may be held responsible both for the confusion and for the appearance of certainty. There is nothing like algebra for inducing a conviction of absolute truth, unless it is the differential calculus, in which some of Douglas's demonstrations were also presented.

The A plus B theorem, once lodged in the mind, was very difficult to dislodge. It had an almost hypnotic quality for those who were disposed to believe it and were not accustomed to close abstract reasoning. And at the time the theory was most widely accepted there were many disposed to believe it, for evidence of glut, unemployment, and unused resources was everywhere. Douglas frequently referred to such evidence; and although it was of course not evidence of the validity of his theorem, readers who were ready to blame shortage of purchasing power for the seemingly endless troubles of the depression easily overlooked this. Again, it was easy to overlook that the theorem proved too much; its logical conclusion was that industry must continually contract and indeed must have been brought to a standstill before now. The only offsetting factors alleged by Douglas involved premises as erroneous as the logic of the original theorem was fallacious: namely that the whole system was becoming increasingly in debt to some persons or institutions outside the system.

It need not be suggested that all those who found merit in the Douglas theory were incapable of understanding a logical analysis of it. But they were not apt to be impressed by even the most able criticism, for the critics were suspect. The orthodox economists were not in a strong position, for they had no very satisfactory explanation of the failure of the economy, and they appeared at least to believe that production automatically provided just the requisite amount of purchasing power. In any case they seemed to accept the moral basis of society, the hypocrisy of which Douglas had quite persuasively demonstrated in his general social critique. The labour and socialist economists were in an equally unfortunate position as critics, being already committed to another, and competing, set of proposals.

The flood of critical analysis had, however, a considerable cumulative effect. Although Douglas never repudiated the A plus B theorem, and continued to make occasional references to it, he pretty well let it go by default. He could afford to do so because a case for social credit could be made without reliance on the A plus B theorem.

§ 5. The Broader Case for Social Credit

The broader case developed naturally from the doctrine of the technological heritage and from the postulate that the nature of capitalist enterprise had been transformed in the last century by the growth of finance to the point where the financiers dominated the whole productive system and manipulated it for the sole purpose of increasing their own power. An extremely persuasive case could be made in this way. The technological potential was far from being realized, though the people had a right to it. Enough evidence of the control of industry by finance was available to make the charge of financial domination impressive, even if one did not agree with that part of the technical theory of credit which purported to prove that the present pricing system necessarily put the whole economy increasingly in the debt of the financiers. Given that the financiers were in control, it was an easy step to conclude that it was the financiers who were preventing the realization of the technological potential, by a permanent policy of restricting credit, and that the issuance of social credit, up to the limit of the utmost potential productivity, could bring plenty and leisure for all without disturbing any except the financiers' interests.

This case had many advantages. In the first place it avoided the vexing intricacies of the technical analysis of money, credit, and prices. It was only necessary to assert that there was an incalculable but vast potential productivity the realization of which was being prevented by finance, without demonstrating by the A plus B theorem that the mechanism of pricing and credit prevented the full use of present as well as potential capacity. Thus most of the orthodox economic criticism, which was criticism of the technical analysis, could be brushed aside. Better still, emphasis on the technological potential enabled the social crediter to meet the one orthodox economic criticism which seemed most damaging.

The criticism, pressed by those who had discovered the fallacy of the A plus B theorem, that the issuance of social credit would be wildly inflationary, could be outflanked without using the technical analysis. Douglas had only to point out that the limiting points to the creation of new credit without inflation are either the disappearance of unused capacity to produce or the satiation of all human wants, and that both these were indefinitely remote.[42] There was no question that the satiation of all wants was a remote limiting point. The disappearance of unused capacity was in Douglas's terms equally remote, for unused capacity here was not the actual unused plant of a period of depression but the potential unused capacity existing in normal times, that is, the whole difference between present capacity and the presumed infinitely greater technologically possible capacity. This is a convincing enough answer to the charge that social credit would be inflationary, if one neglects, as Douglas did, all the other forces which could continue to restrict production.

That the emphasis on potential productivity enabled Douglas and his adherents to avoid or apparently to meet the criticisms of the technical analysis was only one of the advantages of the broad case for social credit. Another, and perhaps more important, was the conclusion that the introduction of social credit, while destroying the financiers, would not interfere with the right of private ownership

[42]Canada, House of Commons, Select Standing Committee on Banking and Commerce, *Proceedings* (1923), evidence of Major Douglas, pp. 477–8. Cf. Major Douglas's evidence to the (British) Macmillan Committee on Finance and Industry (1930), quoted in Hiskett, *Social Credits or Socialism*, pp. 72–3.

of capital or private management of industry or agriculture. The continued exercise of these rights was in Douglas's view desirable in itself. He had a truly conservative attitude towards private property. "Mr. Chesterton and his Distributists, in common with the Catholic Church, were fundamentally right in recognizing stable property tenure as essential to liberty. The terms of tenure are probably far from satisfactory, either now or in the past, but they are most certainly not being improved by being transferred [through nationalization] to the mercy of international usurers, whose policies are rooted in spurious values."[43] Again, "it seems to me beyond question, that unassailable right to genuinely *private* property, and any genuine democracy, are inseparable. I should define private property as anything, no matter what its composition or nature, which, being in the possession of the individual, is necessary to enable him to carry on his normal life without interference. . . ."[44] The contexts indicate that Douglas assumed that shareholders' property was included in the private property necessary for liberty and democracy.

Equally desirable with the right to private ownership of capital was the private management of industry and agriculture, on grounds of administrative efficiency. Private responsibility for results was from his engineer's point of view more efficient than management by committees or by delegated public authority. For these reasons Douglas was completely opposed to any form of socialism, collectivism, or nationalization of industry.

Not only were private ownership and management of industry considered desirable in themselves; what was more important, their maintenance was held to be perfectly compatible with the distribution of a vast unearned increment to all members of the community through the introduction of social credit. Social credit would destroy the financiers' over-all control of industry but need not affect the rights of ownership and management, for these rights had already become separated from financial control. The capitalist entrepreneur, intent on making profits on his capital, was an extinct species. Profit was no longer of any importance. "This process [making profits] probably contributed largely to the rapid accumulation of wealth in the hands of the *entrepreneur* at the beginning of the nineteenth century . . . but the profit-making system is certainly not to any

[43]*The Fig Tree* (a Douglas quarterly, issued from June 1936, to March 1939), June 1938.

[44]C. H. Douglas, "Whose Service is Perfect Freedom," *The Social Crediter*, Nov. 4, 1939. *The Social Crediter*, official organ of the Social Credit Secretariat, has been published in Liverpool weekly since September 17, 1938. See note 21 above. It has no connection with *The Canadian Social Crediter*.

great extent responsible for the present situation, since profits have ceased to form an outstanding feature of business."[45] The capitalist entrepreneur's search for profit no longer drove or regulated the economic system; the entrepreneur had been reduced to an administrator and a recipient of dividends; control of the economy was now in the hands of the financiers, whose incentive was not profit but power through the imposition of scarcity and the reduction of the mass to perpetual labour.

Governments, under the domination of the financiers, had rendered the private ownership of capital meaningless. That the implements of production are at present the private property of individuals "is a pure fiction, because every country reserves to itself the right to make all sorts of rules, not only as to the methods by which they shall be used, but the extent to which they will be taxed and so forth. What is really left to the individual under our present system, is the power of administration within this framework which is set down by the laws of the country."[46]

The inability of Major Douglas to see the essential nature of capitalist enterprise is nowhere more strikingly shown than in the following statement, in which his method of disposing of a problem by redefining the terms is also apparent. "The system under which the whole of the world, not excluding Russia, carries on the production and distribution of goods and services is commonly called the Capitalistic system, which system, contrary to general opinion, has nothing, directly, to do with the relations of employers and employed, which are administrative relations. The fundamental premises of the Capitalistic system are, first, that all costs (purchasing power distributed to individuals during the productive process) should be added together, and recovered from the public, the consumer, in prices; and second, that over and above that the price of an article is what it will fetch."[47] " 'Capitalism' is not a system of administration at all; it is a system of fixing prices in relation to costs."[48] The convenience of asserting that capitalism has nothing directly to do with the relations of employers and employed is evident; it enabled Douglas to propose a reform of capitalism without an alteration in the relation of labour and capital. To do this, of course, it was necessary to overlook the fact that wages are prices; recognition of this would have

[45]Douglas, The Monopoly of Credit, pp. 24–5.
[46]The Douglas System of Social Credit: Evidence Taken by the Agricultural Committee of the Alberta Legislature (Edmonton, 1934), evidence of Major Douglas, p. 85; cf. p. 104.
[47]Douglas, The Control and Distribution of Production, p. 14.
[48]Ibid., p. 77.

brought the relation of employers and employed squarely back into the centre of his own definition of capitalism.

This oversight was not incidental. The possibility of implementing social credit was based on the possibility of separating the internal administration of industries, including apparently the determination of wages, from the fixing of prices. The former was to be left in the hands of private enterprise, the latter was to be placed in the hands of the community.[49] This arrangement was expected to satisfy both the present owners of capital and the community, for the owners were assumed to have lost already all the real attributes of ownership, either to finance or to governments subservient to finance, and to have been left with only *rentier* rights and administrative rights. Neither of these would be adversely affected by the introduction of social credit. Indeed the administrative rights would be strengthened, for the directors and managers would have a freer hand to increase the efficiency of the firm and would no longer be troubled by trade unions. With the release of industry from financiers' control, "and the abolition of the distinction between Capital and Labour as regards Financial Credit, the present exclusively proletarian Trade Union ceases to be necessary . . . the former Trade Union, based on the antagonism of Labour and Capital, and organized, not in the interests of Production, but as a weapon of defence and offence against the Capitalist class as such, disappears. . . ."[50]

The far-reaching importance of the Douglas thesis that financial control had become divorced from beneficial ownership of industry and actual management of production is apparent. It enabled him to uphold private ownership and enterprise while denouncing those attributes of capitalism which were widely detested already—the compulsion to continuous labour, the creation of artificial scarcity and artificial demand, the concentration of economic power. All these were perversions of private ownership and enterprise by finance. The financiers became the scapegoat. Social credit, by removing control from the financiers to the community, would provide new plenty for all without touching existing private ownership. Social credit was the alternative to socialism.

No doctrine could have been better designed to appeal to the middle class, whether independent producers, small shareholders, or managers and professional people; even wage-earners were offered a vision of shorter hours and an unearned income. The magnitude

49Douglas, *Credit-Power and Democracy*, pp. 149, 175–6.
50*Ibid.*, pp. 168–9.

of the promised unearned social increment was such as to cover up all difficulties.

It was never explained, for instance, how the financiers' control was to be taken from them without affecting their property rights, or how a line was to be drawn between legitimate ownership rights and financiers' ownership rights, although in one of his early books Douglas suggested that a beginning might be made by confiscating all individual war bond holdings in excess of £1,000.[51] So convinced was Douglas that the financiers' power depended on their ability to manipulate other people's property, rather than on their ownership of legal titles to property, that he saw no problem. Presumably once their power over others' property was destroyed by the introduction of social credit, they could safely be left with any remaining rights they might have as owners. The new wealth which was to grow up beside the old would overshadow it and render it insignificant.

Again, it was never explained how the maintenance of the existing property rights of shareholders was compatible with the widespread distribution of unearned income to the wage-earners and with the widespread withdrawal of labour which was intended to follow. If people were to work less and less, how was the rate of profit on invested capital to be maintained? It is doubtful if Douglas saw any problem here for he had only a confused notion of the source of profits and of exchange values. He saw, at times, that both value and profit were based on scarcity and on human effort, but he did not see that to diminish scarcity and diminish the expenditure of human effort, as social credit was to do, would diminish exchange values and profits.

Reasoning from the single firm or industry, where profit can be increased by replacing labour with machinery, he failed to understand that in the economy as a whole technological improvement and capital increment contribute to profit by increasing the productivity of employed labour, not by dispensing with labour. He did not, therefore, see that the maintenance of the rate of profit at any stage of technological development presupposes the employment of the whole normal working force at the normal length of the working day and at the level of productivity per unit of labour that has been achieved by the existing level of technology and existing accumulation of real capital.

His failure to grasp this is evident throughout Douglas's economic writings. It comes out clearly in his revision of the orthodox economic

[51]Douglas, *Economic Democracy* (1921), p. 126.

theory. The "early Victorian political economists" ascribed all values to land, labour, and capital. Douglas allowed that this might have been accurate before the industrial revolution, but "there is now a fourth factor in wealth production, the multiplying power of which far exceeds that of the other three," namely, the technological heritage or "progress of the industrial arts."[52] It was on the existence of this fourth factor that Douglas based his claim that the whole community has a right to the unearned technological increment. But this is to add as a fourth factor of production something which, under capitalist enterprise, is included within the other three. The present value of land, labour, and capital is due to the productivity conferred on them by the present utilization of the technological heritage. The right of ownership of land and capital has its present value because their employment yields the present rate of profit; and it would not yield that profit if it did not include the right to the benefit of the techno-logical heritage.

Moreover, the maintenance of a rate of profit sufficient to keep capitalist enterprise functioning has required, and may be assumed to require in the future, continual technological improvement; hence if existing ownership rights in capital are to maintain their value in the future they must include, as it were, a mortgage on the social heritage which is still to be realized. It is not simply that under the capitalist property system the technological heritage is all privately owned already; but that present ownership rights, to maintain their value, must absorb the future technological increment at a rate at least as great as at present. But this problem was no problem, and was not even seen as a problem, if one assumed with Douglas that the potential technological increment was of infinite magnitude.

Enough has been said to show how the belief in an incalculable, even an infinite, potential technological increment of production enabled the social crediter to overlook or dismiss all the difficulties inherent in social credit. Equally essential to the social credit case, as we have seen, was the belief that capitalist enterprise had already been reduced to a fiction by the rise to power of the financiers. The concept of a group of financiers standing outside the productive community at once provided an enemy and disposed of the socialist case, for capital and labour were given a common interest against finance.

Belief in the cultural heritage and in the role of the financiers became the two pillars of the social credit faith. So strong were they that the monetary theory was scarcely needed, and as its fallacies

[52]Douglas, *Social Credit* (1924), p. 56.

were exposed it could be pushed into the background. There, its very intricacy became an asset, for the mere knowledge of its existence gave the adherents of social credit a sustaining feeling that all the mysteries of economics had been probed, even if they could not fully understand them.

This curious relation between the technical analysis and the broader case facilitated the peculiar relation between leader and followers which came to characterize the social credit movement both in England and later in Alberta. The A plus B theorem and the rest of the technical analysis of money and credit played a large part in the recruitment of the original English movement. But as the movement expanded, the monetary theory became a matter of widespread public debate and came under increasingly severe critical fire. Douglas, convinced that he had got at the fundamental truth, could not admit the fallacies in the technical theory. Nor could he repair them. He was therefore compelled after a time to take the position that the technical theory was not a matter for discussion.[53] Soon the whole social credit movement was committed to this position. The leader and his small group of experts became the acknowledged and sole custodians of the mysteries; the function of the followers was to have faith in the cultural heritage, in the power of the people to overthrow the financiers, and in the wisdom and expert ability of their own leaders.

We have finally to notice that the whole social credit case, and especially its emphasis on the technological heritage and the role of the financiers, had the effect of converting the economic problem into a political problem. To the convinced social crediter there were no economic problems left: the Douglas theory provided solutions for them all, and the necessary technical devices could easily be worked out by the experts. The only problem was the political problem, how to get the political power without which social credit could not be introduced. As the Douglas following increased in size this problem came to occupy most of Douglas's attention. The solution he pronounced in 1934 gave a new turn to the movement and intensified the distinction between leader and followers which was implicit in the social credit theory.

Some description of the way the English movement developed, and of its political theory and practice, will be useful in understanding the development of the political movement in Alberta.

[53]*Social Credit*, Dec. 6, 1935; quoted in Hiskett and Franklin, *Searchlight on Social Credit*, pp. 6–7.

CHAPTER FIVE

English Social Credit: The Political Theory and Practice to 1935

-»»«««-

§ 1. The Non-Political Character of the Early Douglas Movement

The English social credit movement was conceived in disappointment. When Douglas first propounded his ideas he had no intention of founding a movement, political or otherwise. He believed his analysis of the flaw in the accounting and pricing system to be so readily understandable by trained minds, and his proposals to be so plainly beneficial to society, that it was only necessary to make them known to the right people in the Treasury and the City. No organized movement or political action would be needed; the proposals could be implemented at a technical level.

For the first eighteen months or two years, Douglas recollected many years later, "I had the idea that I had got hold of some specific technical information and I had only to get it accepted: I had the idea that I was like a clever little boy and that I had only to run to father and he would be very pleased about it."[1] One of the prominent early social crediters has recorded that the criticism of finance in Douglas's *Economic Democracy* (1920) was received with "incredulity, obloquy, and finally silence on the part of those from whom the appropriate action was at first confidently expected," namely "the economists, the bankers, and the Treasury experts."[2]

There was nothing for it then but to attempt a persistent propaganda campaign and seek a body of public supporters. The development of a social credit movement was thus from the outset a somewhat distasteful contrivance. The movement was never as real or important to Douglas as his own ideas; it was a necessary evil, a fallible in-

---

[1]Talk by Douglas to some social credit associates, December 1938, reported in *The Social Crediter*, Jan. 14, 1939.

[2]W. L. Bardsley, "The Social Credit Movement 1918-1939," *ibid.*, Dec. 23, 1939.

strument for the propagation of his word. The very need to seek
public support was a perennial reminder of the failure of his initial
concept of social credit as an engineering solution to an engineering
problem. Douglas did not trouble to conceal his disdain for the
intelligence of the ordinary man, and was after a time increasingly
unable to conceal his disdain for his own followers. The character of
the English social credit movement throughout its life has reflected
this origin.

Three stages in the development of Douglas social credit in England
may be discerned. In the initial period no public movement was
contemplated; the appeal was to those influential circles which, it
was thought, could have Douglas's ideas put into effect. In the
second period, from about 1920 to 1934, efforts were made to build
up an extensive public opinion among educated readers, through
weekly journals, books, and discussion groups. The following which
was thus built up was not, however, organized as a political unit;
until 1934 the Douglas movement was a purely propagandist affair,
its energies being devoted to forming a pervasive public opinion
without yet any specific organization for political pressure. In 1934
a political strategy was worked out, designed to turn social credit
opinion into an effective political pressure group. At no time did
Douglas favour creating an electoral organization which would
nominate social credit candidates in the British elections.

In the first section of this chapter we discuss the development of
the Douglas movement to 1934, and in section 2 the rudimentary
political theory of Douglas's writings during the same time, leaving
to section 4 the theory and practice of political action inaugurated in
1934.

Douglas's critique of the economic system made its first appearance in 1917 in articles in the *Organiser,* then edited by Holbrook
Jackson,[3] and reached a more influential though still limited circle
of readers when Austin Harrison published several articles by Douglas
in the *English Review* between December 1918 and October 1919.[4]
In the meantime Douglas had been introduced by Jackson to A. R.
Orage, the editor of the *New Age,* a lively intellectual weekly which
had for some years been the unofficial organ of the guild socialists.
Orage was a brilliant journalist and an effective social critic, moved

[3]Philip Mairet, A. R. *Orage, a Memoir* (London, 1936), p. 74.
[4]"The Delusion of Super-Production," December 1918; "The Pyramid of
Power," January and February 1919; "What is Capitalism?", August 1919;
"Exchange and Exports," October 1919.

by an antipathy to capitalist society that had much in common with Douglas's. Orage's critique of the capitalist economy and society anticipated Douglas's to a remarkable extent, and was considerably more penetrating.[5] By 1919 Orage had become troubled by serious doubts about the adequacy of the National Guilds scheme, particularly in relation "to the existing, or any prospective, scheme of money."[6] He assimilated the Douglas analysis of finance and in 1919 became completely converted to the Douglas theory.

Writing some years afterward, Orage recorded the extent of his conversion: "Douglas to the best of my consideration has got to the very bottom of economics. There are literally no more insoluble or even doubtful problems in the whole range of economics; and this, needless to say, includes the daughter 'science' of politics."[7] Orage brought over with him "part of the Guild Socialist entourage who became the nucleus of the Social Credit movement,"[8] and devoted his energies to seeking recognition for the Douglas economic policy in responsible quarters and to publicizing social credit ideas. The columns of the *New Age* were opened to Douglas at the beginning of 1919[9] and the whole paper was soon committed to social credit. Orage was to some extent a collaborator in the further formulation of the social credit theory.[10] Social credit study and propaganda groups were formed; by the end of 1920 there were about thirty groups in various cities and towns.[11] A house organ entitled *Public Welfare* was started in 1920, and in October 1921 the first conference of social

[5]A. R. Orage, *An Alphabet of Economics* (London, 1917). The sections on Credit, Interest, and Money contain striking anticipations of the social credit technical analysis. Elsewhere, for example, on Division of Labour, and the Right to Work, the similarity of the two critiques is evident.

[6]A. R. Orage, "An Editor's Progress," *The Commonweal* (New York), Feb. 17, 1926.

[7]*Ibid.*, Feb. 24, 1926.

[8]Bardsley, "The Social Credit Movement 1918-1939."

[9]Douglas wrote the editorial "Notes of the Week" in the issue of Feb. 6 and Feb. 27, 1919, and articles by him appeared in the issues of Jan. 2, 1919 ("A Mechanical View of Economics," reprinted as chap. 4 of his *The Control and Distribution of Production*, London, 1922), and May 1, 1919 ("The Control of Production," reprinted as chap. 3 of the same book). Douglas's first book, *Economic Democracy* (1920) first appeared serially in *The New Age*, June 5–Aug. 7, 1919.

[10]Orage refers to Major Douglas's first book, *Economic Democracy*, as "a volume in which I more or less collaborated with Douglas himself" (*Commonweal*, Feb. 17, 1926). Cf. Douglas, *Credit-Power and Democracy, with a Draft Scheme for the Mining Industry*, with a commentary on the included scheme by A. R. Orage (London, 1920). Cf. Mairet, *A. R. Orage, a Memoir*, pp. 75–6.

[11]Bardsley, "The Social Credit Movement 1918–1939." Thirty-two local groups are listed in *Public Welfare*, December 1921.

crediters was held, devoted to discussion of the economics of social credit.[12] In 1921 and 1922 the social credit doctrine attracted considerable attention in the British press and earned the opposition of socialist writers.[13] Within the ranks of organized labour it made some headway in the early years. After the publication of the Douglas-Orage "Draft Scheme for the Mining Industry," the Scottish Labour Advisory Committee recommended that the Miners' Federation of Great Britain "be asked to investigate Major Douglas's scheme for introducing social credit reform via the mining industry."[14] The Labour party executive thought the matter sufficiently important to appoint, in 1921, a committee of high-ranking members[15] to examine and report on social credit. The report of this committee, accepted by the Labour party executive, and published in July 1922,[16] was adverse. Its conclusion was that the social credit scheme was "theoretically unsound and unworkable in practice" and that it was "out of harmony with the trend of Labour thought, and indeed fundamentally opposed to the principles for which the Labour Party stands."[17] This effectively ended the hopes which some social crediters had had that they would get extensive support in labour circles.

Whether because of this rejection by the Labour party, or because, as Douglas suggested, social credit ideas were getting such wide publicity that "the interests threatened by them became considerably alarmed and took . . . effective steps to curtail their publicity,"[18] public discussion of social credit declined, not to revive until the impact of the depression in the early 1930's. Orage threw up the campaign and the editorship of the New Age in September 1922 and abruptly retired from journalism. He explained subsequently that he had become convinced that there was no hope of getting Major Douglas's ideas accepted. "The Douglas positive proposals were as impeccable as his analysis, only they could not be carried

[12]An account of the discussion at the conference appears in Public Welfare, December 1921.

[13]Articles critical of the Douglas economic analysis and policy appeared in The New Statesman by Pethwick Lawrence, in The Socialist Review by J. A. Hobson, and in The Communist by Maurice Dobb.

[14] C. H. Douglas, These Present Discontents and the Labour Party and Social Credit (London, 1922), p. 20.

[15]C. D. Burns, F. C. Clegg, G. D. H. Cole, H. Dalton, A. Greenwood, J. A. Hobson, F. Hodges, C. M. Lloyd, Sir Leo C. Money, R. H. Tawney, S. Webb.

[16]The Labour Party, Labour and Social Credit, a Report on the Proposals of Major Douglas & the "New Age" (London, 1922).

[17]Ibid., p. 11.

[18]C. H. Douglas, Warning Democracy (London, 1931), p. 138; quoted in Philip Mairet, ed., The Douglas Manual (London, 1934), p. 48.

into effect owing to the stupidity of the community that needed them."[19]

Douglas and his followers continued their propaganda work mainly through the *New Age*, which remained faithful to the social credit cause and absorbed the house organ of the Douglas movement in January 1924.[20] Douglas published two more books and several pamphlets in the 1920's.[21]

There was, however, no substantial increase in the size or influence of Douglas's following, which remained "a sprinkling of scattered groups of earnest students,"[22] until about 1930 when the depression created favourable conditions for the spread of his doctrine. Douglas was invited at the request of a group of his supporters to testify before the Macmillan Committee on Finance and Industry, which he did in May 1930.[23] The revival of interest in social credit was reflected in the volume of correspondence to the press; in 1931 "scores of letters, many of them as long as leading articles, poured into every newspaper office."[24] Orage returned to political journalism in April 1932, launching the *New English Weekly*, which greatly invigorated social credit propaganda, although it is significant that to finance the new paper Orage had to get almost all the money from friends in America, where he had already created a social credit group.[25] Two new books by Douglas were published in 1931[26] and a new edition of *Social Credit*, with a draft social credit scheme for Scotland, appeared in 1933.

During this time, Douglas and his supporters had concentrated on expounding and defending their economic analysis and proposals, leaving the political problem in abeyance. But although no political strategy or theory of political action emerged until 1934, a political

[19]A. R. Orage, "An Editor's Progress," *Commonweal*, Feb. 24, 1926.

[20]The title of the house organ had been changed from *Public Welfare* to *Credit Power* in November 1922.

[21]*The Control and Distribution of Production* (London, 1922) and *Social Credit* (London, 1924); pamphlets, *The Douglas Theory, a Reply to Mr. J. A. Hobson* [1922], *These Present Discontents and the Labour Party and Social Credit* (1922), *The Breakdown of the Employment System* (1923), *Social Credit Principles* (1924).

[22]Mairet, *A. R. Orage, a Memoir*, p. 111.

[23]His memorandum to the Committee, and his Addendum after his examination by the Committee, are published as Appendix I to his *The Monopoly of Credit* (London, 1931). The report of the examination is reprinted in W. R. Hiskett, *Social Credits or Socialism* (London, 1935), chap. 4.

[24]Kingsley Martin, introduction to W. R. Hiskett and J. A. Franklin, *Searchlight on Social Credit* (London, 1939), p. vii.

[25]Mairet, *A. R. Orage, a Memoir*, pp. 109–10.

[26]*Warning Democracy* and *The Monopoly of Credit*.

theory was implicit, and its assumptions were explicit, in Douglas's writings throughout the 1920's.

§ 2. The Rudimentary Political Theory of the Early Douglas Writings

Douglas's early concern with political concepts was evident in the titles of his first two books on social credit: *Economic Democracy* and *Credit-Power and Democracy*, both published in 1920. In them, as in his next major work, *Social Credit* (1924), his concepts of the state and of the nature of democracy were plainly if briefly set forth. His analysis at this stage was mainly critical; he had not yet tackled the problem of political reform.

We have already seen that Douglas was persuaded that society in all its aspects was dominated by the financiers whose aim was to increase their own power by reducing all individuals to complete subservience. To Douglas the state was simply a part of the mechanism by which this was done, the rest of the mechanism being economic and psychological: the maintenance of scarcity, the compulsion to unremitting toil, and the inculcation of the moral ideas and beliefs which would secure a servile society. Among these ideas was the exaltation of the state as an authority from which there was no appeal, or an entity having purposes superior to those of its citizens. Douglas rejected any idealist interpretation of the state. The state had no concrete existence apart from those who operate its functions.[27] The state was merely the government, an apparatus of coercive power at the disposal of the real hidden holders of power. No matter how democratic the constitution, the ostensible government was merely a tool in the hands of the real government which was vested in the financiers.[28] In the British representative system the electors never got any benefit "from more than the minutest fraction of the activities of their representatives," but "a small number of very opulent gentry of international sympathies, who were not elected, and represented no one but themselves, did in fact sway the whole deliberations of the elected assembly."[29]

The modern state, in short, was simply a manifestation and an instrument of the will to power of the active few. The financiers did not stand alone; they had as their willing or unconscious helpers politicians of all parties. The objective of socialist and labour parties was the same as that of finance, namely, the domination of a

[27]*Economic Democracy* (1921), p. 12.
[28]*The Control and Distribution of Production*, p. 106.
[29]*These Present Discontents*, pp. 144-5.

system over all individual dissent by reducing individuals to economic dependence on the controllers of the system.[30]

This view of the nature of the modern state is not to be ascribed merely to Douglas's failure to get his technical proposals accepted by the government or the Labour party or the financiers, although no doubt that was what directed his attention to the political problem. His view of the state followed logically from the technological and social assumptions we have already seen. It was assumed as self-evident that all individuals wanted more freedom, leisure, goods, and security.[31] These they had notoriously failed to get, democratic institutions notwithstanding. On the technological postulates of potential abundance and technical knowledge of the means to achieve it, these objects were technically obtainable. On the engineer's assumption of the purposive nature of society,[32] the people's failure to achieve their objects was attributed to some human agency opposing their will. The state, as the ultimate coercive power in society, must then be a part of the mechanism used by that agency.

The basic political assumption, which is simply a variation of the assumption of a natural harmony of individual interests, is the existence of a general will. Like Rousseau and the nineteenth-century *petit-bourgeois* social thinkers, Douglas attributed to undifferentiated humanity a virtually unanimous real will for certain broad objectives. For Douglas, with his technological postulate, the objectives were individual freedom, plenty, and economic security. If the people were ever consulted about these ultimate objectives they would be nearly unanimous on them, although they might be divided on the means to be adopted. The distinction between objectives (or "policy") and methods became a shibboleth of social credit theory, and was the point of departure of Douglas's critique of existing democratic institutions.

Democratic government was supposed to provide the channels by which the will of the people would prevail. Why did it not do so? Douglas was not content with the usual explanations of the power of money to dominate political parties and the press, or of the tendency toward bureaucracy within any party. Nor did he find the "new despotism" argument sufficient, although he was emphatic that cabinet or party responsibility was a screen behind which an administrative bureaucracy gathered into its hands the power to make the

---

[30]*Credit-Power and Democracy* (1921), p. 145.
[31]*Social Credit* (1924), p. 10.
[32]See above, Chap. IV, sect. 2, p. 100.

decisions.[33] Broad issues "such as, for instance, whether the aim of the industrial system is to produce employment, or whether it is to produce and distribute goods, are matters of policy, and it is very noticeable that such matters are kept as far as possible from the purview and decision of the general public. In fact the aim of the political wire-pullers is to submit to the decision of the electorate, *only alternative methods of embodying the same policy.*" The essence of the party system was "to direct public attention to a profitless wrangle in regard to methods."[34] Not only was it profitless, it was the means by which the people were divided and ruled. For while the majority could be trusted to be right on matters of broad policy, they were not competent to judge questions of method. "To submit questions of fiscal procedure, of foreign affairs, and other cognate matters to the judgment of an electorate is merely to submit matters which are essentially technical to a community which is essentially non-technical." On such matters, in so far as they are not merely matters of precedent, "it is quite certain that . . . the majority will always be wrong,"[35] since the majority can have no grasp of the problem.

Thus the democratic party system was seen as a means of thwarting the real will of the people by ensuring that they voted only on issues about which they were not competent to judge their own interest. And, adding insult to injury, every effort was made to delude the people into thinking that their will did prevail, by fostering the belief that democracy is the rule of the majority. "Democracy is frequently and falsely defined as the rule of the majority. . . . As so defined, it is a mere trap, set by knaves to catch simpletons; the *rule* of the majority never has existed, and, fortunately, never will exist. If such a thing were possible, it would be the ultimate Terror, beside which the worst individual despot would seem a kindly patriarch.'"[36]

Recoiling from the implications of any complete democracy, Douglas offered his own definition:

Real democracy is . . . the expression of the *policy* of the majority, and, so far as that policy is concerned with economics, is the freedom of an increasing majority of individuals to make use of the facilities provided for them, in the first place, by a number of persons who will always be, as they have always been, in the minority.[37]

The essential nature of a satisfactory modern co-operative State may be broadly expressed as consisting of a functionally aristocratic hierarchy

[33]*Social Credit* (1924), p. 144.
[34]*Ibid.*, pp. 142–3 (italics in the original), 190.   [35]*Ibid.*, p. 142.
[36]*Credit-Power and Democracy* (1921), p. 7.   [37]*Ibid.*, p. 8.

of producers accredited by, and serving, a democracy of consumers. . . .
The business of the public, as consumers, is not only to give orders, but
to see that they are obeyed as to results, and to remove unsuitable or
wilfully recalcitrant persons from the aristocracy of production to the
democracy of consumption.[38]

The implications of this view of the desirable state were scarcely
considered. The existing relation between parliament, the cabinet,
and the permanent civil service was rejected but nothing was yet
put in its place. All that was asserted was that the people should be
consulted only about the broadest objectives, and that all else,
including foreign policy, fiscal policy, etc. (which are not "policy"
in Douglas's sense, but merely methods), being beyond the competence of the people, should be left to the experts, subject only
to the people's right to remove the experts who failed to produce
the results.

Nor was much attention given to the problem of how the existing
political system could be reformed to the desired pattern. The question whether parliamentary methods or some variant of the direct
action principle should be used was raised but not settled.[39] An
immediate political objection was "the defeat of the power of political
caucuses to draw up the agenda of an election." To this end, "the
invalidation of an election, if less than say fifty per cent of the electorate voted on the issues submitted to them, would no doubt be as
good a method as any other."[40] But apart from the fact, which he
did not mention, that such a constitutional change could scarcely
be effected until after the defeat of the party caucuses, Douglas was
very doubtful if an election on a "genuine" issue such as "Do you
want employment, or do you want goods?" would get the people
what they wanted, for the powers of obstruction through patronage
would still be formidable. For these reasons he was inclined to
think that parliamentary machinery was not a suitable agency for
political reform.[41] What form the alternative or supplementary
method of direct action would take was not discussed.

But whatever kind of action was to be taken to bring about
political and economic reform, it would certainly require a strong
popular movement convinced of the need for such reform. This set
Douglas an almost insoluble problem. If social credit was to get
anywhere politically, a body of convinced supporters large enough

[38]*Ibid.*, pp. 94–5. Cf. *Social Credit* (1924), p. 143: "The domain of policy
comprises the removal of executives if the results achieved are unsatisfactory."
[39]*Social Credit* (1924), p. 194.   [40]*Ibid.*, p. 195.   [41]*Ibid.*, pp. 195–6.

to be an effective political pressure group, if not a political party, would have to be built up. The only apparent way to build it up was to expound and seek support for social credit principles and proposals. But social credit principles and proposals were clearly matters of technique and method, which, he insisted, the majority of the people were incompetent to judge, and which they must not be permitted to consider.

Until about 1930 there was not a wide enough interest in social credit to make this a serious problem; the few who took it up could be assumed to be members of the intellectual minority which was competent to discuss technological matters. But already in 1924 the lines along which the problem was to be settled were indicated.

The solution was to build up an *élite* "who know what to do and how to do it . . .; it is even desirable that skeleton plans should be in existence to meet the situation as it can be seen to exist; but nothing can be more fatal to a successful issue than the premature publication of cut and dried arrangements which are likely to be completely out of date long before their adoption can be secured."[42] The *élite* should consist not of sentimental reformers or of those who had been successful in business, but of those who had "always been free from financial anxiety" and were yet familiar with the technique of the modern world, and those whose incentive to work was largely artistic, including "practically all persons of really scientific temperament."[43]

This *élite* could, Douglas thought, make an effective appeal to a large majority of the people, but not by expounding social credit principles. "It is my considered opinion that the right way with most people is to discountenance severely any discussion of the general advisability of such matters as we have been considering [that is, social credit principles], and, as far as possible, to put the appeal in the form: 'Suppose that you yourself were offered certain conditions, such as we suggest, under which to carry on your business or your own personal economic life, would you accept them?' "[44]

Not only was discussion of the technical theory of social credit to be avoided in appealing for mass support; even discussion of social ideals was to be avoided[45] as being more confusing than helpful to an understanding of the clear and simple choice with which the voter was to be confronted.

[42]*Ibid.*, pp. 217–18. [43]*Ibid.*, pp. 220–1.
[44]*Ibid.*, p. 221. [45]*Ibid.*, p. 222.

In effect Douglas thus recognized that there was only one way out of the social credit political dilemma. To get popular support for a doctrine an essential part of which was the insistence that the people are not competent to discuss it, the only way was to promise everything and discuss nothing, to assert that you had all the answers and demand to be taken on trust. Thus the nature of the doctrine determined the autocratic form of the movement, and foreshadowed the subsequent social credit theory of a plebiscitarian state.

Before examining these developments we must notice the emergence of a rival social credit movement which had some effect on the direction the Douglas movement took. While Douglas left the political problem in abeyance in the early 1930's and continued his propaganda at an intellectual level designed to appeal to the educated middle class, the depression was creating a new and more restless audience for doctrines which promised rapid relief from poverty and economic distress. In these circumstances social credit did not remain a monopoly of middle class intellectuals, nor did it remain outside the political arena. Alongside the Douglas movement, never affiliated with it though for a time enjoying its approval, was the Green Shirt social credit movement, flourishing from 1933 to 1936, more activist, less intellectual, and very vocally proletarian.

§ 3. The Green Shirts—a Political Movement

The Green Shirt movement was, more conspicuously than the Douglas movement, dominated by its founder and leader. John Gordon Hargrave had for more than a decade before the appearance of the Green Shirts sought an outlet for his restless and forceful personality in creating a nature cult for the "little man," the rejects and misfits of post-war industrial England. But it was not until the mass unemployment of 1933 that Hargrave found adequate scope for his talents by taking over and merging with his own following a militant organization of unemployed which was ripe for such leadership.

Hargrave's first organization, founded in 1920, had the suitably ritualistic name of "Kibbo Kift, the Woodcraft Kindred." Hargrave had been prominent in the Boy Scout movement, and the nucleus of his own movement was "a number of scout-masters, ex-scouts, campers and thinkers"[46] whom he brought with him when he broke with the Scouts. The Kindred was an open-air movement whose members sought to break away from the standards of industrial civili-

---

[46]John Hargrave, *The Confession of the Kibbo Kift, a Declaration and General Exposition of the Work of the Kindred* (London, 1927), p. 58.

zation by embracing woodsmanship and handcrafts with appropriate ritual and uniform costume. Its avowed purpose was to help the little man "to emerge from mass bondage to individual self-expression."[47] In 1924 Hargrave became interested in social credit and introduced it to his organization, which adopted social credit as its economic policy in 1929.[48] By 1927 Hargrave's writings reflected much of Major Douglas's philosophy and economic analysis, without acknowledgment.[49] He repudiated the legend of the nobility of work and the worship of the nation state, rejected the Fabian and Marxian analyses, regarded class conflict as "a side show promoted (unconsciously perhaps) by . . . a manipulator of financial abstractions" and held that the real oppressor of the workers "is not a living being but an abstract formula of calculation."[50] In place of the rejected analyses he offered a rudimentary social credit analysis and solution.

His political analysis was more extreme and outspoken than Douglas's. He was strongly antipathetic to the democratic idea and the parliamentary system. "The theory and practice of democracy is today a reactionary movement. . . . it keeps us in mass formation when our whole aim is to break free and individualize. The ideology of democracy holds up the image of the Average Man. . . . This Average Man idea can, and does, drive whole nations . . . to unindividualised identity, until at last we have the psychological myth of a mass-ego, and its political counterpart in the myth of a 'mass will.' . . . to make laws in the name of the Average Man is to legislate for no one at all, to the very great private gain of hidden financial interests."[51] Hargrave was emphatic about the political incompetence of the mass; the mass has no will but can be given a will. At present that will is given by the controllers of press, radio, and film. To give the mass a new will, by which it could free itself from bondage, must be the work of a few disciplined leaders. To supply such leadership was to be the function of Hargrave and his movement.

The political strategy outlined in 1927 foreshadowed that of the Green Shirts; the Kibbo Kift "must become a political force *outside the House of Commons* . . . [receiving] its impetus *direct from the people*, forging its political technique in such a way as to become actional by its influence over the heads of the 615 members of parliament."[52] The political technique was to be "non-violent"; the use

[47]*Ibid.*, p. 148. [48]*Social Credit*, Nov. 1, 1935.
[49]Major Douglas is not mentioned in Hargrave's book of 1927.
[50]Hargrave, *The Confession of the Kibbo Kift*, pp. 149, 150.
[51]*Ibid.*, pp. 215–16. [52]*Ibid.*, pp. 200–1; italics in the original.

of violence was rejected not on the ground that it was always wrong or inexpedient but that it was expedient only for building up a strong pyramidal state, to which Hargrave was opposed. It was by this rejection of violence that Hargrave distinguished his movement from the Fascist movement and countered the charge that his organization was fascist.[53] While his strategy was based on the rejection of the parliamentary system, Hargrave did not reject the possibility of running a candidate for the House of Commons in order to use the house "as a pulpit from which to demonstrate the helplessness of any and every government which fails to take control of Credit-Power."[54]

Under Hargrave's leadership the Kibbo Kift was transformed into the Green Shirt movement in 1933, after it had been influenced by the Legion of Unemployed,[55] which was founded in Coventry in January 1931 by George Hickling, later the editor of Social Credit. The Legion's manifesto, published in February 1931, demanded a national credit office, the just price, and the national dividend. Candidates were run in the municipal elections in 1932 on a social credit platform. Hargrave was greatly interested in the Legion and introduced into the Kibbo Kift much of the Legion's open-air propaganda technique—meetings with banners and the systematic asking of awkward questions at others' meetings. When Hickling decided to adopt green shirts as the Legion uniform these were supplied from the Kibbo Kift equipment stores, and when the daily press began to refer to the Legion as "the Green Shirts" Hargrave seized on the popular possibilites of the name. The Legion of the Unemployed came to an end in 1933, and Hargrave became the leader of the Green Shirt movement in the same year, launching a weekly paper in the summer entitled Attack! against the Bankers' Combine for the People's Credit.[56]

The Green Shirt movement, employing such titles for its offices as the "London Green Shirt Command" and "National Headquarters, Green Shirt Movement" in 1933 and 1934, was a militant organization

[53]Ibid., pp. 202, 231ff.
[54]Ibid., p. 200.
[55]Social Credit, Nov. 1, 1935.
[56]Variations in the frequency of publication reflect the fortunes of the Green Shirt movement. Attack was published weekly, with one gap of a fortnight, to no. 22 (Dec. 9, 1933); then only once every other month until June 1934 (no. 25); subsequent issues are undated; the last issue (no. 41) appears to have been published late in 1936. In 1937 a paper entitled The Voice of the People, incorporating Attack appeared, also undated, but no subsequent issues of this appear to have been published.

directing its appeal chiefly to the unemployed and to factory workers.[57] "We use an unarmed military technique that calls forth willing discipline under direct leadership—and allows of no sham Democratic committee 'wangling.' "[58] Hargrave urged the unemployed to refrain from sporadic local outbursts which would lead to batons and broken heads, but to join the Green Shirts and undertake "disciplined mass action by way of street demonstrations."[59] His contempt for parliamentary institutions was outspoken. In urging "workers and unemployed" to "come out on the streets" when the Hunger Marchers were due to arrive in London in February 1934, he wrote: "Voting is useless. . . . The Bankers' Combine and its megaphone at Westminster is not afraid of voting papers or shouts of 'Work or Maintenance.' . . . *We must repudiate and fight those who would mislead us by having us believe in the power of the vote. Our struggle must be fought outside Parliament, on the streets and wherever the enemy appears.*"[60] As early as September 1933 Hargrave was suggesting that such a mass movement might culminate in a *coup d'état*. The political proposals of the movement, entitled "The Green Shirt Line of Action," were listed as follows: "1. Take control. 2. Close the 'chatterbox' at Westminster. 3. Take over the Bank of England in the name of the people. 4. Open the national credit office. 5. Issue the national dividend to every citizen. 6. Enforce the scientific price. 7. Set up local hundreds [consultative assemblies] in every district to give expression to the will of the people throughout the country. 8. Put down any counter-revolutionary 'fascist' activity, or any attempt to overthrow the party of the people's credit [that is, the Green Shirts]. 9. Defend the victorious social-credit revolution from international financial sabotage."[61] In February 1934 point 2 was extended to read "and set up a Central Council of Control deriving its authority from the Local Hundreds."[62] It is apparent from Hargrave's propaganda of this period that he was competing with the Communist party for the attention of the unemployed, and he occasionally displayed a superficial familiarity with the ideas of Marx and Lenin.[63]

[57]"At least 80% of our membership is composed of unemployed workers 'on the dole,' " wrote Hargrave in *Attack*, no. 12, Sept. 30, 1933. In February 1934 it is stated in the same paper that 80 per cent are either unemployed or factory workers.

[58]*Attack*, no. 24, April 1934.   [59]*Ibid.*, no. 12, Sept. 30, 1933.

[60]*Ibid.*, no. 23, Feb. 1934.   [61]*Ibid.*, no. 12, Sept. 30, 1933. ·

[62]*Ibid.*, no. 23, Feb. 1934. The term "hundreds" for local assemblies was subsequently used by Mr. L. D. Byrne.

[63]*Ibid.*, no. 29 (?April 1935): Marx needs to be brought up to date; Lenin's *Imperialism* is "a masterly analysis of the finance-capitalist system."

Major Douglas was at first appreciative of the valuable propaganda work being done "amongst the unemployed and that section of the community generally known as 'the workers'"; in January 1933 he wrote to Hargrave that he would feel honoured if the green tartan worn by his (Douglas's) family were used for the facings of the Green Shirt uniform.[64]

The Green Shirts' political strategy during 1933 and 1934 conformed to their contempt for parliamentary methods. They urged the people to "return a Green Shirt Government to power by your direct mandate,"[65] but they did not nominate candidates in by-elections. They proposed to develop a propaganda campaign at each by-election and to try to get people to sign "Direct Mandate Forms," giving a mandate for a Credit Office, a National Dividend, and the Scientific Price, and thus to "take the 'vote' of the electors before the voting begins." "By this means we intend to short-circuit the banker-infested political system of sham democracy—and get a Direct Mandate to Act from the British People."[66] The Green Shirts remained aloof from any ordinary electoral activity until September 1935 when they suddenly constituted themselves the Social Credit Party of Great Britain, with the avowed purpose of preventing the confusion and weakening of social credit by the appearance of independent irresponsible candidates who were coming forward in the absence of a responsible party.[67] They announced that they intended to put up only one candidate at the next general election, in order to test the electorate and to send a Green Shirt into Parliament as a wasp.[68] The Green Shirts' attempt to set themselves up as the leaders of all social credit electoral activities failed, and with its failure the Green Shirt movement petered out.[69]

§ 4. The Douglas Theory and Practice of Political Action, 1934–5

The phenomenal rise of the Green Shirt movement in 1933 and 1934 served to demonstrate that a mass following could be got by promising an immediate fight for social credit slogans and enrolling recruits for direct political action. The Green Shirts, independently of Douglas, succeeded in claiming public attention at the level of the popular press to an extent never achieved by Douglas. It was clearly time

[64]Social Credit, Nov. 1, 1935.   [65]Attack, no. 16, Oct. 28, 1933.
[66]Ibid., no. 17, Nov. 4, 1933.   [67]Ibid., no. 33, (?)Nov. 1935.
[68]Ibid., no. 32, (?)Oct. 1935.

[69]All that is left of it is a small fantastic cult of nature-worshippers with delusions of grandeur. See Thomas Driberg, "A Touch of the Sun," Cornhill, May 1944.

for Douglas to develop a political strategy of his own. The limitations within which such a strategy could be devised have already been indicated. Douglas believed no more than Hargrave in the competence of the mass to judge the value of social credit principles and proposals. But having no taste for the flamboyant methods of Hargrave, he found it necessary to provide a rationale which would enlist supporters while explaining why he could not explain social credit to them, or rather, why they need not ask to have it explained. He also had to devise a series of tactical measures which by giving supporters something hopeful to do would enlist and maintain their interest without the stridency of the Green Shirt street marches.

Douglas announced the new theory and tactics in a speech at Buxton in June 1934[70] and reiterated and elaborated them in speeches and pamphlets and in the columns of his weekly paper during the next few years. The new theory and tactics were a logical extension of the rudimentary political theory we have already examined. The essence of that theory, as we have seen, was that the people were competent only to express their will for the broadest general objectives —freedom, plenty, security—and were totally incompetent to judge any of the matters which were now submitted to them by political parties; that the party system was a device for confusing, dividing, and ruling the people; that, consequently, a true democracy must be so constituted that the electorate would be consulted only as to ultimate objectives, while the choice of methods and the power to put methods into effect would be left to experts, subject to the people's right to have the experts removed if they failed to produce the desired results.

The new theory announced in 1934 re-emphasized all this and added something on the functions and responsibilities of the members of parliament, the cabinet, and the expert. An elected parliament with sovereign power was to be retained. No change in the basis of representation was needed. Douglas was not interested in any system of occupational representation; what parliament needed was above all a general mandate; it should represent the will of citizens as citizens not as members of this or that class or interest group. But in every other respect the present parliamentary system would be changed out of all recognition, for neither parliament nor the cabinet would retain their functions of debate and decision on the whole range of matters which normally formed the bulk of legislation and executive deliberation.

[70]Published as a pamphlet, *The Nature of Democracy*, in various editions.

The transformation of the parliamentary system followed logically from Douglas's sharp distinction between objectives and methods, and his insistence that the whole purpose of representative institutions should be to transmit and enforce the general will for the broadest objectives. The function of the electorate was to express its will for broad objectives and to demand results; the function of the experts was to devise and put into operation schemes which would give the results; the function of the elected members of parliament was simply to transmit the people's demands and compel the experts to produce the required results. The only means by which parliament could exercise this compulsion was to remove unsatisfactory experts and appoint others until the job was done. In the first instance parliament was to inform the existing controllers of the financial system what results were wanted, and to provide them with expert advisers if requested, "but if they will neither take action within a reasonable period of time, and will not accept advice if provided, then it is the business of the representatives of the people to remove them, whether they are alleged to be operating under a system of private enterprise or as public departments."[71]

The most striking feature of the Douglas proposals, however, was that this provision and removal of experts was to be the limit of parliament's activity. Parliament must refuse to consider or approve any schemes or "methods," indeed any legislation embodying practical measures of economic reform. Members of parliament must be forbidden to vote on any "technical" matter.[72] "We do not want Parliament to pass laws resembling treatises on economics. What we do want is for Parliament to pass a minimum of laws designed to penalize the heads of any great industry, and banking and finance in particular, if they do not produce the results desired."[73]

Two reasons were given why elected representatives should not be allowed to consider or vote upon any of the matters that are now their business. One was that the member of parliament was not competent to understand most of the technical questions which came up in parliament. Douglas made a lot out of this argument although it was not really relevant. It is easy to show that members of par-

---

[71]The Nature of Democracy (Pamphlets on the New Economics, no. 2; Toronto, Wm. Dawson, 1935), p. 14. Douglas presented the same scheme to the Alberta legislature in April 1934: The Douglas System of Social Credit: Evidence Taken by the Agricultural Committee of the Alberta Legislature (Edmonton, 1934), evidence of Major Douglas, pp. 95–6.

[72]The Policy of a Philosophy (Liverpool, n.d. [1937]), p. 13.

[73]The Tragedy of Human Effort (Liverpool, n.d. [1936]), p. 11.

liament, however intelligent, cannot judge all the technical matters that come up in bills, but Douglas made this mean that they were not and never could be competent to judge even the principle of any piece of economic legislation. In his view the principle of such a bill was itself a technical matter.

The other reason was given even more weight. Members of parliament must refuse to endorse or approve any schemes for producing results because refusal was the only way of throwing responsibility for results on the experts. "If, when anyone demands a result, he indicates a method of obtaining it, he automatically takes on himself the responsibility for a failure if the method does not work. There are experts who can be held responsible for such a failure but only if they are left to choose their own method."[74] The experts, whether inside or outside the government service, that is, those who actually run the productive system and decide how the services society requires are provided, must not only be allowed to decide on methods, they must also be held responsible for producing the desired results. And the only way parliament could hold them responsible was to refuse to take any responsibility for methods itself. The function of a legislative assembly, Douglas informed the Alberta legislature, was to tell the experts what results were wanted "and if necessary to remove them or provide them with advice, or anything that may be necessary to see that they do the job. In that way you place the responsibility fairly and absolutely where it belongs. When you discuss how it should be done you take the responsibility which is not properly yours."[75]

The function of the elected representative was essentially to be "a representative of a mass desire"[76] transmitting to the operators of the economic system the electorate's desire for results. The legislature was also to transmit to the electorate the names of the individuals responsible for the attainment or non-attainment of the result, to remove those responsible for impeding the will of the people or those unable to produce the results,[77] and to substitute other experts. The functions of the cabinet were not distinguished from those of the legislature; presumably the cabinet was to act as a committee of the legislature and perform the same functions at a different level. The cabinet, like the rest of parliament, was not to deal with methods

[74]*Social Credit*, editorial, Nov. 1, 1935.
[75]*The Douglas System of Social Credit*, p. 96.
[76]*Ibid.*, p. 95.
[77]*The Nature of Democracy*, pp. 13–14. (The Buxton speech, June 1934.)

or to take any responsibility; it was simply to seek out and choose experts and hold them responsible for results.[78]

Very little was said about the relation of the civil service to the cabinet or parliament. In so far as the higher civil servants in, for instance, the Treasury were in a position to regulate and control economic affairs they were experts, and as such would be treated in precisely the same way as the directors of private finance and industry, that is, be told what results were wanted, be given a free hand to produce them, and be removed if they failed.[79]

It is apparent that the Douglas theory of the role of the expert and the representative, in spite of a superficial similarity to the theory and practice of British cabinet government, is basically different. In both schemes the elected representative and the cabinet minister are not meant to be experts but are meant to shape general policies following the will of the electorate and to require the experts in the civil service to carry them out. But Douglas drew a line between policy and administration which left nothing within the scope of policy except the general will for freedom, security, and plenty, and the power of removing and appointing the experts. Consequently his scheme represents an utter transformation of all the relationships in the prevailing system. Parliament, whose members had been elected on no party platform, and were committed to no measures or principles or programmes, would be divested of its present functions and responsibilities. Almost all the questions which now occupy parliament and cabinet would be left to the administrators. Parliament could not consider any economic legislation even in principle. Since no such legislation could be submitted to it, practically all legislation would become delegated legislation. The civil service would become virtually autonomous; nothing that it did could be touched; there would be no protection from it except by removal of its leading men. The cabinet was to renounce responsibility for almost all substantive legislation and administrative measures. No longer would the cabinet minister be responsible to parliament, and indirectly to the electorate, for all that was done by his departmental officials; the essence of Douglas's scheme was that the officials, not the minister, would be responsible. But in this shift of responsibility something was left out. The minister at present is responsible for everything—principle and detail, but the expert in Douglas's scheme would be responsible only for the broad results. No one would be responsible to the electorate for the actual operations of any scheme; neither minister nor parliament could

[78]*Social Credit*, Oct. 14, 1938.   [79]*The Nature of Democracy*, p. 14.

approve or disapprove of "methods." Thus Douglas's proposal for
destroying the irresponsible power of the permanent official, by
making him personally responsible and no longer permanent, is
virtually self-contradictory.

The same may be said of his scheme viewed in its other aspect,
that is, as a way of making parliament an effective instrument of the
people's will. Parliament was to be freed of every function and responsibility except expressing the general will of the electorate and
keeping up adequate pressure on the adminstrators. But since parliament would have no responsibility for what was done or not done,
either by way of legislation or by way of administration, members
of parliament could not be tested by their record in the usual way.
The only record they could submit to the electorate would be their
vociferousness in pressing the demands of the popular will for results
and their show of activity in removing and appointing administrators.
These are qualities in which it is not difficult to appear proficient.
Once the experts were made responsible and removable, the representatives might well become irremovable as well as irresponsible.

We need not examine the hypothetical effect of the Douglas system
of democratic government any further. It can be called democratic
only in the sense that a plebiscitarian dictatorship is democratic. No
other outcome was possible for a theory which began from the
assumption that the people could never be competent to form intelligent opinions on public affairs.

The same assumption determined the political tactics which Douglas
laid down for his movement in 1934. No attempt was to be made to
form a political party, for that would mean competing with existing
parties on their terms, that is, seeking support on a platform of
specific social credit proposals. This would violate both of the political
principles on which Douglas was most insistent: that the electorate
should not be asked to consider economic methods of achieving
freedom, plenty, and security, and that the member of parliament
should not take any responsibility for methods. Instead, the members
of the social credit movement were to devote their energies to
persuading the voters, by a house to house canvass, that they could
have what they wanted if they united in demanding results only.
This was referred to as "the task of purifying the desires of the general
population, by which I mean the integration of popular will to a
united objective without specification of mechanism. One of the most
effective methods is by explaining what would be the result of
Social Credit as compared with those we know to rise out of the

present system."[80] "One by one the voters should be asked whether they are in favour of a larger personal income, with absolute security, via the National Dividend; and sufficient information should be placed before them to show that this is possible. This is a job for the rank and file. The electors should then definitely be asked for a pledge to vote for no candidate who is not prepared to demand that dividend."[81] In addition, "every sitting Member of Parliament . . . should be asked whether he is prepared to proceed along certain lines which will be explained to him, and informed that he will not be supported unless he is. If any sitting Member of Parliament is not willing to give such an assurance, a new candidate should be nominated,"[82] as a non-party candidate, demanding the National Dividend, and that only, without saying how the dividend could be issued.[83]

What Douglas called the Electoral Campaign was developed on these lines during 1934 and 1935. Whether he ever had any hope that it would succeed or whether it was a desperate expedient to give his followers something to do is not clear. He knew that the pledge to be exacted from members of parliament and candidates was inconsistent with party commitments. " . . . Members of Parliament must be elected on the clear understanding that they will disregard the Party Whips at any time or all the time in favour of the instructions of their constituents."[84] Since no organization was proposed by which the instructions of the constituents could be transmitted to them, a few party candidates might sign the required undertaking, but it was not a very effective way of undermining the party system.

The Electoral Campaign did not come up to expectations. Three candidates in the general election of November 1935 signed the candidate's undertaking; one was a Labour party candidate and two were independents, referred to as National Dividend candidates.[85] By April 1936, eighteen members of Parliament were reported to have signed the less exacting member's undertaking.[86] While enthusiastic accounts by door-to-door canvassers in the constituencies during the campaign indicated that in some districts at least it was easy to get many signatures for the elector's pledges, it was admitted later[87] that this canvassing had not had the desired educational effect of making the voters realize their own power when united behind a simple and clear demand.

[80]*Ibid.*, p. 13.   [81]*Ibid.*, p. 15.   [82]*Ibid.*
[83]*Social Credit*, editorial, Nov. 1, 1935.
[84]*Ibid.*, Oct. 25, 1935, article by Major Douglas.   [85]*Ibid.*, Nov. 1, 1935.
[86]*Ibid.*, April 24, 1936.   [87]*The Policy of a Philosophy* (1937).

After 1936 the Douglas movement declined in size, prestige, and intellectual content. We need not here follow the political activities of the English social credit movement any further, although the final development of the theory will have to be noticed in a later chapter,[88] for it had repercussions in the development of the Alberta social credit party.

Neither the electoral tactics nor the political theory which Douglas developed in 1934 was at all fully thought out. There was nothing on the method of nominating the necessary non-partisan parliamentary candidates, nothing on the method of conveying the constituents' will to the member of parliament, nothing on the relation of the member and the cabinet, and nothing on the means by which the cabinet would compel the administration to produce results except the extreme method of removing the administration. In the situation for which the theory was devised, none of this was necessary. For in England the problem was to drive a wedge into the solidly constituted party system, and even in the most hopeful expectation there would be plenty of time to work out the problems of representation when the tactics began to succeed.

In Alberta, where the political opportunities and problems of social credit were different, Aberhart accepted and expounded the main principles of the Douglas political theory but modified and supplemented them as he went along. Both in building up his electoral organization and in running the government, Aberhart had to work out new devices and find solutions for all those problems that Douglas had left unconsidered. For the most part his political procedure was consistent with Douglas theory, but in one important respect it was not. In assuming all the usual responsibilities of the premiership and refusing to transfer responsibility to the experts, Aberhart departed significantly from Douglas principles. But those principles were strongly enough held by Aberhart's supporters to enable them to make him return part of the way, at least in appearance, by the threat of a party revolt in 1937. After that, party and government settled down to something like the normal Canadian pattern, but never completely like it, for they retained the plebiscitarian character inherent in social credit movements.

[88]Chap. VII, sect. 2.

CHAPTER SIX

Social Credit in Alberta: Aberhart Theory and Practice, 1932-7

->>> <<<-

§ 1. The Alberta Political Norm

We have now to examine, in this and the next chapter, the changes made in the Alberta pattern of democratic theory and practice by the social credit movement and government, and to consider whether these changes constitute a temporary deviation from the norm or whether in any respect they constitute, or are likely to constitute, a new norm. This will lead to a further inquiry, in the final chapter, as to whether some modification of the orthodox theory is required in the light of the three decades of unorthodox practice in Alberta under the U.F.A. and social credit administrations.

In considering the extent to which the social credit movement and government deviated from the normal theory and practice of party and cabinet government, we must start from the fact that fifteen years of U.F.A. politics had already done something to modify the Alberta norm. We have seen that the U.F.A. in office maintained very largely the usual pattern of cabinet government, in spite of the ideas to the contrary which had dominated the movement at the beginning. Yet the U.F.A. reign left some things different. It left a people accustomed to direct influence on government policy through U.F.A. locals and annual delegate conventions, as well as through constituency organizations and elected members of the legislature. It left a people accustomed to feel that the government was (or should be) their government, their creation, to a degree unknown where the old party system still flourished. It left a people confirmed in their repugnance to the party system, and distrustful of party machines. The two-party system, never at home in Alberta, had become virtually a one-party system. But the one party was never fully integrated with the government nor subordinated to it in quite the degree usually found in an orthodox party. The party retained some of the characteristics of a popular movement: it exerted more pressure on the government through its annual delegate conventions than through its elected members of the legislature.

While the two-party system had been subverted, the cabinet system had retained its hold. The cabinet dominated the legislature in much the usual way, and even dominated the convention. Yet the fact that the cabinet's position within the U.F.A. system was so strong that it could and did refuse to yield to convention pressure in the early 1930's, and instead made the convention yield to its position, was what finished the U.F.A. politically. And the reason the intransigence of the cabinet had this effect was that it thwarted a persistent belief among the rank and file U.F.A. members and convention delegates that the convention was the body which really expressed their will. The belief that policy should be determined by direct delegate conventions had brought the U.F.A. into office in 1921, and although this belief appeared to have lost its strength during the long years of successful U.F.A. administration of the province, it revived clamorously when economic conditions worsened after 1930.

The political legacy of the U.F.A., then, was a system of democratic government significantly different from the normal party and cabinet system. By the time social credit became a political contender in Alberta a new norm had been set: virtually a one-party system, cabinet rule, and a revived tradition of direct delegate democracy.

On to this scene came the Aberhart social credit movement. While it is not our main purpose to account for its rise and rapid growth and its overwhelming success in 1935, we must pay some attention to the conditions which determined the kind of appeal it made, for these conditions shaped the theory and practice of the movement and subsequently of the government. We shall find that a variety of circumstances, economic, political, and ideological, at once made Alberta unusually susceptible to social credit propaganda and required some modification of the English doctrine. The modified theory and practice of social credit, in turn, brought changes in the accepted theory and practice of democracy in Alberta. We have to consider, therefore, the impact of Alberta on social credit, as well as the impact of social credit on Alberta.

In this chapter we shall examine the circumstances in Alberta which required or invited modification of the English doctrine (section 2), and the actual modifications developed by Aberhart in bringing the Alberta social credit movement into politics and building the campaign which gave it victory in the provincial election of 1935 (section 3). The theory and practice of the movement on the eve of the first social credit administration of the province will be seen to have been not substantially different from the Douglas doctrine, and to have implied a system of democratic government markedly different from either the U.F.A. or the orthodox system. Finally (section 4) an examination of the practice of the social credit cabinet and legislation in the first eighteen months of office will show an important but incomplete substitution of orthodox cabinet and party practice for that implied in the social credit theory. In the following chapter we shall examine the resurgence of social credit political theory within the Alberta movement and legislature in 1937, and the results of the subsequent internal divergence of views.

§ 2. Formative Conditions of the Alberta Social Credit Movement

The social credit movement in Alberta may be taken to date from 1932, when William Aberhart became a convert to the English doctrine. Social credit ideas had of course been known in Alberta long before this. They had been assiduously publicized by the U.F.A. newspaper and by some of the leading figures in the U.F.A. for many years.[1] There had been some discussion of social credit, along with other theories of monetary reform, in U.F.A. locals, and there were a few intellectual groups in Calgary and Edmonton devoted to discussion of Douglas doctrine. But it was not until Aberhart took it up that a mass movement was created.

The rapid spread of social credit ideas from 1933 to 1935 need not be attributed entirely to Aberhart's energetic propaganda and organizing. The depths of sudden poverty and insecurity to which almost the whole community had been reduced by the drop in the prices of the goods they produced, and by the consequently overwhelming problem of farm debt, had created an extraordinarily receptive and responsive audience for social credit doctrine. The fact that social credit could be presented not only as a monetary device

[1]Douglas's books and pamphlets were favourably and extensively publicized by The U.F.A. from its beginning in 1922, and the U.F.A. office carried a stock of them all through the 1920's and early 1930's. A U.F.A. Directors' Bulletin (no. 20) was mainly devoted to exposition of Douglas theory with substantial extracts from Douglas's books (cited in Public Welfare, June 1922). William Irvine was a tireless advocate of social credit principles both in Alberta and in Ottawa, where as a member of parliament he was instrumental in getting Douglas to appear before the House of Commons Committee on Banking and Commerce in 1923.

but as an economic theory and a social philosophy made it doubly attractive; not only did it promise economic relief, it also could provide an explanation of the apparently senseless catastrophic world in which more and more Albertans found themselves groping for understanding and hope.

Social credit's remarkable similarities with evangelical religious doctrine, which so many Albertans found the most satisfying, recommended it still further. Combining in itself a root-and-branch denunciation of the world as it was with a magical promise of a new secular life for all who were suffering, social credit had a peculiar affinity to the fundamentalist and prophetic religious gospel of which Aberhart was a vigorous preacher. An evangelist whose mind ran powerfully to prophetic interpretation of the Bible could take the fullest advantage of the social credit doctrine, unhampered by those analytical misgivings which prevented its whole-hearted reception by the more rationalist U.F.A. leaders. There were, indeed, things in Douglas's doctrine that Aberhart could scarcely have comprehended and could certainly not have agreed with. Aberhart's puritanism was too strong to allow him to accept Douglas's denigration of work and praise of abundance not earned in the sweat of the brow; it is doubtful if Aberhart ever grasped Douglas's denunciatory concept of the "work fetish." But he found no difficulty in merging the positive side of the Douglas doctrine with his own prophetic gospel.

Moreover, before Aberhart took up social credit he had already built up a large personal religious following, and had a rapid and effective means of reaching a very wide audience. In Calgary, where he had been a high school principal since 1915, he had organized Bible classes and weekly Bible services in the early 1920's with a skill and fervour which eminently qualified him for the role of radio evangelist which he assumed in the middle 1920's. Tens of thousands of responsive listeners throughout the province were added to the thousands who came under his spell in Calgary. They were not all mere listeners; groups were formed and entered into regular relations with Aberhart's headquarters, the Calgary Prophetic Bible Institute. They were Aberhart's personal following; increasing numbers turned to him for spiritual guidance, and trusted him to lead them. This relationship between inspired leader and mass following was present from the beginning of the Aberhart social credit movement.

Aberhart first encountered social credit doctrine in the summer of 1932. He soon became convinced that it explained economic depression and insecurity, and could cure them, and he prepared systematically to hand on his discovery to as many as would receive it, beginning with his Bible followers. In the autumn and winter of 1932 he introduced social credit into his Sunday radio talks, organized a study group in his Bible Institute, trained other expositors, spoke at neighbourhood meetings, and in the summer of 1933 he made an extensive speaking tour through southern Alberta. Local study groups were soon formed throughout the province, and a central advisory board composed of delegates from the study groups was established. The strength of the movement increased steadily, always under Aberhart's commanding leadership except for two months at the beginning of 1934, when his brief renunciation of the leadership demonstrated his indispensability. The U.F.A. locals were extensively infiltrated, for social credit was not yet a political rival but a doctrine and a method available to any political organization which would take it up.

As such, social credit was extensively debated at the U.F.A. convention of January 1934 which, without committing itself to the Douglas remedy, urged the government to give it careful consideration and take action to introduce it if feasible. Growing pressure within the U.F.A. led to the holding of a legislative inquiry, by a committee of the whole house, into the possibilities of social credit, in March and April of 1934, at which Aberhart was the first and most lengthy witness and Major Douglas himself the final one. The questioning by the government leaders was mainly designed to elicit the unworkability of social credit and the difficulty of introducing it into the province, but although neither Aberhart nor Douglas could be said to have met the implied criticisms, the demonstration that the U.F.A. leaders were hostile or lukewarm gave new impetus to the social credit movement.

By the autumn of 1934 there was strong pressure within the Aberhart social credit movement for forming a social credit electoral organization to contest the 1935 provincial election. In December 1934 Aberhart announced that at the next election "reliable, honourable, bribe-proof business men who have definitely laid aside their party politic affiliations, will be asked to represent Social Credit in every constituency."[2] This step, it was explained, was being taken to ensure that social credit should not become party politics. "In order that the issue shall not be confused, we have insisted that the Social Credit proposals be kept distinct and separate from party

[2]*Alberta Social Credit Chronicle*, Dec. 7, 1934.

politics." This gloss did not deceive the existing parties. When the U.F.A. convention met in January 1935 it heard and questioned Aberhart at great length and finally, by an overwhelming majority, rejected the resolution to incorporate the Aberhart plan in the U.F.A. platform. The way was then clear for Aberhart to turn his movement into a political party. This he proceeded immediately to do.

The organization was based on local social credit groups but there was always strong control from Aberhart's headquarters. A "Preliminary Draft Organization and Discussion of Platform" was sent out to local groups in February and March, 1935, giving instructions for holding constituency conventions. Each group with twenty or more members was to choose three delegates; any polling division without such a group was to have one delegate, to be approved by one of the accredited delegates. Each convention was to be called by the leaders of the district under authority from Calgary headquarters. The constituency conventions were to elect constituency officials, elect seven delegates each to one of the central conventions to be held in Calgary and Edmonton in April, and discuss and propose amendments to the draft platform. They were not, however, to nominate the party candidates for the provincial general election.

Constituency conventions along these lines were held in March, and in April the two central conventions, of the Southern and Northern Alberta Social Credit Leagues, took the final steps in creating a political party. Aberhart was given full powers as leader, was instructed not to stand as a candidate for any seat, but was authorized to assume leadership of the government if the party won a majority of seats. He was also given the final choice in the nomination of the candidate for each constituency. The constituency convention was to nominate three or four contenders for the candidacy, and Aberhart "together with his advisory committee and the seven constituency delegates" was "empowered to decide the candidate from those nominated by the constituency convention."[3]

Following this plan, the constituency conventions met and each nominated three or four prospective candidates. In the interval between this nomination and the final choice of the one candidate, the integrity, ability, and former political affiliation of each of the prospective candidates was thoroughly canvassed. Aberhart and a small advisory committee then went to various centres in the province, met the prospective candidates, and, with the seven constituency delegates, made the final choices. Intensive organizing and can-

[3]Resolution of Southern Convention, April 4–5, *ibid.*, April 12, 1935.

vassing in each constituency accompanied and followed this process of selection.[4] On August 22, 1935, the Social Credit League won 56 of the 63 seats in the legislature.

It will be apparent, from this brief account of the early stages of the Alberta social credit movement and from what has been said earlier, that the circumstances in which the movement and the party developed were very different from those confronting Douglas social crediters in England, either then or at any earlier period. First, because Alberta was so largely a *petit-bourgeois* and debtor community, producing primary commodities for world markets, the effect of the depression was a sudden and drastic reduction of almost the whole community to spiritual and material insecurity and want. There was no Labour party or labour faith to sustain any substantial part of the community, as in England, nor any strong conservative faith; virtually the whole community was set adrift by the collapse of the economic and spiritual values. Secondly, again as a result of the class composition and debtor position in Alberta, there was a long-standing and widespread disposition to turn to monetary cures when economic difficulties became pressing. Thirdly, there was the widespread predilection for prophetic religion, as preached by those who made a point of bringing religion to the people and keeping it there. Of such religious movements, marked by the continual dependence of the followers on the leaders, and the leaders' confidence that they had all the answers, Aberhart's was only one—but much the most successful one.

These three circumstances made Alberta, as a community, far more receptive than was England to a monetary reform doctrine with spiritual overtones. They made it possible for social credit to become a mass movement, and in so doing ensured the vulgarization of the social and economic doctrine of Major Douglas. This presented no difficulty.

Other circumstances combined to lead to modification of the Douglas political theory. Of these the most important was the Albertan experience of active delegate democracy and the lively recollection that a popular movement could be turned into a successful electoral organization. A people who had seen the U.F.A. sweep into office after only a year or two of political organization was not intimidated by the difficulties of building a new organization

---

[4]For an account of the nomination procedure and the campaign, by one of the candidates, see N. B. James, *The Autobiography of a Nobody* (Toronto, 1947), chaps. 21, 22.

for the purpose of capturing political power. Their inclination to do so was increased by the lack of any established party which could command a belief in its ability or willingness to do anything to rescue the people of Alberta from their plight.[5] These circumstances made it possible, as it was not possible in England, to contemplate turning the social credit movement into a political party. Yet although Major Douglas was always opposed to any attempt to create a party, the fundamental principles of his political theory were readily adaptable to the Alberta situation.

§ 3. Aberhart Doctrine and Practice, to the 1935 Election

The social, economic, and political doctrine propounded by Aberhart can be described quite briefly; his own political practice less briefly, for it was a compound of Douglas strategy, Alberta's requirements, and Aberhart opportunism.

The Douglas theory of the cultural heritage, the case against the financial system, and the technical economic analysis of money, credit, and prices, all strained through Aberhart's powerful and less sophisticated mind, issued in a doctrine cruder and more forceful than the original, and always directly related to the immediate Alberta problem. Douglas's diffuse social and economic doctrine was reduced to a few stereotypes of high emotional and low intellectual content, suitable for proselytizing. These were the staple of the study groups, the broadcasts, and the columns of the Social Credit League's weekly paper.[6] The cultural heritage, "A plus B," the unearned increment, the basic dividend, and the just price became the dogmas with which converts were made.

In this process of reduction much of the Douglas doctrine was lost, but it could easily be spared. Some of it was distorted, but the distortion did no damage. The Douglas concept of unearned increment, for instance, was confused with profiteering through price-spreads and became almost unrecognizable. The "just price" underwent a similar change. In Douglas theory it stood for a system of prices periodically

[5]One reason for the sweeping social credit political victory in Alberta in contrast with the C.C.F. victory in the otherwise rather similar province of Saskatchewan may be seen in the fact that Alberta had had a farmers' government for so long that it had become conservative and unable to cope with the farmers' reaction to the depression. The farmers' organizations in both provinces were the backbone of the C.C.F. from its formation in 1932; but in Alberta the farmers' organization was seriously discredited by its conservatism, while in Saskatchewan it had never been in office.

[6]*Alberta Social Credit Chronicle*, published from July 20, 1934, to Jan. 17, 1936.

fixed in order to ensure that everything produced would be bought; it was a matter of impersonal accountancy and in no way excluded profit. In Aberhart's hands it became less an economic than a moral concept; it was a "fair" price which would exclude profit and, instead, allow producers and distributors a "fair return" for their work by such means as a commission on turnover.

Where the Douglas economic theory was not distorted it was narrowed into a presentation of the cause and cure of the local and immediate problem. The cultural heritage became the potential productivity of Alberta's resources, and finally became the allurement of $25 a month. The A plus B theorem became a highly simplified explanation of the cause of the depression in Alberta, or at most of the business cycle, instead of a theory of the secular decline of capitalism.

All these revisions of the Douglas economic and social theory, reckless as they were of its niceties, strengthened the appeal of social credit for Albertans. Indeed, as one astute western observer, Professor McQueen, suggested early in 1933, the pure Douglas theory was too mysterious to succeed in Alberta.

Part of the strength of bi-metallism was that nobody quite understood it in the backwoods, but it did deal with pieces of silver and pieces of gold, and people hesitated to ask questions about such obvious things. They do persist in asking about bank credit when the Douglas scheme is expounded, and then it is immediately obvious that no one, including the speaker, knows anything about that. When the annals of demagoguery are written it will likely be concluded that to be popular a doctrine involving no mystery or too much mystery should always be discarded for one of just the right amount of mystery. Bank credit suffers from too much and debt adjustment hasn't enough of the mystery element.[7]

Aberhart's superb political sense enabled him to steer just the right course between the sober U.F.A. policy of debt adjustment and the miraculous credit doctrine that came to Alberta from a sophisticated urban culture.

As with the economic and social theory, so with the political; Aberhart took what he needed and developed it as the circumstances in Alberta seemed to require. The political theory was the easiest for him to grasp, being strikingly congenial to his talent for leadership and his belief that the people wanted to be led. He believed as strongly as Douglas that there was a general will for the broad

[7]R. McQueen, "Douglas, Dodds, Depression & Co.," originally published in the *Winnipeg Free Press*, April 29, 1933, and reprinted in the *Manitoba Arts Review*, II, 3, Spring 1941.

objective of, as he put it, ending poverty in the midst of plenty, and that that will could be mobilized by getting the people to demand results only.

Very early in his political campaign, and more emphatically as the campaign went on, Aberhart preached the necessity of the people's uniting to demand results and forgoing the divisive discussion of methods and technical theory. Even the social credit groups had to give up the luxury of discussing economic theory. By March 1935 he was publicly lecturing his followers on their duty to drop "A plus B" and devote themselves to mobilizing mass demand for results without explaining the theory. So far, he wrote, the movement has been dominated by "educators" who have devoted themselves to the explanation of technicalities in the belief that "no one is worth having in the movement unless he or she has a grasp of the fundamental technicalities." "The majority of Social Crediters at the present day have got it into their minds that this is the only way to gain support. And so it is if the aim is to make people 'Social Crediters.'" But now the aim is "to obtain a mass expression of the will of the people, i.e. a mobilization of the nation's most urgent desire—the abolition of poverty in plenty. . . . The vast majority of people are not interested in details, and so are satisfied to express their will and let somebody else do the job. . . . We have enough supporters who are technically sound, but you must admit we are short of men and women who can mobilize the will of democracy." What is needed now is not "educators" but "campaigners," no matter how "technically unsound." They are the ones to do the job: "a most brilliant exposition of 'A plus B' don't do it." So Aberhart gave a new directive: "the movement is officially, for the present at any rate, for the 'campaigner'"; the educators must "stand out of the way of the campaigner" and not "hold up the traffic by making demands on group energies and finances."[8]

From then on, social crediters as well as the general electorate were told not to concern themselves with the theoretical economic principles and diagnosis on which the social credit proposals were based; it was not necessary to understand them, but only to vote for basic dividends as the way of ending the depression. As the election campaign reached its climax all the emphasis was put on the people expressing their will for the abolition of poverty without bothering their heads either about the technical theory or about the methods to be used. Aberhart, who had never attempted to

[8]*Alberta Social Credit Chronicle*, March 22, 1935.

explain the technical theory to the electorate, dropped even his attempts to explain the social credit scheme; after saying that a plan could not be drawn up until a government favourable to social credit was in office and could get all the facts, he fell back on the homely analogy he had often used before:

You don't have to know all about Social Credit before you vote for it; you don't have to understand electricity to use it, for you know that experts have put the system in, and all you have to do is push the button and you get the light. So all you have to do about Social Credit is to cast your vote for it, and we will get experts to put the system in.[9]

In the main pre-election article in the social credit weekly paper, followers were adjured to unite in expressing the general will for results only. Aberhart's use of the notion of a general will to get votes for his party is so strikingly displayed in this article that it may be quoted at length.

VOTE FOR RESULTS, NOT SCHEMES

It is for the people to demand what they want clearly and urgently—to DEMAND RESULTS. STAND FAST ON that, for there lies hope. More, this is our might, our power to secure those results.

Consider that vast number of men and women who are electors. Each and every one has his own wishes and desires, hopes for better times, wishes for leisure and enjoyment. Their united WILL—the will of the People—is not difficult to interpret. Let them but grasp that our distresses and worries REALLY CAN be swept away from out our lives, that nature's bounty and man's ingenuity REALLY CAN provide ourselves, our houses and our friends with the good things those dividends would buy; let them but see that, and the thing is done.

RESULTS

Then always vote for the RESULTS you want. For if you vote for any scheme whatsoever you will merely be passing your opinion on it. And you may be sure that there will always be others voting for some OTHER plan, and so nothing vital will be done. But add your WILL to that of other Alberta voters, and together we shall gain power that will move mountains—that most assuredly will abolish poverty—*easily*—for it is just a bad dream. Facts, the REAL things, have only to be straightened up a little, rearranged, and poverty will cease to exist.[10]

This is the voice of a true believer, but Aberhart, the practical politician, was not unaware of the advantage to be derived from the very broad mandate implied in this theory. It was remarkably convenient in preventing constituency resolutions from tying his

[9]Aberhart at an Edmonton meeting, as quoted in the *Albertan*, August 14, 1935.
[10]*Alberta Social Credit Chronicle*, Aug. 16, 1935.

hands. At the Calgary constituency convention of March 25, 1935, for instance, motions making specific recommendations on the policing of the province, on compulsory pasteurization, on public works and relief schemes, on the public health act and on oil production, were all defeated, not on their merits but on the ground that it was not the business of the convention to take a stand on such matters. Aberhart endorsed the convention's refusal to consider these motions, telling the delegates: "A democracy can suggest but it has not the power to execute, and that is what anybody would be doing when you start to decide what your government should and should not do when it is elected. Don't try to tell your government everything they should do. The minute you start to talk about the policing of the country you are out of order. The one great thing you have to do is keep together. . . ."[11] Nothing could be more faithful to the Douglas theory, nor in more striking contrast to the U.F.A. theory of democracy. The plebiscitarian character of the Aberhart movement is sufficiently demonstrated, not by the fact that this theory was held by the leaders, but by the fact that it was outspokenly proclaimed by them and willingly accepted by the followers.

Equally faithful to the original social credit theory was Aberhart's emphasis on the supposedly subordinate role of the politician. He preached the Douglas theory that the function of the politician was merely to be a channel for bringing mass desire to bear on the experts. During the election campaign the voters were encouraged to consider politicians, as well as experts, expendable; if the elected politicians failed to carry out, or to get the experts to carry out, the people's mandate for results, they should expect to be replaced.[12] And Aberhart was prepared to provide machinery for this. His demand for an unlimited mandate was mitigated by a pledge to introduce legislation providing for the recall of any elected member by his constituents. It is of course the commonplace technique of mass leaders to insist that they are utterly the servants of the people and readily dismissable by the people. They are the more ready to do this when they are fairly sure that they are indispensable. A Recall Act was duly passed by the social credit legislature in April 1936, and was repealed in October 1937, retroactively to the date of the original enactment, just when a petition to recall Aberhart himself was gathering signatures in his own constituency.

In all the aspects of Aberhart's campaign that we have noticed so far, his practice was fully in accord with the main principles laid

[11]*Ibid.*, March 29, 1935.   [12]E.g., *ibid.*, May 31, 1935.

down in the Douglas theory. He shared Douglas's assumptions about the capacities of the people and was a far more successful practitioner of the art of leadership which those assumptions implied.

In some matters, however, he departed from the practice required by Douglas's political theory. The most striking deviation was his formation of an electoral machine to contest every constituency in the general election. This was in effect to establish a political party, whereas Douglas, as we have seen, was opposed to any attempt to form a political party. Yet in this, Aberhart's deviation was more apparent than real.

From the beginning of his political activity Aberhart was thinking of it in terms of Douglas's "electoral campaign." This conception was evident in his first announcement, in December 1934, that social credit candidates would be run in every constituency; it accounts for the otherwise peculiar statement that this action was being taken in order to keep social credit proposals separate from party politics.[13] Again, the "elector's pledge" proposed by Aberhart at an early stage in the campaign was modelled closely on the pledge which Douglas had proposed some six months earlier as part of his English electoral campaign. After reciting his will that poverty be abolished by the distribution of basic dividends, the elector was to pledge himself "to vote for any Provincial Parliamentary candidate in Alberta who will undertake, that this, my declared policy, shall be carried out before any other legislation. This candidate to be 100% supporter of Social Credit." The latter stipulation was technically consistent with a candidate's membership in the U.F.A. or any other party, but the next sentence of the pledge (coming, as it did, after the U.F.A. had turned down social credit) made it plain that no other party than social credit could be supported: "If no candidate for whom I can vote will give such undertaking, I will register my vote in opposition to the party representing [*sic*: ?represented in] Parliament who has been in power and failed to recognize Social Credit in their platform, so that all may learn that true democracy enjoins obedience to the will of the people."[14] Aberhart did not bother, as the Douglas movement in England was doing, to obtain signatures to this pledge: it was put forward merely as "a declaration and pledge that every good Social Crediter should be willing to take and keep."

In the Alberta campaign the elector's pledge was merely supplementary, for the movement had already been committed, by its leader, to the nomination of a complete set of social credit candi-

[13]See above, p. 146.　　　[14]*Alberta Social Credit Chronicle*, Feb. 8, 1935.

dates independent of any existing party. It may seem that in these circumstances Aberhart's talk of an elector's pledge was only misleading. But on closer examination it appears that his decision to run his own candidates in every constituency was not inconsistent with the Douglas strategy, for the latter did envisage a final recourse to independent "national Dividend" candidates. Aberhart's action was simply more precipitous, as was required by the pace of the movement in Alberta.

A second apparent deviation from Douglas strategy was, like the one just discussed, more apparent than real. Although Aberhart did not use the technical theory of social credit in his bid for mass support, and even reduced the theory to a subordinate place within the movement, in order to concentrate on mobilizing a mass desire for the abolition of poverty, he found it impossible to build up a popular campaign without a specific scheme for Alberta. It was all very well for Douglas, who had never got to the stage of leading an active mass movement within sight of political success, to say that the electorate should not be allowed to discuss schemes or "methods" of achieving economic security and freedom. It was true that the whole electorate could not be expected to understand the A plus B theorem, but Aberhart saw quite early that the Alberta electorate wanted something more specific than general concepts such as the unearned "increment of association" and the "just price." These had been the stock in trade of the converters and the converted, but they were not enough to persuade a still wider public to support social credit politically. It is evident from, for instance, the questions put to Aberhart, and to Douglas, at the legislative hearings in March and April of 1934, that what was wanted was a specific scheme for the distribution of social credit in the province. How would social credit dividends be paid and financed, how would the flow of credit be kept up, and how would prices be controlled? Aberhart had realized, even earlier, that these were the questions people wanted answered. His first expository pamphlet, *The Douglas System of Economics*, published some time prior to February 1934, was devoted almost entirely to detailed explanation of these points. So, largely, was his presentation of the social credit case to the legislative committee in March 1934.[15] His second pamphlet, the *Social Credit Manual*, issued at the beginning of July 1935, was an even more detailed exposition, a large part of it being devoted to a series

[15]*The Douglas System of Social Credit: Evidence Taken by the Agricultural Committee of the Alberta Legislature* (Edmonton, 1934), pp. 11ff.

of sixty questions and answers, most of them on particulars of the proposed operation of the scheme of dividends and price regulation and credit flow.

Aberhart's campaign, through most of its course, had thus consisted largely in explaining and defending in considerable detail the specific schemes he had formulated for financing and distributing social credit in the province. In campaigning on these proposals, he was apparently asking the voters to endorse "methods" as well as objectives. And in so doing he incidentally made it more obvious than ever that he did not understand Douglas's economic proposals or theory. For instance, although he insisted, following Douglas, that social credit dividends were not to be financed by taxation, he outlined in detail his proposal for financing the issuance of dividends by collecting a levy on commodity transactions, which was in effect a very substantial processing or turnover tax.[16] Douglas publicly repudiated this scheme and suggested that Aberhart had "made the common tactical mistake of elaborating his detail to a general audience to too great an extent."[17] Aberhart replied, by radio, that he was "convinced that we could never have had the astounding results we have had if we continually spoke in generalities and did not bring the subject matter down to the detail of everyday life,"[18] and he repeated all the detail in the definitive *Social Credit Manual* published a few weeks later.

Another distortion of the Douglas theory was evident in the compulsive nature of Aberhart's proposals. Douglas had emphasized that the social credit dividends were to be a distribution of the whole society's unearned increment of wealth and therefore were not to be made dependent on any recipient's contribution to production: "it is as members of the community, tout court, unconditionally, that individuals should benefit by this unearned increment."[18a] Douglas indeed contradicted himself on this point once, by proposing that, for the first five years after the initiation of a social credit scheme, an individual who refused fit employment would be liable to suspension of his dividend.[18b] There was therefore a Douglas precedent for Aberhart's

[16]As an important part of Aberhart's scheme this was given much radio publicity, and can be seen in its final form in Aberhart's *Social Credit Manual* (1935), pp. 29, 37.

[17]Letter to J. F. Lymburn, June 1, 1935, published as an appendix to Douglas's *First Interim Report on the Possibilities of the Application of Social Credit Principles to the Province of Alberta* (Edmonton, 1935), p. 14.

[18]Aberhart broadcast, as reported in the *Calgary Daily Herald*, June 12, 1935.

[18a]Douglas, *These Present Discontents* (1922), p. 13.

[18b]Douglas, *Social Credit* (3rd ed., 1933), Appendix: "The Draft Scheme for Scotland," art. 9.

announcement that if a citizen "persisted in refusing work, his dividends would be cut off or temporarily suspended. Then, as there is no relief or dole, he would be compelled to work."[19] But there was no Douglas precedent for the further announcements that any citizen who "squandered his dividends and was hungry or improperly clothed" would be warned by an Inspector that "he was-abusing his rights and privileges and that it must be stopped or he would lose his dividends,"[20] and that a person who "did not wish to join with the Social Credit idea . . . would not receive any monthly dividends."[21]

These are the most striking of the distortions of the Douglas economic proposals which became prominent during Aberhart's election campaign. They are cited here not primarily as examples of Aberhart's misunderstanding of Douglas's basic economic ideas, but as instances of that emphasis on detail and "methods" which appears as a departure from the requirements of the Douglas political theory. It was not, however, a serious departure. Aberhart, as we have seen, strenuously maintained the Douglas principle that the people should leave schemes or "methods"—the terms are interchangeable—to the expert, so that they should not be diverted from expressing their general will for results. When he came to apply this principle it proved to be unworkable; like so many of Douglas's proposals it was too ill defined to be effectively applied. The fact was that the people demanded a scheme, and Aberhart was not at all averse to giving them one. But he seems himself to have believed that he was not asking for electoral endorsement of "methods." He generally prefaced his exposition of his detailed practical scheme with the cautioning statement that it was not a detailed plan, and that such a plan could only be prepared later by experts.[22] And his emphasis on the practical scheme can be reconciled with the Douglas principle, for Douglas did allow that the electorate should be told enough to show them that social credit could produce the desired results. The Albertans whom Aberhart had to reach wanted more showing than Douglas had anticipated.

The Douglas principle of leaving "methods" to the experts was of course a great convenience for Aberhart, for although he had put forward and defended a specific plan for Alberta and was asking for electoral support on that basis, which implied that he was something of an expert himself, he could always disclaim expertness and avoid its responsibility when pressed too far, as when he refused

[19]Aberhart, *Social Credit Manual* (1935), pp. 33–5.   [20]*Ibid.*, p. 33.
[21]*Ibid.*, p. 47
[22]E.g., *Social Credit Manual*, pp. 3, 5, 59.

the invitation of the U.F.A. government to go to Edmonton and produce a working plan for the introduction of social credit. It need not be suggested that it was only for this reason that Aberhart embraced the Douglas theory of the expert; he seems genuinely to have felt that his own role was primarily to mobilize mass desire for results rather than to provide a plan.

It thus appears that both Aberhart's descent into particularity and his early decision to run social credit candidates in every constituency were valid applications of the Douglas political theory to the circumstances in Alberta, and that Aberhart's acceptance of the Douglas political theory whereby the people were confined to demanding broad results and the experts were responsible for producing them was genuine as well as convenient. But in another matter Aberhart stretched the Douglas theory beyond anything implied in the original. He apparently took it to justify that peculiar device we have already noticed whereby the social credit candidate in each constituency was finally chosen by him and his advisory committee rather than by the constituency delegates in convention. The case the social credit leaders usually made for this device was the empirical one that it was necessary to prevent false social crediters from getting the nomination by stealth or intrigue. Perhaps this case did not sound too convincing; at any rate, they seem also to have taken the position, as a matter of principle, that nomination of a candidate fell within the functions of the expert rather than of the people. The full resolution of the Southern Alberta Social Credit Convention which established this device was as follows:

Whereas we must always maintain the fundamental principles of true democracy; and

Whereas there is a tempting opportunity afforded under the old political lines for candidates to use wire-pulling tactics; and

Whereas we believe that it is fundamental under true democracy that the people directly, or indirectly through representation, are qualified to indicate the general course of their desires, but that execution of them must be left to experts,

Be it therefore resolved that in the nomination of candidates in each constituency we agree to nominate three or four—and that our leader together with his advisory committee be empowered to decide the candidate from those nominated by the constituency convention.[23]

If the third clause of the preamble has any meaning it is presumably that the choice of candidates to represent their general will is not within the competence of the people. Yet even this astonishing doc-

[23]*Alberta Social Credit Chronicle*, April 12, 1935.

trine was not plainly a distortion of the Douglas theory, for Douglas had not carried his theory to the point of stipulating nominating procedures.

Apart from this curious interpretation of the theory of the experts and the people, however, the social credit campaign may be said to have been conducted as nearly as possible along the lines of the Douglas theory. There are only a few recorded instances of social credit spokesmen making commitments on particular matters, such as interest-free production loans and hail insurance coverage for farmers unable to pay for it,[24] which were matters of detail that should not have been put to the people according to the Douglas political theory. In contrast with the U.F.A. and other parties, the social crediters scarcely bothered to draw up an election platform. A platform was published a few days before the election, but it had all the appearance of an afterthought, and contained nothing on social or economic methods. Aberhart properly enough said, immediately after the election, that the social credit party had made only one promise, to end poverty amidst plenty, or, more modestly, "to attempt to provide all citizens with the bare necessities of life."[25] He took it that he had been given the mandate he had asked for, that he had been instructed to provide results by methods to be devised by whatever experts he would charge with that task. The mandate included a time allowance of eighteen months, for Aberhart had repeatedly said that he would need that long to introduce social credit into the province.[26]

In summary, it appears that both of the main apparent deviations from Douglas political theory which were required by the conditions in Alberta—the creation of a political party, and the strategy of "bringing the subject matter down to the detail of everyday life"— were less departures from the Douglas political theory than evidence that that theory was too abstractly schematic to be practical. This was to be expected, for Douglas had developed it in circumstances far removed from the actual requirements of a mass movement. Aberhart's political strategy and theory were consistently opportunistic, but opportunism involved no serious unfaithfulness to the Douglas political theory.

Thus, apart from the distortions of Douglas's economic and social theory, which we have seen to have resulted partly from the circumstances in Alberta and partly from Aberhart's moral preconceptions and intellectual limitations, the impact of Alberta on social

[24]E. C. Manning, reported in the *Albertan*, Aug. 1, 1935.
[25]*Albertan*, Aug. 24, 1935.   [26]E.g., *Social Credit Manual* (1935), p. 62.

credit was to reduce its political theory to immediate practicality, without rejecting its fundamental assumptions and principles: the homogeneous general will, the evocation of the general will by confining the people to demanding results, and the reliance on the experts for "methods."

To the extent that the people of Alberta were caught up in this kind of thinking, the impact of social credit on Alberta may be said to have been to alter the prevailing theory and practice of government, even before the social credit government took office. It substituted the doctor's mandate for the interest group mandate, the general will for the economic group will. It reduced the function of political decision, at the level of the electorate, to the registration of an uninstructed and undifferentiated will for general welfare. The U.F.A. assumption that a homogeneous social interest would emerge once the popular forces had overthrown the rule of the wealthy interests, gave way to the social credit assumption that a homogeneous social interest existed now and could be discovered and made effective immediately. The *petit-bourgeois* concept of society, which had impaired the U.F.A. theory, was now carried to its extreme. Beside the tenuous social credit concept of democracy, the U.F.A. theory appears thoroughly realistic.

§ 4. Aberhart Political Practice: The First Eighteen Months of Office

When Aberhart's Social Credit League won 89 per cent of all the seats in the provincial election of 1935 its political theory was not as clearly defined as that of the U.F.A. had been at the time of its only slightly less spectacular victory in 1921. The U.F.A. had had quite definite convictions about the proper relation between the elected legislative member and the constituency association, between the private member and the cabinet, and between the government and the convention. They had given thought to these relationships because they had assumed that the stuff of politics would continue to be specific demands of different local and economic groups. The problem as they saw it was to provide new channels by which the demands of these groups for particular legislative or executive action could be brought to bear on the government more effectively than by the old party system. Hence the initial U.F.A. emphasis on constituency autonomy, responsibility of legislative members to the constituency association, freedom of legislative members from cabinet domination, and the separation of legislature and convention and of cabinet and U.F.A. executive.

The outlook of the Social Credit League was strikingly different. The social crediters had given very little thought to the relations between elected member, cabinet, constituency association, and convention. Not much thought was needed, for these matters were pretty well all settled by the overriding social credit political theory. The stuff of politics was no longer to be the particular demands of different local and economic groups; it was to be the implementation of the unanimous general will, the undifferentiated mass desire for economic plenty, freedom, and security.

The social credit constituency association represented not that exclusive body of farmers who had been assumed, in U.F.A. thinking, to have a clear and instructed view of their own group interest and of the legislation that would be beneficial to them, but the miscellaneous body of citizens who were assumed to have a clear and uninstructed demand for "results." Neither the elected member of the legislature nor the constituency association was to debate or endorse "methods"; they were merely to be channels for mass desire. The cabinet and the premier were to be reduced, or magnified, to the same position as the whole legislature. Aberhart had said nothing specific about the role of the premier and cabinet but had endorsed the Douglas theory, by which a government was not to have the responsibility of deciding on legislative and executive policies in the ordinary sense, but would confine itself to hiring, exhorting, and firing experts who would have the responsibility and the power of deciding all particular legislation and executive policies. Since the expert was to take all the specific responsibilities there was thought to be no problem of the relative responsibilities and power of cabinet, elected member of the legislature, constituency association, and convention. They all were to share the one task of bringing the general will to bear on the experts. The legislature and cabinet were indeed to have the additional task of deciding what experts to empower, and how long to give them, but in the performance of this function there was no clear differentiation between the duties of the cabinet and those of the whole legislature.

The only proclaimed line of responsibility was that by which elected members of the legislature were to be made recallable by their constituents. The social credit provision for recall was not, as with the U.F.A., recall by the constituency association, but recall by petition signed by a stated percentage of all the voters in the constituency. This was quite in keeping with, though not required by, the social credit notion of a conglomerate electorate in each constituency. It was also quite in keeping with the fact that it was not by the constituency association that the elected member had originally been chosen as the social credit candidate. The assumption of a general will required, as it generally has done, the assumption of an inspired and omnicompetent leader, with a corresponding reduction in the importance of the intermediate delegate bodies.

From the beginning, Aberhart's organization was strongly centralized, in contrast with the U.F.A. His headquarters, not a delegate convention, decided and announced that candidates would be run in every constituency, issued the draft platform and instructions to the constituencies, limited the agenda of constituency conventions, and laid down the procedure for nominations. The central office took the initiative, and kept control of the electoral machinery throughout. The constituency conventions and the central conventions were more than compliant; they gave themselves enthusiastically to the will of their leader. The social credit political theory and the inspirational quality of Aberhart's leadership, which demanded and received the complete submergence of his followers' wills, combined to put any problem of the popular control of the legislature out of sight, or at least in abeyance.

Thus when the social crediters took office as the government of the province they did not have to contend with the centrifugal tendencies which had confronted the first U.F.A. cabinet. There was no demand for constituency autonomy, for responsibility of members of the legislature to constituency associations, or for freedom of members from cabinet domination.

The first social credit government was formed in accordance with the usual practices of the cabinet system. Aberhart had been authorized by the central social credit conventions, four months before the election, to assume the leadership of the government in the event of a social credit victory. There was, of course, no inconsistency in the social crediters' undertaking, prior to the election, to form a government, as there had been in the case of the U.F.A. with its theory of group government. A meeting of all the successful and defeated social credit candidates, within a week of the election, endorsed Aberhart as leader and premier-elect and gave him "an absolute free hand in the selection of such person or persons as he deems necessary for the duties involved in the efficient administration of public affairs."[27] The members-elect then pledged themselves to vacate any seats the premier might wish to have at his disposal in

[27]*Alberta Social Credit Chronicle*, Aug. 30, 1935.

forming the cabinet. One seat would certainly be needed, for the premier-elect had not been a candidate. Thus Aberhart accepted the office of premier with complete freedom to choose his cabinet from within or without the elected legislative party. The premier accepted the usual powers and responsibility for administration, and the cabinet was formed in accordance with the normal conventions.

While none of this was inconsistent with social credit theory, that theory did require that the premier and cabinet should then, in effect, abdicate in favour of responsible experts. There is no evidence that Aberhart ever had any intention of doing so, and although the evidence of his contrary intention is not decisive, it is clear that he put himself in a position where he was compelled to retain responsibility.

Major Douglas was the obvious candidate for the position of expert, the more so as he was already under contract with the government of Alberta (a contract made by, but outlasting, the U.F.A. government) to act as "Principal Reconstruction Adviser to the Government." In the event, this contractual obligation confused rather than clarified matters, for it meant that besides being the acknowledged founder and master of social credit doctrine Douglas was at the same time a mere paid adviser of the government of Alberta. Aberhart took advantage of this to insist that Douglas provide not merely advice, but the kind of advice which would fit in with what Aberhart had already done or determined to do. The exchange of correspondence between Aberhart and Douglas[28] reveals the impossibility of Aberhart's following the social credit political theory to the extent of making Douglas the responsible expert.

One of Aberhart's first actions after the election, even before he was installed as premier, was to cable Douglas: "Victorious when can you come?"[29] This cannot be taken to imply an intention to hand over responsibility to Douglas, for when Douglas replied that he could come in the middle of September, Aberhart gave no definite invitation but instead asked for "full information by letter or preliminary directions."[30] Douglas at once sent proposals for "immediate measures."[31] Of the two specific financial proposals, Aberhart brushed one aside as a matter of detail which could be taken up later,[32]

[28]The complete correspondence for the period August 24, 1935, to March 24, 1936, is published as Appendix III in C. H. Douglas, *The Alberta Experiment* (London, 1937).   [29]Aberhart to Douglas, Aug. 24, 1935.

[30]Aberhart to Douglas, Sept. 4, 1935.
[31]Douglas to Aberhart, Sept. 5, 1935.
[32]Aberhart to Douglas, Sept. 24, 1935.

and rejected the other on the ground that it "would alarm our citizens."[33] From the beginning he consistently rejected Douglas's financial advice, while asking repeatedly and emphatically for a detailed plan or even "definite instructions." But he made it clear that he as premier, and the cabinet, were responsible: "we are awaiting the definite outline of your plans so that we may come to some conclusion as to what is definitely necessary."[34] Douglas made further specific proposals. At the end of October, resentful of Aberhart's neglect of his proposals and of his actions in following an orthodox financial policy and appointing Mr. R. J. Magor, an orthodox financier, as adviser to the government, Douglas proposed the termination of his contract.[35] Aberhart replied a month later, rejecting Douglas's latest specific financial advice, demanding that he fulfil his contract by giving a definite outline of the steps to be taken "when we begin to establish social credit," and warning him that "nothing can be gained by your assuming the position of dictation rather than that of advice."[36]

The positions taken by the two men were irreconcilable because Aberhart would not accept Douglas's main strategy, and apparently did not even understand it, yet continued to demand detailed advice on matters which he considered primary and Douglas considered secondary. The crucial issue was the financing of the provincial debt. Aberhart thought that this could be done along orthodox lines —federal government and bank loans, and provincial governmental economies and a balanced budget—without prejudicing the introduction of social credit, and he proceeded to act along these lines. Douglas, quite accurately, said that this kind of action would seriously prejudice the possibility of introducing social credit, and that the first step that must be taken to introduce social credit was for the government to "emancipate itself from the power of banking and international finance" and to challenge "the monopoly of credit." "A policy," he wrote "which apparently aims at defeating the banks with the assistance of the banks themselves, under the supervision of an agent of the banks, seems to be so dangerous that I do not feel it has a reasonable chance of success. . . ."[37]

In fact, Aberhart's policy was not social credit at all in any sense that Douglas could recognize; but Aberhart was reluctant to per-

[33]Aberhart to Douglas, Sept. 24, 1935.
[34]Aberhart to Douglas, Sept. 24, 1935.
[35]Douglas to Aberhart, Oct. 29, 1935.
[36]Aberhart to Douglas, Nov. 27, 1935.
[37]Douglas to Aberhart, Oct. 29, 1935.

ceive it. The cause of his reluctance takes us to the heart of the matter: he was unwilling to challenge the financial powers because he had accepted responsibility for administering the province and he needed money to do it. Once he had accepted this responsibility, he had to rely on outside finance in order to carry on the government. This made it impossible for him to accept Douglas's advice. A *fortiori*, it was impossible for him to give Douglas the powers of the responsible expert envisaged in the social credit political theory. Aberhart made his position clear in informing Douglas: "I personally do not intend to sink my right as Premier to express my opinion upon your advice or that of any other person in the employ of the government. I am responsible to the people, and I of course shall be called to account for any mistakes that are made."[38] The reduction of the expert to an employee, and the assertion that the premier was responsible to the people for any mistakes that might be made, was a direct negation of the social credit political theory.

Having abandoned the social credit theory of the roles of the politician and the expert, Aberhart from the outset of his administration assumed for himself and his cabinet all the usual functions. Since the cabinet took responsibility it had to sponsor all sorts of particular legislation and steer it through the legislature. And although there was practically no opposition group in the legislature to keep the social credit members together, the social credit ministers did not have as much difficulty from members' independence or from constituency autonomy in the first session as the U.F.A. cabinet had had in its first session. Long and frequent caucuses produced virtually unanimous agreement; there were few cases of private members voting against the government until the 1937 insurgency. This was to be expected in view of the members' indoctrination. They were there to demand results, not to debate "methods," and their plain duty and interest was to support the government and give it a chance to produce results. Also they were dependent to an unusual extent on the person of Aberhart. They were mindful of the fact that he had chosen each of them as the social credit candidate. And if some of the social credit members of the legislature did not regard him as their inspired leader, at least they were aware that his prestige was an essential asset of the party, while many, perhaps most, of the members had submerged their wills in his and needed to keep up their faith in his leadership.

Two things, then, combined to give the cabinet unusual authority

[38]Aberhart to Douglas, Jan. 24, 1936.

over the legislative party: the followers' acceptance of the leader as inspired, and the party's indoctrination with the theory that it was not the business of an elected legislature to discuss "methods" but only to demand results. But as we have seen, while the followers were still guided by this theory, Aberhart had rejected the complementary theory of the proper relation between experts and politicians. In other words, while the private members of the legislature were nothing but "representatives of mass desire," the cabinet rejected this role for itself and assumed the responsibility for formulating legislation. In so doing it conformed to the orthodox pattern of cabinet government.

This pattern was substantially retained during the first year and a half of the administration, but even during that period there were noticeable deviations from it, indicative of an underlying relation between cabinet, legislature, and electorate rather different from either the orthodox or the U.F.A. pattern of democratic government. From the beginning of his premiership Aberhart made it a point not to speak in the legislature. Apart from one brief intervention in the debate in the special session in 1936,[39] in reply to an opposition taunt that he had fallen down on his promise to pay a $25 monthly dividend, Aberhart made no speech in the house until 1939, when he spoke for an hour and a half in defence of the government's record. Referring to this as "probably my maiden speech in the house," he said:

I have departed from my usual policy and I wonder if I have accomplished anything. I am sure our members are fully aware of everything I have said. I am equally sure that the opposition will not accept anything I have said. The public I can reach by radio, so why take up the time of the house with a long address? There is an old Chinese proverb, "crowing hens lay no eggs." If I must choose I would rather be a hen that lays eggs for the good of mankind than a hen that crows and never takes any action.[40]

The assumption that legislative debate is an alternative to action was entirely characteristic of Aberhart. The whole statement quoted suggests a complete lack of understanding of the orthodox theory of the function of parliamentary debate. But there was no reason why he should have troubled to understand the orthodox theory, much less have accepted it, for the ordinary theory hardly applies to a house in which one party has nine-tenths of the seats, and where the leader has his own radio station which can reach practically his whole electorate.

[39]On Aug. 27, 1936.   [40]*Edmonton Journal*, Feb. 18, 1939.

In fact, Aberhart had rejected the orthodox theory of the functions
of legislative debate in accepting, for the private members, the
Douglas theory on the function of the elected representative. In social
credit theory, the function of the members of the legislature was to
be representative of mass desire. Obviously, that function could only
be performed by those who took that view of it and had pledged
themselves to it, namely, the social credit members. It clearly could
not be performed by the few opposition members, who did not share
that view of their function. It was, then, quite logical for Aberhart
to neglect the legislature and to expect the legislature's function to
be performed instead by the caucus of the social credit members.
The legislature's sessions became for Aberhart a necessary evil, needed
only to pass legislation through the legally required stages. The
social credit caucus virtually took the place of the legislature's sessions. In the first session after the election the caucus was said to
have met four nights a week throughout the session.[41] In the first
two weeks of the 1937 session it was reported that the social credit
members had spent about eighteen hours in legislative session and
more than twice that long in caucus.[42]

Aberhart's indifference to the legislature called forth some un-
favourable comment, but only from opposition members and from
outside. His own followers in the house were apparently content.
They had no cause to complain, for they had the benefit of his
active presence in caucus. They may even have welcomed his
abstention in the house, for it gave them more scope for speech-
making to a full press gallery. The one function the legislative
sessions still did perform was the production of speeches suitable
for publicity in the members' constituencies.

We may see, in Aberhart's studied neglect of the legislature and
his reliance on party caucus and radio, an unconscious confusion
of the functions of party and state. This confusion was even more
noticeable in another deviation from normal practice: the use of
party machinery for the performance of governmental functions. The
government saw nothing incongruous in arranging that some of the
work of official registration of citizens for the promised social credit
basic dividends should be carried out by the party machinery. "The
work will be conducted by the campaign machinery set up by the
Social Credit party for the last general election. Men who served
the party at that time will prepare the way for registration by

41*Ibid.*, April 6, 1936.
42*Ibid.*, March 10, 1937.

organizing each constituency for registration. The work will be voluntary and will cost the Government nothing."[43]

On the whole it appears that in the first year and a half of his administration, Aberhart followed the orthodox theory of the relation of cabinet to private members, and did not need to trouble himself, as the U.F.A. had had to do, about the relation of elected member to constituency association or the relation of the government to the provincial convention. Paradoxically it was because the private members accepted the Douglas theory that they should not discuss "methods" but merely serve as representatives of mass desire, that the premier was able to depart from the Douglas theory and assume the normal responsibilities of cabinet government. But he was able to do so only as long as there was a reasonable expectation among the members that his policy would produce the results they were there to demand. After eighteen months, that expectation appeared no longer reasonable to a substantial group of the social credit members, and a revolt known in social credit circles as "the insurgency" broke out during the 1937 session of the legislature. The insurgent members, true to the Douglas theory, did not even then presume to debate "methods," but they did feel entitled to demand results; their complaints were not about this or that government measure, but about the absence of any government action to break away from orthodox finance and move toward social credit.

[43]Statement by Acting Premier Manning, *Alberta Social Credit Chronicle*, Sept. 13, 1935.

CHAPTER SEVEN

Social Credit in Alberta: The Recrudescence and Decline of Douglasism

->>-<<-

§ 1. Political Implications of the 1937 Insurgency

Having failed to call in Douglas or take his advice, Aberhart not unnaturally could show no progress toward social credit results by the end of the eighteen months he had allowed himself. It was not only that he had not yet actually started any flow of social credit dividends; that might have been forgiven, in view of various difficulties that had been encountered. What could not be forgiven, by those of his following who had absorbed the rudiments of Douglas's theory, was that Aberhart was apparently making no effort to do any of the fundamental things required by that theory. Nor could the fact that he was not on good terms with Douglas be entirely concealed.

From the beginning of the 1937 regular session of the legislature it was apparent that no major move towards the establishment of social credit had any place in the government's programme for that year. The speech from the throne, on February 25, foreshadowed an orthodox budget and the postponement for another whole fiscal year of any budgetary provision for social credit in the province. For the government to come before the legislature with such a negative programme without admitting failure was, to the more ardent social credit private members, galling evidence of the government's presumption as well as its ineptitude.

Before the rebellion of private members began in the legislature Aberhart took the offensive, by appealing, over the heads of the elected representatives, to the social crediters in the constituencies. In a Sunday broadcast from the Calgary Prophetic Bible Institute on February 28, he announced that he was unable to redeem his election pledge to establish social credit in Alberta within eighteen months. He then asked for a vote of confidence from the constituency associations.

He asked them to pass resolutions at constituency association meetings, advising whether they wished him to resign or continue his efforts toward a new economic order for Alberta. . . .

He told them he had no intention of resigning unless the people desired a change, either in leadership or in party.

The premier suggested no association votes be taken until the first week in June "when the roads and weather conditions are improved and after the legislation of the present session of parliament is made known."

"I shall expect the president of each constituency association . . . to call zone meetings of all Social Crediters now registered and have them express, by resolution, their decision in this matter."

"I am not asking our opponents what they think, for they had nothing to do with our election and had nothing to do with my promise."[1]

There was, of course, no reason why he should have asked his opponents for their opinions. But in pointedly not asking the elected social credit representatives what they thought, Aberhart was carrying one stage farther his subversion of the legislature. Not only was he passing over the legislature, which was in session then; he was also passing over the social credit caucus. Even the caucus was apparently regarded as unworthy of the one function allowed the legislature in Douglas theory, the representation of mass desire. Aberhart's appeal to the constituency associations was also a manoeuvre for time; he wanted their decision postponed for three months.

A substantial group of the elected representatives took their function more seriously. The first public indication of revolt was a statement by A. L. Blue (S.C., Ribstone) in the budget debate, on March 16, that he would not support a vote of money for the government to carry on until it had introduced social credit. A week later the existence of an insurgent group was known. The attack in force opened on March 23 with a speech by A. V. Bourcier (S.C., Lac Ste. Anne) denouncing the government's fiscal policy as the very opposite of social credit, and objecting to the regimentation involved in the proposed government bills on licensing and regulation of trade as inconsistent with social credit principles. Other social credit members attacked along the same lines. Their intention was to delay the passing of the budget until some legislation providing for the establishment of a social credit programme for the province had been introduced. On March 24 the government met its first defeat, though only on a procedural motion: an insurgent motion to adjourn rather early in the day was carried, against Aberhart's protest, by 27 to 25. Aberhart refused to regard this as a vote of want of confidence, and gave notice that he would

[1]*Edmonton Journal*, March 1, 1937.

move closure of the budget debate on March 29. The insurgent attack continued in the following days to such effect that Aberhart thought it wiser not to risk the life of the government by putting the budget to the vote of the house: in his Sunday broadcast on March 28, after denouncing the insurgents' financial proposals as confiscatory, he announced that he would withdraw his closure motion and ask for a temporary money vote, without taking the budget debate to a conclusion.

When the house met on March 29, Aberhart sought the unanimous consent of the house to the withdrawal of his closure motion, which was refused. The motion was then put and defeated, without a recorded division. The insurgents announced their determination to defeat the government's scheme of getting a temporary money vote passed, and said they were assured of enough support to defeat the motion for provisional estimates whenever it was made.

In caucus the same night Aberhart prevailed on the insurgents to meet the government half-way. What this meant was revealed in the house next day, March 30, when Aberhart, having introduced a bill entitled the *Social Credit Measures Amendment Act,* was allowed to proceed with an interim supply resolution and bill. The Social Credit Measures Amendment bill provided for the appointment by the legislature of a board of from five to seven members with authority to appoint a commission of experts to plan and implement a system of social credit. The government indicated that the house would be expected to adjourn for six to ten weeks after voting interim supply and passing the new bill. The interim supply, for three months, was voted the following day without dissent. But the Social Credit Measures Amendment bill ran into heavy weather. It was not acceptable to the insurgents. Neither were the complementary bills providing for the licensing and regulation of trade and industry.

A week later, on April 8, the Social Credit Measures Amendment bill was withdrawn, and the provincial treasurer, Solon Low, introduced a new comprehensive bill, entitled the *Alberta Social Credit Act.* The Act provided for the creation of "Alberta Credit" to the amount of "the unused capacity of industries and people of Alberta to produce wanted goods and services," the establishment of credit houses for the distribution and transfer of this credit, and the payment of subsidies to producers and distributors in support of a system of price discounts. It established a Social Credit Board consisting of five private members of the legislature who were named in the bill, and empowered the board (1) to appoint a commission of from three to five experts, each to hold office for ten years, to operate the system of credit creation and distribution, (2) to appoint additional technical experts, (3) to examine social credit legislation and "make recommendations for legislative action in respect thereof." The commission was given considerable authority but in some important matters its decisions were subject to the approval of the board, and in others (for instance, setting the date at which the payments of monthly dividends were to begin, and establishing classifications of persons entitled to the dividends) the board was given sole authority.

The feature of this bill, as of the bill it superseded, which attracted most attention in the opposition press, was the extent to which the cabinet had abdicated in favour of a board composed of a few private members of the legislature. In each bill it was the board, not the cabinet, which was given the responsibility of finding and appointing the experts who were to operate the scheme.

At first the government put a bold face on it. Aberhart said, in reference to the first bill:

It has been thought wise to remove the direction of Social Credit as far as possible from the realm of political influence. So we have already introduced an amending act calling upon the legislature to appoint a board of from five to seven members which will have full authority, apart from the lieutenant governor in council, to appoint a commission of qualified men to put into operation the plan and to have the advice of technical experts appointed or secured by the board.[2]

When the second bill, which had been introduced on April 8, came up for debate on April 13, the government admitted an even more striking renunciation of its responsibility. The provincial treasurer explained that although he had introduced the bill he took no responsibility for it. The bill, he said, "was drawn up by a committee [of insurgent members] without the interference of the cabinet."[3] Dr. Cross, as minister of trade and industry, made a similar statement: since the government's bills had not been accepted by the backbenchers, these men had been told to go ahead and prepare their own legislation. Mr. Manning, speaking as a member of the cabinet, said in extenuation that the cabinet had not tried to shirk its responsibility: "the idea of transferring responsibility to a board had come from a majority of the members and not from the cabinet."[4]

It might appear that the victory of the insurgents was complete, but it was far from being so. Indeed it was to meet insurgent criticism

[2]Sunday broadcast, April 4, as reported in *ibid.*, April 6, 1937.
[3]*Ibid.*, April 14, 1937.   [4]*Ibid.*

of this bill that the cabinet admitted, or rather, asserted that it was not responsible for the bill. But according to the insurgents the cabinet was not as innocent of responsibility as it had made out. Some of the insurgent members claimed that the bill as introduced in the house was not recognizable as the one prepared by the insurgent committee, but had been "mutilated and distorted by the government since it was handed over to it."[5] Specifically it was charged by one of the insurgent leaders, H. K. Brown, that in the insurgent committee's draft, the Social Credit Board was intended to be merely a temporary body for the selection of experts, whereas in the bill presented in the house the board was to be a permanent body. But another insurgent, G. L. MacLachlan, who was named in the bill as chairman of the proposed board, denied, as chairman of the insurgent committee which had drafted the bill, that there had been any major changes in it since it had left the committee's hands. Whether by accident or astuteness, the government had divided the insurgents in naming some of them to the proposed board. The extent to which they were divided is indicated by the fact that two amendments were proposed by individual insurgent members, one by A. J. Hooke that the tenure of the board be only until the prorogation of the present session, and one by Mrs. Rogers that the duties of the board be transferred to the cabinet, and both were defeated. The bill was passed on April 13, and the house adjourned on April 14.

The spectacle of a government introducing but disclaiming responsibility for a crucial bill was astonishing enough. Even more remarkable was the admission that the transfer of responsibility from the cabinet to the board, contained in the bill, had been dictated by the insurgents. The bill seemed to represent a complete capitulation of the government to the insurgents. The government was allowed to stay in office not merely at the price of having its immediate policy dictated by the insurgents, in accepting a bill for which it refused to take responsibility, but also at the price of handing over to a group of private members the continuing power of finding and appointing experts.

The insurgency, and this solution of it, were, to all appearances, applications of the original Douglas theory. The representatives of mass desire, or a sufficient number of them, had spoken. They had asserted that Aberhart had taken no steps to break away from orthodox finance and introduce a social credit scheme. They had demanded that this be done forthwith and that proper experts be brought in. They had drafted a bill in which the responsibility of finding and ap-

[5]*Ibid.*

pointing the experts was removed from the cabinet, and they had made the cabinet accept it. The cabinet's renunciation of this responsibility appeared to be a complete abandonment of the orthodox theory of cabinet responsibility, and although not required by, it was not inconsistent with, the Douglas theory, for Douglas had never drawn a clear line between the responsibility of the legislature and that of the cabinet for the appointment of experts.

But the *Alberta Social Credit Act* was not by any means a transfer of responsibility for "methods" and administration from elected legislators to appointed experts as required by Douglas theory. In the first place, the Act prescribed in considerable detail such machinery and methods—credit houses, retail trade discounts, and so forth—as the legislators could think of, instead of simply empowering experts. In the second place it divided the responsibility for administering the scheme between (*a*) the expert commission, (*b*) the non-expert board composed of elected members of the legislature, and (*c*) the government. The powers of the board have already been mentioned. As for the government, although it did not appear to have much authority under the Act, it was specifically stated to be "the responsibility of the Provincial Government to see that the deposits brought into existence pursuant to this Act can be validated" (sect. 32 (2)), and it was the provincial treasury board, not the Social Credit Board or Social Credit Commission, that was given the power and responsibility of reducing the amount of credit outstanding "whenever in its judgement, acting upon the records of the Commission, an unduly expanded credit condition exists or is impending" (sect. 35 (1)). In the third place, the Act anticipated that both supplementary orders and further legislation would need to be made, but it did not give the required power either to the board or the commission. The power to make orders to alter or supplement the provisions of the Act was specifically given to the cabinet (sect. 42), and the power to pass new legislation was of course left with the legislature, the board having authority only to make recommendations (sect. 3 (3c)).

Thus the Act was neither a thoroughgoing application of Douglas political theory nor a complete capitulation of the government to the insurgents. It served the strategic purpose of dividing and defeating the insurgency, and it was not long before the bulk of the social credit legislative party was again united behind the cabinet. During the six weeks' adjournment of the legislature, several of the insurgents toured the province to state their case, but rather to justify their temporary rebellion than to ask for a further mandate. In effect, once they had voted for the *Alberta Social Credit Act* they had to allow their electors to suspend judgment on the government until a reasonable time had been given for the experts to be found and the system inaugurated.

In his Sunday address of April 18, immediately after the adjournment, Aberhart told the social credit groups: "You should definitely instruct your M.L.A. whether he should cross the floor in opposition to the present government or not. It is surely evident that there should be no serious criticism from the government side of the house."[6] When the house reassembled on June 7 none of the insurgents crossed the floor. In the first recorded vote in the house, on an opposition no-confidence amendment during the budget debate, the government was sustained by a vote of 40 to 7. The 40 included all the social credit members present (except one who had been ousted by the caucus), but 13 insurgent members were absent. It was apparent from this division, and from another on June 17, when the speaker's ruling blocking an insurgent amendment which called for a royal commission to investigate highways expenditures was upheld by only 35 to 24, that the government could not yet count on the unqualified allegiance of the insurgents. However, the budget was passed and the legislature prorogued on June 17, with a promise that a special session would be called in August to implement the decisions of the experts.

Although the insurgency had been weakened and held in check by the creation of the Social Credit Board, no settlement could be expected until the board found experts and the experts produced, if not results, at least the appearance of working towards results. The first steps toward this had been taken during the April-to-June adjournment. MacLachlan, as chairman of the board, had gone to England to try to get Douglas to come; Douglas had declined, but proposed two of his lieutenants, G. F. Powell and L. D. Byrne, who arrived in Alberta in June. The initial prestige of the Douglas emissaries was considerable, for their presence was a token of the speedy action which had been long awaited. Their first action, which their very presence made possible, was to arrange for an impressive show of unity between insurgent and non-insurgent members of the legislature. Each member of the legislature was invited in June to sign a pledge or "agreement of association" binding him "to regard it as my first and foremost duty to the people of Alberta in general, and my electors in particular, to uphold the board and its technicians whilst means are devised by the latter whereby the will of the people of Alberta [de-

[6]*Ibid.*, April 19, 1937.

fined in the agreement as "a secure sufficiency of the amenities of life in freedom . . . in the form of a dividend of $25 a month for all bona fide citizens"]shall prevail throughout its institutions of production and distribution," and to "avoid recriminations and provocative utterances . . . regarding all others who associate themselves with me to achieve this . . . objective." The agreement was to hold until the time when "the board's specialized technicians have submitted suggestions for action which will begin the assertion of the people's autonomy and sovereignty in relation to their own credit, and when such suggestions are supported by the board as . . . meriting the consideration of a new agreement for association."[7] This agreement was signed by 49 of the 56 social credit members of the legislature, including the premier and all the cabinet. Six others, without signing this pledge, wrote to Powell assuring him of their support for Major Douglas "until such time as his plans have been completed."[8] The one other social credit member, who signed nothing, had been read out of the party in the previous winter. None of the seven opposition members signed.

This pledge inaugurated the period of the greatest influence achieved by the board and the lowest level of prestige of the legislature and cabinet. Interpreted strictly, it bound the majority of the legislature, including the whole cabinet, to subservience to the board during the board's pleasure. In effect it did no more than measure the immediate relative prestige of board and legislature. The low point which the legislature reached during the first months of the board's activities is indicated by the fact that instructions were publicly given to the members of the legislature by the board. A prominent instance of this was the publication in the social credit weekly paper of a letter, curtly addressed "To Interested Parties among M.L.A.'s" and signed "Social Credit Board" instructing the M.L.A.'s to take immediate action in their constituencies to secure publicity and support for the government's letter to the banks.[9] However, as soon as the board and its technicians produced plans which required legislative action and government sponsorship, power shifted back to the cabinet, although the power which the legislature lost it never regained.

By August the Douglas experts had prepared the first of a contemplated series of legislative measures designed to bring "finance" to

[7]*Today and Tomorrow*, June 17, 1937 (semi-official social credit weekly founded December, 1935; official organ of Social Credit League from June, 1943, until superseded by *Canadian Social Crediter*, October, 1944).
[8]*Social Credit*, July 9, 1937.   [9]*Today and Tomorrow*, Aug. 5, 1937.

heel. These included the *Credit of Alberta Regulation Act,* which required every banker and bank employee to obtain a licence from the Social Credit Commission, and which put every bank under the control of a local directorate the majority of whose members were to be appointed by the Social Credit Board; the *Bank Employees Civil Rights Act,* which would prevent any civil action being taken in the courts by any bank which had not submitted to the controls and so obtained the licence required by the first Act; and the *Judicature Act Amendment Act, 1937 (Second Session),* which prohibited any action or proceeding concerning the constitutional validity of any enactment of the legislature being taken without permission of the lieutenant governor in council.

These bills were presented to the brief special session of the legislature (August 3 to 6) and rapidly enacted. At the beginning of this August session a new pledge was distributed to the members of the social credit caucus, superseding the June pledge. The August pledge included the same undertaking to support the board and its technicians, but no longer during the board's pleasure. Instead, it asserted the necessity of passing "a succession of legislative acts" to control financial institutions "until we achieve our immediate objective . . . that each institution within the province of Alberta shall carry on their business so that the will of the people of Alberta can invariably be implemented." It then bound the member to support the government, not the board, until that objective had been achieved: "So I promise, for so long as a majority of my electors concur in my so doing, to vote consistently for a government which does give continuous and unremitting legislative priority to such procedure until our above declared immediate objective has been achieved; and I will vote consistently against any government which does not."[10] This pledge was signed by 50 of the social credit members; the six who refused to sign it were disbarred from the caucus.

The August pledge left the private member of the legislature completely subordinate, but now to the cabinet rather than to the board or commission. He was pledged to support the cabinet as long as it went on giving priority to legislation designed to control financial institutions, until such time as all institutions in the province should be so operated that "the will of the people of Alberta can invariably be implemented." The pledge, of course, gave adequate shelter and comfort to the expert commission, at least as long as that body was considered to have a monopoly of authentic expertise. The pledge was less

[10]*Edmonton Journal,* Sept. 23, 1937.

a binding instrument than an indication of the real dependence of the social credit M.L.A.'s on the experts and on Aberhart for the production of plans and legislation which would enable the members to face their constituents.

The duration of the legislature's impotence was, to say the least, indefinite. In the nature of the case, any legislation which seriously attacked the position of the chartered banks and other financial institutions in the province would be invalidated by the courts as *ultra vires*, or by the federal government through its power of disallowance, or by the lieutenant-governor by his power of reservation. From this time on, every successive piece of legislation enacted on the recommendation of the Douglas experts to break the grip of "the financiers" was invalidated by one or more of these federal devices, beginning with the disallowance of the three August Acts mentioned above within two weeks of their enactment. The invalidations were a positive advantage to the Aberhart government and to the experts, for they could be presented as a demonstration that forces outside the province, readily identified with finance, were blocking the valiant attempt of the government and the experts to implement the sovereign will of the people of Alberta.

Nor was the invalidation of these legislative measures unexpected, at least by the Douglas experts who had prepared them. The pontifical Douglas weekly in England, in reporting the invalidation of three of the Alberta bills in 1938, said: "In case any of our readers should feel depressed by the apparent setback . . . we have the highest authority for stating that not only was the course of events anticipated, but that it is regarded as being highly satisfactory and inevitable to the eventual and desired outcome."[11] Mr. Powell, in the same year, told a social credit conference in England that "the disallowed Acts had been drawn up mainly to show the people of Alberta who were their *real* enemies, and in that respect they had succeeded admirably."[12] This statement was not, as might be thought, an indiscretion, although its obvious implication was that the Douglas experts in Edmonton had never believed that their measures could be made effective. It was, rather, a straightforward reflection of the thinking of the English social credit leadership. Douglas had by this time developed the implications of his earlier belief in a world plot to the point of holding that the conversion of the people to this belief was more important than any other action that social credit leaders might undertake. The exposure and defeat of the plot were prerequisites of any realization of social credit. In using the Alberta movement to further

[11]*Social Credit*, March 11, 1938.   [12]*Ibid.*, Sept. 23, 1938.

his design Douglas was quite logical, and he did not mind the Albertans knowing how they were being used since it was for their own good.

To understand this, and later developments within the Alberta party which effected its practice of democracy, it will be necessary to consider, in the following section, the development of Douglas theory from 1937 on.

§ 2. English Social Credit Doctrine, the Last Phase, 1937-49

The extravagances of Douglas's theory in this period merit description as much for the light they throw on the fundamental nature of social credit thinking as for their direct effect on the Alberta movement. The political interpretations and proposals of the 1940's, some grotesque and all bizarre, were perfectly logical extensions of the original principles. As such, they reveal strikingly the quality, at once pathetic and vicious, discernible in social credit thinking from the beginning but made obvious only when failure and despair brought it to the fore.

The Douglas movement in England had fallen on evil days with the failure of the "electoral campaign."[13] Similar measures on a smaller scale were developed in succeeding years, but with little effect. In 1936 and 1937 a "local objectives campaign" sought to remedy the defects which had appeared in the electoral campaign. Social credit groups were instructed how to develop the united action of a majority of ratepayers on some matter of local dissatisfaction. Specific objectives—the improvement of a certain road, the installation of traffic lights at a particular point, the replacement of a footbridge, the improvement of a school or a bus service—were formulated as democratic demands embodying the will of the electorate, demands which the elected representatives would fail to carry out at their peril. The desired changes were put forward as demands, not as petitions, to emphasize that the elected representative was on each specific issue a servant of the voters. In this way the social credit leadership sought to develop at the local level the same "sovereignty of individuals over their institutions"[14] that they had hoped to evoke nationally by their electoral campaign. The debility of the social credit movement was incidentally disclosed by Douglas's explanation that the campaign had also a more important purpose, namely, to provide discipline for the members of the movement. Morale was low because the members

[13]See above, Chap. V, sect. 4.
[14]*Social Credit*, May 14, 1937.

would not work; they did not realize that "everybody cannot take executive positions" when something has to be done.[15]

The local objective campaign was extended to broader issues in a "rates campaign" in 1937 and 1938. Ratepayers in some cities were brought together in a series of demands for lower rates and lower assessments with no decrease in social services, "in effect a demand for a local dividend."[16] Ratepayers' dissatisfaction with governmental proposals for altering rating assessments in the winter of 1937-8 was seized upon, and the Douglas headquarters claimed credit for the government's decision in February 1938 to postpone action. In 1938 and 1939 the same technique was applied to certain national issues connected with preparation for war. A campaign was developed against proposals for billeting evacuated civilians and householders during war or crisis, on either a voluntary or compulsory basis; instead, a demand was made for the building of proper billets without raising taxes or rates. The social credit headquarters congratulated itself on the government's announcement in February 1939 that a million pounds was to be expended on the provision of camps for evacuated civilians. Another campaign was undertaken against the government's voluntary service enlistment campaign; the social credit demand was that all should be paid for their services.

These attempts to win public support on particular issues followed the decline of interest in social credit as a universal scheme of economic reform. Douglas admitted in 1937 that social credit was "on the downgrade, at any rate temporarily" and attributed this to the economic prosperity of the time.[17] But none of the campaigns stayed the disintegration of the English movement.

A serious schism in the leadership in 1938 indicated basic weaknesses. At the peak of the movement's activity, in 1933, a permanent headquarters, named the Social Credit Secretariat, had been set up in London, for developing and directing political action and general propaganda, with Major Douglas as chairman. A new weekly paper, *Social Credit*, had been established as the official organ of the secretariat, the first number appearing in August 1934. Through it, policy was announced and instructions given to the movement. The *New Age* and the *New English Weekly* continued as journals of opinion devoted to social credit principles but within a few years their independence of

---

[15]C. H. Douglas, *The Policy of a Philosophy* (Liverpool [1937]), p. 8.

[16]"Political Strategy, 1934–38" by "H. E." (Director of Political Strategy of the Secretariat), *The Fig Tree*, Sept. 1938, p. 147.

[17]Douglas, *The Policy of a Philosophy*, p. 3.

the secretariat showed itself in outspoken criticism of its dictatorial attitude and of the official policy.[18]

The constitution of the secretariat made dictatorship easy. The chairman's authority, derived from popular election, was unlimited; there was no regular elected body to share in authority or even to serve in an advisory capacity.[19] The directors were appointed by the chairman, were responsible to him, and held their appointments at his discretion.[20] In September 1935 a limited company, the Social Credit Secretariat Limited, was formed "as a convenient method of carrying out and managing portions of the business of the Social Credit Secretariat."[21] At the end of 1937, after his re-election as chairman of the secretariat, Major Douglas replaced a number of directors of the secretariat who, however, remained directors of the company. The schism developed in September 1938. Some members of the company challenged Douglas's conduct of the secretariat. Douglas attempted to remove the control of the weekly paper, *Social Credit*, from the company, and having failed to do so, resigned from the chairmanship of the company on September 12, renounced all connection with it, and took most of the directors of the secretariat with him. They carried on as the Social Credit Secretariat, set up new headquarters in Liverpool, and began to publish a new weekly, *The Social Crediter*, on September 17.[22] The company continued to publish *Social Credit* for another six months but was forced to go into liquidation in April 1939, its revenue from social credit groups and from donations having failed since the withdrawal of Major Douglas.[23] The schism was attributed by the company to Douglas's refusal to do anything to remedy its financial situation, and to his autocratic behaviour both in depriving some directors of departmental authority in the secretariat while they remained legally responsible as directors of the company, and in handing over authority to persons who had no responsibility in the company but whose actions involved the company in expenditures and liabilities.

[18]See passages quoted by W. R. Hiskett and J. A. Franklin, *Searchlight on Social Credit* (London, 1939), p. 9 and p. 12 from *New English Weekly*, July 23, 1936, and *The New Age*, June 17, 1937.

[19]The chairman was elected by a council of representatives, which was elected by the members of all affiliated social credit groups, and which was dissolved as soon as this function (and the ancillary function of assisting the chairman in his selection of the other members of the executive board) was performed.

[20]Statement by L. D. Byrne, retiring Director of Organization, *Social Credit*, March 13, 1936.   [21]*Social Crediter*, Sept. 17, 1938.

[22]The Secretariat has remained in Liverpool since that date, and *The Social Crediter*, published there, has continued as the official organ.

[23]*Social Credit*, March 24, 1939.

As the political and intellectual content of the movement declined, popular support dwindled, membership fell off, and the movement ceased to attract new recruits of the desired calibre for leadership. Criticism of the secretariat by intellectuals who had been adherents of social credit for many years became more outspoken. The *New English Weekly* published a series of articles by several such dissident social creditors early in 1940, linking the "eclipse" of social credit to the decline of the "habit of intelligent discussion of social credit issues which has disastrously dwindled, not only in these columns but elsewhere, discouraged by dictatorial pronouncements, irrelevant fanaticisms, and that insensate repetition of clichés which has driven out old supporters and driven off new ones."[24]

The outbreak of the war hastened the decline of the movement. The virtual suspension of normal political party life and the necessary subordination of domestic problems left no opportunity for continuing any of the Douglas "campaigns." It was, however, still possible to keep up a running commentary on world events from the standpoint of social credit theory, and to extract support for that theory from a consideration of the trends which those events could be interpreted as disclosing. The *Social Crediter* was given over to this commentary and generalization during the war and post-war years; some of it was published also in pamphlet and book form.[25]

Since one of the most obvious effects of the war on the British economy and society was the rapid growth of governmental power and the reduction of individual freedom, Douglas had no lack of material. He had believed, for some twenty years, that there was a world-wide drive to diminish individual freedom, that this was a plot directed by hidden international financiers, that war was simply an instrument of this policy, and that the world was moving rapidly towards a final attempt to destroy freedom permanently. The climax seemed to have arrived. The war itself; the regimentation of whole populations; the schemes for post-war international regulation and control of credit, resources, and trade, with their diminution of national sovereignty; the ascendancy of planning at home; and the emphasis on "full employment" as the goal of domestic policy—all this, and more, was interpreted as clear evidence of the progress of the

[24]Maurice B. Reckitt, "Social Credit Today and Tomorrow," *New English Weekly*, Jan. 4, 1940.
[25]E.g., the following, all by C. H. Douglas: *The Big Idea* (Liverpool, [1942]); *The "Land for the (Chosen) People" Racket* (Liverpool, [1943]); *Programme for the Third World War* (Liverpool, [1943]); *The Brief for the Prosecution* (Liverpool, 1945).

world plot. Douglas's belief in British character and British traditions enabled him, consistently enough, to support British participation in the war; since the enemy states were in a more advanced stage of totalitarian rule, they must be defeated before any restoration of freedom in Britain or the world could be hoped for. But he was obsessed with the urgency of persuading the British people that the real and continuing enemy was the world plotters. And he became convinced that the only way to do so was to name certain groups, individuals, and organizations as responsible. It was no longer enough to demonstrate that there was a conspiracy against individual freedom, nor even to show exactly how the conspiracy was operating. The only way to arouse the people to their own defence was to tell them *who* was encompassing their enslavement.

To unmask the world plotters thus became Douglas's overruling passion. He had no doubt who they were. At the centre were the leaders of world Jewry; the plot was a relentless Judaic conspiracy against Christian civilization. International Jewry controlled both international finance and international bolshevism; the leaders of finance and of communism were consciously working together to enslave the world. "The Powerful Banking Interests which rule the American government are also the power which governs Russia."[26] "Anyone who has contemplated the changes of front of the Communist movement must be satisfied that it is an extension of international financial intrigue although quite possibly its dupes would react violently to the suggestion"[27]—a typical Douglas sentence. The inner ruling group of Nazi Germany was another partner in the conspiracy. Nazi persecution of the Jews notwithstanding, "that the genuine *higher* policy of Germany is anti-Jew is patently absurd";[28] the persecution was useful as a means of "forcing the barriers of immigration laws" and placing "refugees" behind the enemy's lines.[29]

The indisputable fact is that there is a coherent Jewish policy everywhere. At the present time it can be seen in full operation in practically every country in the world, *and on both sides of the fighting-line. It is the conditions which are inseparable from total war which alone make possible the erection of the bureaucratic state alike envisaged by the Jews and the Great German General Staff as the instrument of World Dominion. Hence, so long as this influence is allowed to operate, we can expect one war after another until someone has enslaved the planet.*[30]

The spurious *Protocols of Zion* were frequently cited, but even they

[26]*Social Crediter*, April 29, 1939.
[27]Douglas, *The Brief for the Prosecution*, p. 81. [28]*Ibid.*, p. 41.
[29]*Ibid.* [30]*Ibid.*, pp. 41–2 (italics in original).

were inadequate. "What many readers of them do not grasp is that 'Big Business,' Socialist Government, and World Politics are merely components of Jewish Freemasonry."[31] "The link between the International Jew Financiers and such politicians as can be easily identified as having facilitated this plot (whether knowingly or because it is part of the equipment of a successful politician) is undoubtedly secret societies such as Grand Orient Freemasonry and the New York B'Nai B'rith."[32]

Having brought freemasonry, Jewry, finance, communism, and nazism together in one conspiracy, Douglas had no difficulty in adding trade union and socialist party leadership. "History has no more amazing spectacle than this Socialist–Communist–Finance-Ring–Trades-Union–Cartel combination. . . . "[33] Even the co-operative movement was implicated: "One of the factors in this world plot is the Co-operative Wholesale Society. . . . It stands out a mile as one of the tools of high and international finance. . . . "[34] While the C.W.S. might be let off as a tool, the trade unions were not: the *Social Crediter* insisted that "Red Socialism and High Finance, with International Big Business and Trades Unionism, are . . . completely, and in their higher ranks, . . . consciously part of one world organization. . . . The ultimate objective is simple and clear—it is to reduce the main body of the world's population to the status of cattle. . . ."[35]

There was some unwillingness within the movement to accept the theory of the Jewish world plot, but Douglas insisted that it was an integral part of social creditism. Followers were told, in 1945: "Those people, and they are many, and some of them are sincere, who brand as 'negative' efforts to isolate and exhibit the forces and persons who are effective on the present situation are, to put it conservatively, a dangerous nuisance."[36] Three years later reluctance among the followers was still a problem. The *Social Crediter* surmised the existence of "a small number—loyal and valued members of our public, who although, because of their loyalty, they accept our views on certain aspects of the Jewish race, yet have an idea that these are an excrescence on 'Social Credit' and, they feel, might have been left unnoticed." This "very excusable failure of comprehension" was set right by emphasizing certain propositions: "both Judaism and Social Credit are rooted in philosophies . . . ; Social Credit is Christian . . . ; Judaism is implacably anti-Christian . . . ; both philosophies have a policy and

[31]*Social Crediter*, June 4, 1949.   [32]Douglas, *The Big Idea*, p. 50.
[33]*Social Crediter*, March 31, 1945.   [34]*Ibid.*
[35]*Ibid.*, Nov. 18, 1944.   [36]*Ibid.*, April 14, 1945.

these policies cannot live together." Hence the "vocation" of the official movement was to expose the enemy forces and "unmask their aims."[37]

The extravagance of Douglas's conclusions should not be allowed to obscure the logic of his position. It was, indeed, logical in two senses. In the first place the existence of a world plot was a logical and necessary deduction from his first assumptions. As we saw before[38] his earliest social theory assumed (a) that society was entirely purposive—that all social events were the desired results of assignable wills; (b) that there was a natural harmony of individual interests—a nearly unanimous general will for individual freedom, security, leisure, and plenty; (c) that these objectives were now technologically attainable; and (d) that there could be no valid dispute about the means, because means were a matter of technical knowledge. From these assumptions it followed that a world of war, regimentation, insecurity, incessant labour, and poverty was the result of the conscious policy of a few seeking to enslave all the rest. So much was a necessary conclusion. The identity of the plotters was not, it is true, necessarily implied, but Douglas's choice of the main plotters was the obvious one in view of their tried and tested serviceability as scapegoats.

In the second place, belief in and insistence on exposing the plot was, by this time, the only logical course the English social credit leadership could take. In view of the failure of all its other efforts, a world plot was a necessary hypothesis for the survival of the movement. Douglas himself saw this, though he presented the matter in a slightly different light. "The first point on which to be clear is that if we are *not* faced with a long-term policy, our position is quite hopeless. If every step in the industrial arts merely confronts us with more devastating wars, more restrictions and controls, and, except in the United States, a lower standard of life, mankind is so hopelessly perverse that his only tolerable future lies in early annihilation. . . . But if we are facing a Satanic policy, our position, although very serious, is not necessarily irremediable."[39]

The insistence that the whole social credit movement be committed to the exposure of the plotters followed with equal logic. "Policies *in vacuo* are a contradiction in terms. Policies embody strategies; you do not fight a strategy, you fight the human beings who are carrying out that strategy. . . . The best defence is attack."[40]

[37]*Ibid.*, Feb. 7, 1948.   [38]Chap. IV, sects. 2 and 3.
[39]C. H. Douglas, "The Great Betrayal," *Social Crediter,* May 22, 1948.
[40]*Ibid.*

To such straits was social credit thinking reduced. There was no choice but to despair finally of the sanity of mankind or to embrace a phantasy. And to such straits was the social credit organization reduced that nothing less than the supposition of a world plot would now justify its existence, excuse its failure, and give it something further to do.

Along with the world plot, complementary to it, and following equally logically from Douglas's first assumptions and from the position to which the movement had been reduced, went a remarkable extension of the Douglas theory of democracy. It will be recalled that the political theory of the movement in the 1930's, while denying that the people, or the majority, were competent to decide on "methods," asserted that the majority could be trusted to be right about objectives.[41] The whole theory purported to show how the real will of the people could be made sovereign. But we have seen also[42] that Douglas from the beginning had had the strongest reservations about the rights of the majority. He had always rejected majority rule, as being equivalent to despotism. "Real democracy," he had declared in 1920, "is . . . the expression of the *policy* of the majority, and, so far as that policy is concerned with economics, is the freedom of an increasing majority of individuals to make use of the facilities provided for them, in the first place, by a number of persons who always will be, as they always have been, in the minority."[43] Already implied in this definition of democracy was the rejection of the majority principle in the 1940's. Democracy, in effect, was the expression of the will of the majority provided that the will of the majority was what Douglas thought it must be, namely, a will for increasing individual freedom to make economic (and other) choices separately, not collectively. The essence of democracy was individual liberty, rather than majority will; and liberty was simply "freedom to choose or refuse one thing at a time."[44]

While there was still any hope that the people might be awakened, by social credit propaganda, to a realization that this was their will, the principle that the majority had the right to determine objectives was consistent with the more basic Douglas concept of democracy as the realm of personal freedom. When this hope could scarcely be entertained any longer, the right of the majority to determine policy had to be put aside, at least until some devices could be found to correct

---

[41]See Chap. V, sect. 2.   [42]Chap. V, sect. 2.
[43]C. H. Douglas, *Credit-Power and Democracy* (London, 1920), p. 7.
[44]C. H. Douglas, *Social Credit* (London, 1924), p. 43.

the prevailing expression of majority will. The failure of the people to respond to any of the Douglas campaigns designed to evoke their real will was taken as evidence that "whether as a result of mass 'education' or from some deeper cause, the political instinct of the average inhabitant of these islands is deteriorating."[45] That the people's will had not emerged was of course owing to the policy of the world plotters: since the social crediters' "tactical successes against this policy are entirely inadequate . . . the entire conception of democracy has to be recast if the world is to survive."[46]

The recasting of the Douglas theory of democracy began as early as 1942. Emphasis was shifted from the validity of the real will of the people back to the pre-eminence of individual rights. Individual freedom and responsibility were declared to be the essence of democracy, to the exclusion of any other principle. The individual was to be responsible for minding his own business only. "Groups are inferior to individuals. Majorities have no rights . . . they are abstractions to which it is impossible to impart the qualities of a conscious human being. The attempt to construct a system of human relationships on the 'rights' of majorities is not democracy. If it were, democracy would stand self-condemned."[47] It was even asserted that there was no difference between the majority principle and the "Führerprinzip": "it is obvious that a majority is only a specialized and deceptive word for the 'Führerprinzip.' No majority can act without a Leader. When an individual resigns power, he resigns it *primarily* to be used against him."[48]

So the majority principle was found to be the contrary of democracy. Genuine democracy was "essentially negative," and could be reduced to the right of the individual to "contract out" of the decisions of the majority.[49] Douglas concluded that "a majority ceases to have any validity when it is led to an objective its component individuals do not understand, or when a dissentient minority is forced to accompany it."[50] Little theoretical basis for this rather striking conclusion was provided at the time; when it was forthcoming it did not make the case much clearer.

One basis offered was the natural right of an *élite* to be exempt from majority will; this led to a general demand for an area of individual freedom exempt from social control. Douglas suggested that "minorities have obtained privileges by natural selection" and that it would

[45]*Social Crediter*, March 24, 1945.
[47]Douglas, *The Big Idea*, p. 55.
[49]*Ibid.*, p. 55.
[46]*Ibid.*, Jan. 11, 1947.
[48]*Ibid.*, p. 57.
[50]*Ibid.*, p. 57.

be "a gross interference with the process to penalize it." Hence, "the primary perversion of the democratic theory is to identify it with unrestricted majority government. . . . Nevertheless, the democratic idea has real validity if it is separated from the idea of a collectivity. It is a legitimate corollary of the highest conception of the human individual that *to the greatest extent possible, the will of all individuals shall prevail over their own affairs.* Over his own affairs, the sanctions of society must be restored to the individual affected."[51] This echo of John Stuart Mill did not carry matters much further, since the scope of the individual's "own affairs" was not defined.

Another basis for rejecting the majority principle was found in a curious theory of society as a contract. A nation "is an association to pursue individual ends by common rules . . . an association is a contract, and the unilateral abrogation of a contract is universally condemned."[52] Without suggesting what the terms of the contract were supposed to be, Douglas asserted his conclusion: the doctrine that "the will of the people must and shall prevail" as Asquith had said in supporting the Parliament Act of 1911, "is, of course, an affirmation of essential lawlessness—the right to break a contract unilaterally."[53]

Behind this concept of the nation as a contractual association stood the idea of the nation as an organism growing in accordance with some transcendent natural law which was not to be thwarted by any mere majority. "The real British constitution . . . is an organism."[54] The concept of an objective law inherent in the universe, to which individuals must accommodate themselves or perish, had permeated Douglas's earlier social theory.[55] Social credit, he now emphasized, was only one manifestation of it, Christianity was another. Two further specific principles were also required by it: the supremacy of common law over parliament, and division of power between king, lords, and commons. He urged that both the common law and the House of Lords should be restored to their former power in order to destroy the present supremacy of a bare majority of the House of Commons. Only so could the contractual-organic structure of society be secured against unrestricted majority government.[56]

[51]*The Brief for the Prosecution,* p. 72 (italics in original).
[52]*Ibid.,* p. 67.   [53]*Ibid.,* p. 68.
[54]C. H. Douglas, "Realistic Constitutionalism," *Social Crediter,* May 24, 1947; reprinted in *Canadian Social Crediter,* June 19, 1947.
[55]E.g., *Credit-Power and Democracy* (London, 1921), p. 18; *Social Credit* (1924), p. 87; *The Use of Money,* p. 4.
[56]*The Brief For the Prosecution,* p. 68; "Realistic Constitutionalism," *Social Crediter,* May 24, 1947.

It would be difficult and scarcely profitable to attempt to give these latter-day forays into political theory a coherence they lack in the social credit literature. The central idea is clear enough: the assertion of the supremacy of individual rights and responsibilities, whether thought of as historic, organic, contractual, divine, or natural, over the decisions of any numerical majority. It cannot be emphasized too strongly that this was Douglas's position from the beginning: he was an individualist first and last, and a democrat only when he believed that the real will of the majority would be a will for individualism. When he saw the majority willing the welfare state he dropped the general will and drew new conclusions from his old individualism.

The culmination of this attack on the majority principle was the denunciation of the secret ballot, which emerged plainly in English social credit literature in 1946. The secret ballot made the expression of opinion anonymous and irresponsible, and thereby contravened the first principle of individual responsibility; it put "the rules of society . . . at the mercy of an anonymous, irresponsible and politically ignorant vote."[57] Abolition of the secret ballot was directly proposed in March 1946, along with other measures, as a way of restoring individual responsibility. The proposals were:

(*a*) The secret ballot to be abolished and replaced by an open, recorded and published vote.
(*b*) The Party system to be retained.
(*c*) Prior to an election, each Party to put forward an outline of any legislative proposals together with both the cost to the taxpayer and a designation of the interests and specific individuals affected.
(*d*) The cost of Legislation by the successful Party together with the proved loss to any individual not having voted for the successful Party, to be borne solely by those having recorded votes for the successful Party, and any reduction of taxation directly attributable to specific legislation to be shared as to 25 per cent by recorded supporters of the unsuccessful Parties, and 75 per cent by the supporters of the successful Party so long as it may remain in power, after which the gains shall be equalized.[58]

The essence of this proposal, it will be seen, was to remove from the individual citizen the obligation of paying for any social undertaking which he had not demanded by his recorded vote. And not only was the individual not to have to pay, neither was he to be subjected to the controls involved in such undertakings. The "substitution of the open ballot for the secret franchise, and allocation of taxation

[57]*Social Crediter*, Feb. 23, 1946.
[58]"The Light Horse," Part 3, *Social Crediter*, March 16, 1946; reprinted in *Canadian Social Crediter*, Nov. 7, 1946.

according to the recorded voting for a programme which incurs a nett loss" were to be accompanied by "a large measure of freedom to contract out of legislation of a functional character, with a consequent discouragement of the spate of so-called Laws which are little more than Works Orders."[59]

How far individuals were to be able to contract out of any scheme for which they had not voted was not clear, but Douglas insisted that "it is necessary to provide individuals, as *individuals*, not collectively, with much more opportunity to judge political matters by results, and to be able to reject, individually and not collectively, policies they do not like. . . ."[60]

The right to contract out of compulsory legislation, and the allocation of taxation according to recorded votes, were openly advocated as ways of destroying the welfare state. "Defence, Justice, and Foreign Relations . . . properly belong to the political system. The load which can be shed (i.e. where cost can be reduced) is in economic experiments and social legislation."[61] Each voter would be more careful about conferring a mandate for schemes requiring increased taxation, for he could no longer hope to vote himself benefits at the expense of his neighbours. With "the elector knowing that he would not be taxed for what he did not 'buy,' and able to contract out if he did not want to join in," political parties would be compelled to offer less and less social legislation, smaller and smaller budgets,[62] until the welfare state had disappeared.

So novel and ingenious were these proposals that their continuity with earlier social credit principles was easily overlooked. Yet the demand that the elector should "not be taxed for what he did not 'buy', " was simply an extreme corollary of the social credit concept of political society. Douglas had consistently held that politics should be a process by which each individual could successfully demand the services he had independently decided were worth his buying. The analogy between casting a vote and making a purchase in a shop had been a social credit favourite for many years. The consumer by the act of purchase was said to be "voting" with his money and thereby determining what goods would be produced. Conversely, it was held that the money voting of the consumer was the ideal type to which political voting ought to be made to conform, on the ground that the former was the more effective in getting results. This analogy between money and the ballot had been much used after 1934 in support of the view

---

[59]Douglas, "Realistic Constitutionalism," *Social Crediter,* May 24, 1947.
[60]*Ibid.*   [61]*Ibid.,* Feb. 7, 1948.   [62]*Ibid.*

that the elector should vote for results, not methods, just as the consumer was said to do in casting his money ballot.

What is relevant here is not the convenience of the analogy for the "results vs. methods" case, but the continuity of the basic concept of politics. The same assumption underlay the earlier money-ballot analogy and the later demand for the open ballot, namely, that the political relations between individuals were properly the relations of the market. The one difference came from a change in estimation of how the market could be organized. In the earlier argument, virtually all individuals were assumed to have the same wants; accordingly, a majority decision as to the results wanted could be trusted to represent virtually all individual wills. In the later argument, this unanimity of wants was not assumed; each individual was to be left to choose between policies at the prices at which they were offered, and pay for his own choice. In both cases, voters were consumers, and politics was trade; but when the proposed co-operative buying—the mobilization of mass demand—failed, Douglas's concept of politics reverted to the simple pattern of the competitive price system.

All the proposals for confining and whittling away the substance of contemporary democracy—from the limits to be placed on the power of a majority of the Commons to the abolition of the secret ballot and the establishment of an individual right to contract out of compulsory legislation—were presented as expedients which would have to serve in place of an outright attack on the concept of democracy. "Short of a *coup d'état*," Douglas wrote in 1947, with the frankness which comes of desperation, "I do not think that the idea of democracy, which is of course very nebulous, can be abruptly abandoned. It has been too much propagandized, and means too many things to too many men."[63] The best that could be done was to restrict the majority will and try to render it harmless by making each voter an independent buyer of services. Presumably, if this could be done, democracy as "the expression of the policy of the majority" would again be acceptable, as being consistent with individual freedom. The will of the majority could be trusted if it were merely a collection of separate individual wills for "freedom to choose or refuse one thing at a time."

The abolition of the secret ballot was taken up with characteristic impetuosity. The speech in which Douglas elaborated the proposal in 1947 closed with the assurance that, if the destinies of England were to be settled by "appeal to an anonymous, irresponsible, and uninstructed ballot-box democracy, . . . the outcome is a mathematical

[63]"Realistic Constitutionalism," *Social Crediter*, May 24, 1947.

certainty—our final eclipse."[64] Two years later the *Social Crediter* recorded its conviction, in the context of a discussion of the world plot, that "five minutes' consideration of this subject, which is either pure moonshine or the most vital subject which affects us on earth, ought to convince anyone that a ballot-democracy can only be advocated by two kinds of persons—the abysmally ignorant or the consciously traitorous."[65]

In summary, the extension of the Douglas political theory after 1937 comprised, first, an overwhelming concern, mounting to an obsession, with the supposed world plot; second, an increasingly outspoken rejection of the majority principle; and finally the denunciation of the secret ballot. Each of these was a consistent development of the earlier philosophy of social credit, and each was required by the declining fortunes of the English movement.

The world plot thesis had been announced, though not emphasized, in the Douglas writings of the 1920's. That the social crediters should devote their energy to its elaboration and exposure in the late thirties and the forties was, as we have seen, a logical consequence of their failure to win the mass support they had expected.

The rejection of the majority principle, though inconsistent with the earlier belief in a general will which would be expressed by the majority, was consistent with the still more fundamental belief that the essence of democracy was individual freedom. Of the two concepts which had initially been entertained together—the supremacy of individual choice and responsibility, and the supremacy of the general will—the latter had to be sacrificed when, after two decades of social credit attempts at evoking it, the general will was farther than ever from demanding the supremacy of individual choice and responsibility.

The campaign against the secret ballot, finally, was a last attempt to reverse the trend toward a collective welfare state without denying democracy in name. The proposal that the individual's tax liability be limited to what he had "bought" by his signed ballot, reveals the essence of the Douglas social theory. Society is reduced to a retail market in which each individual fends for himself and buys only what he wants at the going price. Defence, justice, and foreign relations apart, no one is to be obliged by the rest in the name of the purposes of the whole society. Freedom is equated with "consumer's sovereignty." The price system is enshrined as the true measure of political obligation.

[64]*Ibid.*
[65]*Social Crediter,* June 4, 1949.

§ 3. *The Failure of Alberta Delegate Democracy: Cabinet, Board, Legislature, and Convention, 1937-9*

In Alberta as in England it was failure of social credit action that led to extension of theory. Failure of action in Alberta was neither as early nor as complete as in the English movement. While Douglas was driven to extreme theoretical positions by his failure to make any mass appeal, there was no doubt that Aberhart had obtained mass support in 1935 and again, jointly with the experts, in 1937. Only when it became evident, as it did by 1939, that all their efforts to introduce social credit were fruitless and that they had been forced to a standstill, did they find the world plot thesis attractive. And, as we shall see, it was then more attractive to the experts and their sponsors, the Social Credit Board, than to the cabinet and party leaders. The roots of the divergence between the party leaders and the Douglas men in Alberta, which ended in an open break in 1947, go back to 1939. We shall examine that development in the next section of this chapter, but here we must notice the relations between cabinet, board, legislature, and convention between 1937 and 1939. Those years marked the failure not only of social credit but also of delegate democracy in Alberta.

Of all the relations within the Alberta political structure it was the relation between the cabinet and the Social Credit Board and its experts that attracted most attention in 1937 and 1938. There was considerable speculation in the outside press about their relative authority. It was widely thought that the cabinet had become mere puppets of the board and the experts. A leading eastern financial paper early in 1938 published excerpts from apparently private governmental correspondence as evidence of this view.[66] It was obvious enough, without any documentary revelations, that the cabinet had begun to parrot the Douglas experts, but whether the experts were dictating to reluctant ministers or whether the ministers were in full agreement with the experts and therefore leaning heavily on them could only be a matter of conjecture. The question, which was master, was not well conceived; in fact they needed one another. Not only could each use the other to its own advantage; each depended for its life on the other.

Moreover, there was no serious reason for discord between them. If some members of the cabinet suffered at first from natural pique at being overshadowed by the board and experts they soon recognized the value to themselves of being able to shift responsibility. Cabinet and experts found it mutually advantageous to preach the standard

---

[66]*Financial Post*, Jan. 8, 1938.

Douglas theory that the elected representatives should demand results only and leave responsibility for methods to the experts. This position sufficed for a year or two, while the experts and the government together went on producing social credit plans and putting them on the statute books, until it became plain that there was no hope of getting any of them past the federal government's veto.

Amidst the speculation about the relative authority of the cabinet and the board, the real and important shift in power after the establishment of the Social Credit Board and the arrival of the Douglas experts was commonly overlooked. The cabinet and the experts together had reduced the legislature and the delegate conventions to insignificance. That this should go unnoticed outside was natural enough. The subordination of representative bodies was less likely to be noticed by the financial press than was the supposed ascendancy of the Douglas experts, which threatened confiscatory legislation.

We have already seen[67] how by August 1937 the cabinet had not only subordinated the legislature to itself but had stripped the social credit members of the legislature of any function except that of maintaining the enthusiasm of their constituents. By its settlement of the insurgency the government had put itself in a stronger position than before. It could now, while appearing to follow the Douglas theory, hide behind the experts. It could claim that it was restricted to the same role as the legislature, that of demanding results only, and it could make this claim more effectively after than before the insurgency, for now the existence of Douglas experts at work in Edmonton could be demonstrated. In short, in settling the insurgency by appearing to accept the Douglas political theory and bemusing his supporters with it, Aberhart had restored the supremacy of the cabinet and reduced the legislature to a position of subservience from which it never recovered.

We have still to notice that the party, that is, the Alberta Social Credit League, was reduced to the same insignificance as the legislature, and by the same process. Loss of function led to atrophy at all levels, from the local groups to the provincial convention.

The locals, nurtured on the A plus B theorem and the apocalyptic vision of the results that could be theirs by uniting their wills, were deprived of function by their very success in electing a social credit government. Although attempts were made from time to time to revive group discussion of social credit economic theory, which had been dropped during the 1935 election campaign, the locals could not

[67]Section 1 of this chapter.

live by stale "A plus B" in its simple form, and the complexities of the technical theory were generally beyond their grasp. The broader and less technical case for social credit could of course still be taught, but while it was an excellent campaigning case it was scarcely fuel for continuous local activity. Of what use to go on discussing the need to displace the financiers, and asserting the people's right to their technological heritage, when they had just installed a government and experts who were seeing to all that?

Finally, the groups were of course enjoined from discussing the specific steps to be taken in applying social credit principles to the provincial economy. "The people," Aberhart told some of them at a social credit picnic in August 1937, "need not bother how [their] aims might be accomplished—leave that to the experts chosen to do it. Don't let the details bother you, ask for results. For goodness sake don't get an inferiority complex. You cannot get anything if you don't think you can get it. How? That is something you don't need to bother about. You go ahead with your farm work."[68] There was, indeed, nothing else for them to do as long as they continued to believe in the social credit theory. They *had* asked for results, in 1935 and again in the insurgency. They might be excused for thinking it pointless to go on asking when they obviously had to wait. But in fact their faith in their leaders was firm enough to enable them to believe that they would be fulfilling some function in merely continuing to demand results.

The constituency associations soon found themselves in the same position as the local groups. By their acceptance of social credit political theory and their support of the government and experts they had divested themselves of any useful function. They had had their fling during the insurgency, when they had been invited by Aberhart to instruct their M.L.A.'s whether to give the government a new lease of life after its avowed failure to introduce social credit. Once the government had got its new lease and had publicly turned it over to the experts, there was nothing more for the constituency conventions to do, except every four or five years to nominate a panel from which the leader and his advisers would choose the party candidate for the constituency.[69]

68Speech by Aberhart at social credit picnic at South Cooking Lake, near Edmonton, as quoted in (mimeograph) "Basic Facts Service" by R. J. Deachman.

69The same method of choosing social credit candidates as in 1935 was used for the 1940 general election. Aberhart justified its use in the following words in 1939: "Candidates are chosen from a quota of three or four selected by the people in a general convention. From these three or four, the individual candidate is selected by a committee of representative men from the various parts of the

The atrophy spread, naturally, to the highest delegate body of the league, the annual provincial convention, though not rapidly enough to suit the government. The league's leaders, who were also the government leaders, had to discountenance the introduction and debating of resolutions on specific matters of provincial administration. Convention delegates, whose schooling in Douglas political theory might be sufficient to warn them off the arcana of social credit "methods", did nevertheless think it their place to discuss the prosaic day to day business of provincial administration. The government was, after all, administering a wide range of provincial services and regulations which had nothing to do with social credit, and was putting through the usual crop of statutory amendments at every session of the legislature. Not unnaturally the conventions assumed that they had the right to bring their own experience to bear on all these matters in the form of recommendations to the cabinet, just as the U.F.A. conventions had done.

They were informed otherwise. Mr. Manning opened the annual provincial convention of the Social Credit League in January 1938 by telling the delegates with what they might concern themselves and with what they might not.

The original platform of the Alberta Social Credit League was a truly democratic one, Mr. Manning stressed. "It dealt with broad general principles essential to the securing of the results the citizens required." He advised the convention to keep that policy in mind when deliberating. "Confine your deliberations to the major policies involved," he urged.

"Your government is the most unique government in the world," he said later, "in that you people charged us with a double responsibility—the responsibility of administering provincial affairs and the responsibility of completely changing our economic system. You can deal profitably with the latter phase but not with the first."

The speaker urged upon his listeners the importance of carrying back to their constituencies the important information which would be given them through the various addresses on the program.[70]

Thus admonished, the delegates listened to addresses by the two Douglas experts, Powell and Byrne, reiterating the theory that

---

constituency. To secure unity throughout the province, and to prevent skullduggery of any kind, an advisory committee chosen by the board of management of the Social Credit League sits in with the representatives from the various parts of the constituency to advise them in their choice. I am persuaded that this is the most democratic method of choosing candidates that has ever been established in this country." (Edmonton *Bulletin*, Feb. 18, 1939). The method, however, was not used for any of the general elections after 1940.

[70]*Today and Tomorrow*, Jan. 20, 1938.

"methods" should be left to the experts while the people and their representatives sustained them by expressing a will for results only. On the second, and last, day of the convention Aberhart drove home the lessons the delegates were meant to learn. While Manning had warned the delegates off concrete discussion of provincial administration, he had left them the right to "deal with" the government's "responsibility of changing completely our economic system." Aberhart made it plain that they were to deal with this matter by faith rather than works.

Mr. Aberhart urged the delegates to recognize the importance of an absolute necessity for the cause. "No cause, no esprit de corps," he warned them. "You must be convinced that there is only one remedy and that is contained in the philosophy of Social Credit. When you are convinced, no power can stand before you."[71]

Faith was, indeed, to issue in works, but only in a most attentuated way: the delegate's task was to transmit to his local group the inspiration he had shared and the precepts that had been handed down at the convention.

The importance of the information given to you by Powell and Byrne was stressed. "See that you take this information back to your groups. And remember, that the great work of the premier, cabinet and M.L.A.'s of this province is to see that there is never a break in your ranks. Give your experts a chance to do the things you want," he challenged.[72]

In spite of this effort to keep the convention to inspirational and theoretical generalities, of the 105 resolutions which had been presented 48 were discussed and of these 37 were adopted. The adopted resolutions were to be placed before the cabinet; those which had not been dealt with were to be turned over to the appropriate government departments.[73]

Succeeding annual conventions were increasingly diverted from debating specific resolutions, and told, both by their own leaders and by the experts themselves, how little standing anyone but the experts had under the social credit dispensation.

To secure effective action [Byrne told the 1939 convention] . . . the people must assume their sovereignty. To do so they must unite, under proper leadership, for the results they want in common. . . . It is not necessary for the people or their representatives or the Government to know how these results can be secured, any more than it is necessary for them to know how armaments are built in order to give the nation adequate defence from ex-

[71]*Ibid.*   [72]*Ibid.*   [73]*Ibid.*

ternal aggression. It is sufficient for them to know that it can be done—
that is is physically possible.[74]

No clearer indication of the decline of the delegate convention since
the days of the U.F.A. is needed.

Although it did not prove feasible to do away with all specific resolutions, the executive gradually established a pattern for conventions
by which resolutions were minimized and their discussion was kept in
hand. The hundreds of resolutions coming from locals were ruled out,
as dealing with local demands. Informative and inspirational addresses were given preponderance, and came to occupy two-thirds or more
of the convention's time. The informative part of the programme included talks by various experts, in agriculture, welfare, and other
fields of provincial administration, who were often members of the
staff of a government department, though not usually deputy ministers.
These talks were frequently arranged to coincide with the subject-
matter of resolutions, which the executive saw in advance of the convention; in these cases the talk would be given first, setting the tone
for the discussion of the resolution. No vestige remained of that working delegate body which had earned for the U.F.A. convention the
name of "the farmers' parliament." The social credit convention had
become a secular revival meeting, with carefully provided adult education admixed.

We may now sum up the relations between the cabinet, the legislature, and the convention as they emerged after the settlement of the
insurgency. The cabinet, or more accurately the premier and those
other members of the cabinet who were also leaders of the party, had
established their supremacy over both the legislature and the convention to an even greater degree than any U.F.A. cabinet had done.
Legislature and convention were not only subordinated; they were
rendered almost vestigial. This was a natural result of their acceptance
of the Douglas theory that the people and their representatives should
demand results only.

The cabinet, on the contrary, established its supremacy by quietly
rejecting in fact the role assigned to it by Douglas theory, while taking
advantage of the protection which that theory gave it. The government
could forestall any querulous disposition of caucus or convention
simply by flourishing the Douglas teaching. Caucus and convention
were bound to accept it, for both caucus and league had, in the settlement of the insurgency, subscribed in effect to the doctrine that the

[74]*Social Crediter*, March 18, 1939.

experts should be responsible and should have time to produce a workable social credit plan.

One curious incident showed that the cabinet was prepared to shelter behind the Douglas doctrine of ministerial irresponsibility even in matters of administration unrelated to social credit. Towards the end of the 1938 session of the legislature the opposition introduced a resolution based on the findings of a provincial Royal Commission on highway construction. The resolution recited abuses in the administration of the Department of Public Works and called for a change in the methods and policy. Mr. Fallow, the minister, introduced an amendment (which was subsequently carried) which not only completely altered the operative clause of the resolution but also substituted, for the last clause of the condemnatory preamble, the statement that "the inquiry proved to the satisfaction of the ordinary layman that said inefficiency and carelessness was due to the refusal or inability of the Departmental officials to carry out the policy of the Government."[75]

Without denying the abuses, the minister thus denied responsibility for them, and in this he was supported by the solid social credit majority. This device for saving face, not usual in the practice of cabinet government, was exceptional even in Alberta social credit practice, and can scarcely be cited as an application of Douglas theory. But it is evident that in support of the government's whole position the Douglas theory was very useful. It was not without reason that the government leaders continued to preach, and allow the Douglas experts to preach, that the government had no responsibility except to support the experts. As long as this theory was accepted by the movement as a whole, it left the government in fact the master and rendered both legislature and constituency organization useless in respect of contributing to the formation of government policies, useful only in sustaining the enthusiasm of the social credit electorate.

The Douglas theory, then, which was to have restored to the people a sovereignty they had lost under the old party system may be said scarcely to have fulfilled its promise. As a working system of democracy it was supposed to ensure that the elected representative became the servant of the electors, effectively transmitting their will. But it was an essential part of the scheme that the people's will should be stripped of all definition, leaving nothing concrete enough to be

[75]Alberta, Legislative Assembly, *Journals*, XXXVIII, 1938, pp. 94–5; cf. *Edmonton Journal*, March 16, 1938.

represented. True, it had not been possible in Alberta to keep the people's will quite as undefined as Douglas's formulation of "a secure sufficiency in freedom." The Albertan people's will could not steadily be prevented from being as precise as a will for $25 a month. This will could indeed be transmitted, but it could not be made effective as long as the people accepted the social credit theory, and as long as the government and experts could make a show of finding ways to bring in the new economic order.

Since it was thus difficult for the representative to transmit the will of his electors to the government, all that was left him was to transmit the will of the government to the electors. He became public relations man for the government, his trade the purveying of confidence. The sovereignty of the people turned out to be illusory; the more it was proclaimed by the government, the less the people were permitted to exercise it. In giving up the right to express their will on specific issues and concrete problems, social credit followers had exchanged the substance of influence for the shadow of sovereignty.

This result was not due to Aberhart's modification of the Douglas political theory; it was inherent in the original theory. Whether the responsibility for "methods" was given to the experts, as required by Douglas and pretended by Aberhart, or to the government, as in practice it was in Alberta, was of no consequence beside the fact that the people and their delegates and representatives, in convention and legislature, had lost the right to give either advice or instructions about anything substantial, or to participate in any way in the administration.

§ 4. Douglasism vs. Cabinet Government in Alberta: The Last Phase, 1939–49

We have seen that the dominance which the cabinet and experts had established over the legislature and convention after the insurgency rested on two conditions: first, on the social crediters in the legislature and in the province continuing to accept the theory that their function was merely to demand results; second, on the ability of the government and experts to keep up some expectation that they could produce results, specifically, that they could subdue the financiers. The first of these conditions could not easily be met without the second, but as long as there were any avenues left to explore in proceeding against "finance" the cabinet and experts were fairly secure. We have seen too that the harmony between the government and the Douglas men depended on the same conditions. While there were any

Douglas tactics left which could be made to appear feasible in Alberta the government needed the Douglas men, for Aberhart had nothing of his own to propose.

It followed that when all conceivable legislative devices for bringing the power of finance under control had met the same fate at the hands of federal agencies, the authority which the cabinet and experts had established for themselves in 1937 began to crumble. With it went the identity of interest of government and experts. No longer could they jointly count on finding refuge in the people's acceptance of the duty of leaving methods to the experts. A new basis of authority had to be found, and in the search for it the government and the Douglas men proceeded along divergent lines. The government came to rely more and more on its record of good administration, while continuing to recite the standard Douglas political theory; the experts came to seek refuge in the later Douglas theories.

These changes began to be noticeable by the beginning of 1939. It was apparent by then that the immediate tactical resources of government and experts were exhausted. The power of the federal government had proven insurmountable by the powers at the disposal of the Alberta government and the experts. Without some new basis in wider popular support, or some new methods of making the popular will prevail, they could do nothing more in their battle with finance. This was acknowledged by the government in the 1939 session of the legislature. The speech from the throne was silent about social credit, and of the 105 bills introduced during the session none sought to defeat "the money power" or implement social credit. The rationale of this position was given in Manning's speech on the budget.[76] Referring to the existence of a small group of "international money monopolists," he cited, as confirmation of their power, the fact that "every outstanding Act passed by the people's duly elected representatives in this Legislature which challenged that financial monopoly and claimed for the citizens of Alberta the right to exercise some measure of control over matters so vital to their welfare, has been either disallowed by the Federal Government or declared *ultra vires* by the Courts." Confronted with this treatment of its efforts, the government had not abandoned its just claim. "No government with the welfare of its people at heart could consider submitting to such an injustice. We do not purpose to be unreasonable nor to press our demands with undue haste, but the longer our claim is denied the more irresistible

[76]March 6, 1939. Published as a pamphlet entitled *Financial Tyranny and the Dawn of a New Day* (n.d., n.p.).

becomes the onrushing avalanche of public opinion, and the more indignant the demands of those whose united voices remain unheeded in a country, for the so-called democratic rights of which their fore-fathers bled and died."[77] In other words, the government would do nothing more to implement social credit until it had more support. To rely on a continuing and cumulative growth of popular resentment while calling a halt to the drama which had evoked and heightened it was rather optimistic, but having exhausted the possibilities of single combat the government had no alternative. The same quietism was apparent in the programme of the 1940 session of the legislature. Since this was an election year some gesture in the direction of social credit was to be expected. New legislation, mainly an act to set up a pro-vincial bank, was passed but was not seriously regarded as an assault on the financiers.

How long a social credit government could have maintained itself by taking such a position, had not extraneous events worked in its favour, cannot be known. The outbreak of the world war before the expiry of the government's mandate effectively postponed the time of judgment, by making it perfectly proper for the government to sub-ordinate contentious measures to a policy of co-operation with the federal government in the prosecution of the war. How nearly the government had come to paying for its inability to establish social credit in its first term is indicated by the fact that in the provincial election of March 1940 it lost a substantial proportion of seats, emerg-ing with 36 out of the 57 seats, or 63 per cent as compared with its previous standing of 89 per cent of the legislature.

War removed from the government leaders the burden of action, but not of speech. They were still social crediters. But they were also the government of the province of Alberta. They could therefore speak of their good administration of the province, and did so at great length. At the same time they constantly reminded their audiences of the basic principles of social credit political theory. Democracy meant government which would give the sovereign people the results they wanted; the people were really united in their will for results, but had no way of expressing it under the party system or of asserting it under the domination of finance. In the main this was simply a repetition of the earlier Douglas theory, especially of its critical aspects, but need and convenience required a somewhat different em-phasis than before.

Complaint about the domination of financiers became acceptance of a modified form of Douglas's world plot theory. One of Aberhart's

[77]Manning, *Financial Tyranny*, pp. 27–8, 39.

last broadcasts before his death in 1943 was entitled "The Plan for World Control." It was an impassioned attack on the recently announced British and American plans for a post-war international monetary system. "By giving over control of finance to some alien dominated international dictatorship, [the people of Canada] would be giving that authority complete control over every aspect of their national life . . . the final result would be a slave state, worse than anything yet proposed by our bombastic dictators." The people should therefore "oppose, expose and resist . . . this audacious and evil conspiracy by the Money Powers to set up a World Slave State."[78]

Aberhart's politics had always been dramatic; it is not surprising that he turned to Douglas's world conspiracy for those elements of drama which he was no longer able to provide by himself. Here was conflict and suspense on a world-wide scale, and although the Albertans' connection with it might at first seem remote, the very immensity of it might catch them up and sweep them along. But Aberhart took only what he needed; neither he nor Manning believed in or would propagate the Douglas theory of a Jewish world plot.

New difficulties attended the critique of the party system; it was still preached but with some differences. Government and party leaders continued to discourse on the futility of the people's being asked to decide about "methods," and the importance of their uniting to demand results. The emphasis now was, of course, not on the ability of the experts to produce results; it was on the inadequacy and viciousness of the party system which, by asking the people to choose between methods, ensured that they would never get results.

Even this much of the standard Douglas theory could not be expounded as freely or relied on as heavily as before. In the first place, it was difficult to denounce the party system without denouncing party organization as inherently undemocratic, and this could not be done very convincingly, since the Alberta Social Credit League was now virtually indistinguishable from a party, despite protestations to the contrary. It was as much controlled from the top as any orthodox party; indeed, both in the choice of candidates and in the formulation of policies, the social credit leaders had an authority, and a freedom from constituency control, that might well be admired by the leaders of the old parties. It was therefore difficult for Aberhart and the government to take the line that party organization as such was an evil. Even to criticize parties for being committed to platforms and "methods" was not likely to be altogether convincing, for the Social Credit League was committed to social credit monetary reform as the

[78]*Social Crediter,* June 26, 1943.

method of ameliorating the condition of the people, and the government had been elected and supported on that platform.

In the second place the alternate-party system, as far as Alberta politics was concerned, was something of a straw man. Except in the two large cities the old parties had no organization worth speaking of, at least for the provincial elections, and everybody knew it. In spite of this, the case against the alternate-party system, as the means by which special interests confused, divided, and ruled the people, had not lost its effectiveness. For the old party system was still in operation in federal politics; the federal government which consistently thwarted the will of the Alberta electors was a product of that system and could be exhibited as an embodiment of all its evils. The campaign against the party system was therefore still relevant, provided that it was directed against federal parties.

Aberhart became president of the Democratic Monetary Reform Organization of Canada, and in that capacity expounded throughout 1942 the old social credit political theory. The party system was "a vicious and alarming negation of democracy in its true essence."[79] The people should abandon party affiliations and unite to demand results. All this talk did not surmount the inherent difficulty of distinguishing between such a "union of electors" and a political party. If the old party machines refused to bow to the non-party expression of the will of the people for results, there was no way to proceed except to put up "union of electors" candidates. That much was recognized. But it was not admitted that to do this would turn the union into a party competing with other parties. Only if the union succeeded in sweeping the other parties out of existence could it claim to be other than a party itself. For the most part the social credit leaders and organizers lived on just this plane of optimism, though recurrent doubt is suggested by the emphasis with which they asserted that their new federal organization was "NOT 'just another political party.' "[80]

Their position was indeed confusing. They could see that in organizing beyond Alberta they would have to proceed by putting up their own candidates in competition with other parties. Yet they believed not only that the union of electors was basically different from a party, but also that it was capable of superseding the alternate-party system. This belief was based on what they had done, and what they thought they had seen happen, in 1935. As it seemed to them, they had swept Alberta in 1935 by telling the electors to abandon party and unite their

---

[79]"The Democratic Monetary Reform Organization of Canada," text of statement by Aberhart as National President, *Social Crediter*, March 7, 1942.
[80]*Ibid.*

wills for results. The electors had done so, and there was now no semblance of an alternate-party system in the province. Since the Social Credit League had been conceived as a non-party union of electors, since it had annihilated other parties in Alberta, and since its leaders did not admit that it had taken on the internal characteristics of party, it was natural for the leaders to think that they had discovered a new species of political organization and to attribute their success to it.

What the social credit leaders failed to notice was that there never had been an alternate-party system in Alberta. The people had not abandoned a party system in 1935; they had merely abandoned the U.F.A. for the Social Credit League. In overlooking this, the leaders overestimated the efficacy of their slogan and method of organization. They did not see that it was the relatively homogeneous social composition of Alberta that had kept the alternate-party system out of provincial politics from the beginning, and that only if all Canada were an equally homogeneous community could a union of electors expect to supersede the party system in federal politics.

The social credit leaders could therefore think of replacing the federal party system with unions of electors. They did not, of course, want to see any change in Alberta. Having their own party organization there, they were not anxious to press for an Alberta union of electors, and it was made clear that the new federal organization was in no way to supersede the Alberta league. The D.M.R.O. was to be an initiating and co-ordinating body; initiating electoral organization from the bottom up in provinces where there was no such organization, and assisting and co-ordinating the work of the provincial bodies. But the autonomy of existing provincial organizations was stressed; they would "not be asked to submerge their identity."[81]

In all this critique of the prevailing party system of democracy, as presented by the government and league leaders, there was no hint of the doctrine which Douglas was developing from 1942 on. The sovereignty of the people's will was not questioned; there was no suggestion that democracy was essentially negative or consisted in the right of individuals and minorities to contract out, no suggestion that the majority principle was a faulty or vicious basis for democracy. Naturally not, for Aberhart and Manning had a majority.

At Aberhart's death in May 1943, Manning[82] succeeded as premier and leader, by choice of the caucus, and announced continuation of

[81]"Organization for Democracy in Canada," *Social Crediter*, March 21, 1942.
[82]E. C. Manning before the rise of the social credit movement had been associated with Aberhart in the work of the Prophetic Bible Institute. In the 1935

the Aberhart policy: full co-operation in the national war effort, un-relenting struggle "to secure for each and every citizen of this province the permanent social and economic security and freedom which are rightfully theirs" by capturing "effective control of the monetary system," and "sound, honest and efficient administration in every de-partment of government."[83]

Before the end of the war, when it would be necessary again to take up the crusade for social credit, a new issue on which the govern-ment could develop support was found in the threat of socialism. In the Alberta general election of 1944 the struggle against socialism conveniently replaced the struggle for social credit. On this issue the government was returned with a larger majority than ever before. If it lost some of its radical supporters to the C.C.F., it gained many more from the business community, which was now convinced, with good reason, that Manning's social credit was no menace to private enterprise but the best protection against the growing strength of the socialist C.C.F. The menace of socialism became and remained the staple of the official Alberta social credit propaganda.

The crusade against socialism required no break from the standard social credit theory; on the contrary, it could quite properly be pre-sented as an integral part of social credit strategy. Douglas had always stood for private enterprise and against socialism, and never more strongly than in his war and post-war writings where he asserted the complicity of socialist parties in the world plot against freedom. Manning and his cabinet colleagues, without accepting the extreme formulation of the world plot, could with good conscience go along with that part of it which linked socialism with high finance. They soon convinced themselves that in attacking socialism they were attacking the international financiers, indeed, that the only way now to attack financiers was to attack socialism. This conclusion followed from the premise that the financiers, having been driven out of their first position by the social crediters' exposure of their manipulation of the monetary system, had now resorted to socialism as the means of maintaining their grip on the world's wealth. As the *Canadian Social Crediter* put it:

---

election campaign he usually appeared on the same platform as Aberhart and was appointed, on the formation of the social credit government, provincial secretary and minister of trade and industry.

[83]Speech at Edmonton, June 11, 1943, reprinted from the *Edmonton Bulletin*; in a pamphlet (published by the English Social Credit Secretariat) *Aberhart: Manning; a Contemporary Account . . . with a Public Declaration of Policy . . .* (Liverpool, 1943).

The Banking Monopoly . . . have changed battle tactics: they have decided to beat us by another method [other than concealing the truth about the money system]. What is that method? They intend to take control of real wealth. The safest and best way of doing that is by socialism. The state will take all; and those who control the state will control all.

[Hence, social crediters were told,] The battle against monopoly—particularly against state monopoly, the most devilish of all—must be waged today. The battle against taxation and control must be fought in grim earnest. (But in this respect, battle chiefly against the federal government, since provincial governments are almost hog-tied.) [84]

This was an extremely convenient doctrine, well designed to appeal to the independent small producer, who was inclined to be equally fearful of socialism, high finance, and monopoly. His fears, heightened, were used to divert his attention from the lack of social credit in Alberta and focus it on the present and future menace of the socialist C.C.F. and the capitalist federal government, who were made equally agents of the financiers.

This line was developed intensively from 1945 on, with outstanding success, although for a time it appeared that it might not be sufficient. For with the end of the war, there were renewed demands by constituencies that the government again take up its struggle for social credit in the province. Something of the old crusading fervour reappeared at the annual convention of the Social Credit League in December 1945. The main resolution cited the federal government's disallowance of all essential social credit legislation, and its apparent intention "in conjunction with the financial corporations and advocates of state dictatorship" to pursue "the same disastrous policies" as before the war, and called on the provincial government "to take such action as it deems necessary, in face of any and all opposition, to institute the necessary democratic reforms, in accordance with Social Credit principles, to free the people from the growing threat of dictatorship."[85] Before the vote was taken the attorney-general, Mr. Maynard, emphasized what this resolution meant, and warned the delegates to be "very sure of what you are voting for." "We've had disallowances and ultra vires. We had war on our hands before this war. If you pass this resolution, it means another declaration of war on those who oppose the will of the people." Reminding the delegates of the recent apathy of the league, he asked: "Do you really want drastic action now? . . . Do you really mean an unlimited campaign against finance? Do you mean going beyond the law, if necessary? Do you mean going beyond the constitution? . . . In the fight we had before 1939, two of our boys went

[84]*Canadian Social Crediter*, Jan. 23, 1947.   [85]*Ibid.*, Dec. 13, 1945.

to jail. Do you want to go that far again? . . . I'm prepared to go to jail."[86] Manning spoke briefly of the importance of respect for laws and constitution, but did not dissociate himself from his attorney-general's position. The result was a foregone conclusion: the resolution was passed unanimously, with much cheering and the singing of the social credit marching hymn, "Onward Christian Soldiers."

Although this was generally represented as the result of a spontaneous surge of demand from the rank and file, it is evident that the leaders had striven for this effect. The lack of any substantial pressure from the constituencies is indicated by the size of the convention; the most that could be reported of it was that "over 180 delegates" attended,[87] and this in spite of a very generous permitted ratio of delegates to members of the league.[88] The constituencies had indeed become apathetic, and the league had reached a low ebb of membership; some striking show of activity was needed if it was to be revived.

Armed with this mandate from the convention, the government introduced new legislation which would give it control over the banks and enable it to issue social credit to the people. Grandiosely entitled *The Alberta Bill of Rights Act,* the bill declared that every citizen had the right to enjoy the various civil and property rights he enjoyed under existing law, and in addition that he had the right to a social security pension if gainful employment was not available or if he was physically incapable of gainful employment, and in any case when he reached the age of sixty. The pension was to be not a fixed amount for each eligible individual but only that supplementary amount necessary "to ensure an annual income of not less than six hundred dollars a year." This was a far cry from the original promise of a monthly dividend of $25 to every citizen. Now, only the unemployed, the incapacitated, and those over sixty were to be eligible for benefits, and even they, after being subjected to a means test, would get only the amount necessary to bring their income up to a subsistence level.

Part II of the bill provided for a whole apparatus of licensing and control of banks, and creation and circulation of additional credit, by a government board. This was to make available to the consuming public sufficient purchasing power to buy all the goods produced. The additional purchasing power was to reach the consuming public by

[86]*Ibid.*   [87]*Ibid.*

[88]Publicized before the convention (*Canadian Social Crediter,* Nov. 8, 1945), the allowance was two delegates from every group of ten members, with one additional delegate for every additional ten members. It was also provided that where there was no organized group one member from each poll might attend the convention as a voting delegate.

way of the social security pensions, educational and medical benefits, reduction of taxation, and subsidies to consumers' goods' industries.

Since an essential feature of the bill was the same licensing and control of banks that had been invalidated, in all previous bills, by the federal government, there was never much doubt as to the fate of this bill. The only wonder is that the government could think that its supporters would be much aroused by it, especially as the bill provided that it was not to go into effect unless and until its constitutional validity had been passed by the courts. The bill itself, with promotional commentaries, was printed in various attractive forms by the government and by the league and widely distributed, but there is no evidence that it evoked much enthusiasm. It was duly declared *ultra vires* by the Supreme Court of Alberta in 1946 and by the Privy Council in 1947. By this time, however, the tide of post-war prosperity, heightened by the new provincial revenues from the discovery and opening up of enormous new oil deposits, had put the government effectively beyond the need of any further effort to subdue the financiers or otherwise implement social credit principles.

The various shifts by which the social credit government maintained its support after 1939, when its legislative efforts to control finance and introduce social credit dividends had virtually to be abandoned, may now be seen in perspective. From 1939 to 1945 the war was an adequate reason for the government to postpone social credit operations in the province, while keeping the theory alive by exercises in criticism of the federal party system and federal government as tools of the world financial plotters. Before this breathing spell ended, the growing strength of the C.C.F. provided a new issue. From 1944, the struggle against socialism practically replaced the struggle against the financiers, while being represented as the same thing. This strategy won the election in 1944 but did not arouse the league to any great enthusiasm. An attempt to arrest the decline of the league by building up a renewed demand for social credit action in the province in the 1945 convention, and by producing the Alberta Bill of Rights in 1946, was of doubtful success. But before its saving effect on the fortunes of the government could be measured or put to a test, Alberta struck oil and the government reaped a steady golden harvest.

Through all these shifts of line, the government had one constant continuing claim for support. Aided by wartime prosperity it had provided satisfactory and even improved administration of the normal provincial services—health, education, welfare, and so on. It could thus claim the favourable notice of the electorate for the quality of its administration, even if it could not produce social credit dividends.

The Social Credit Board and the Douglas experts, however, had no such line of retreat. The board had been established and the experts appointed with only one avowed purpose—to produce social credit in Alberta by taking the control of the people's credit away from the financiers. Confronted with failure they had, unlike the government, no natural alternative employment. Unable to disavow their responsibility or to cover it over with other functions, they had to resort to more and more extreme theoretical positions to explain their failure. Since their failure was as complete as Douglas's in England, they were more drawn to his later theories than was the government, which was not in as great need of them. Only the world plot in its extreme form served to justify the board's failure, and the preaching of it gave them a full-time occupation.

The board thus became a pure propaganda body. Its annual reports to the legislature came to contain practically nothing about the work for which it had been established, on which indeed there was nothing to report, but more than made up for this, in length, by elaborate restatements of the world plot thesis. In this propaganda the Board was vociferously supported by the *Canadian Social Crediter*, by a few other members of the Alberta legislature, and by several of the social credit members of parliament at Ottawa. They followed the full Douglas line, even to the explicitly Jewish world plot; their performance in this respect needs no further description here.

For a time the board was cautious about following Douglas's denigration of the majority principle of democracy. This was natural enough. For in the first place the board consisted of members of the legislature and of the social credit caucus in Alberta. And in the second place, there were still thought to be possibilities of organizing "unions of electors" in Canada as a whole; while this belief persisted, the Canadian Douglasites could not conveniently follow their master in abandoning the concept of the sovereignty of the majority will.

However, in its annual report for 1946, presented to the legislature in 1947, the board, while still advocating the union of electors and asserting that the people are really united in the results they want, came out against the secret ballot, and in favour of an open signed ballot with the voter's liability limited to paying for the schemes for which he voted.[89] The substitution of an open for the secret ballot had, following Douglas, been mooted some months earlier in the

[89]Alberta Social Credit Board, *Annual Report 1946, Presented to the Legislative Assembly . . . at its 1947 Session* ([Edmonton, 1947]), pp. 16–17.

Canadian Social Crediter,[90] but its public presentation in the official report of the board to the legislature, without the prior knowledge of the caucus, brought matters to a head.

As if the proposal to do away with the secret ballot was not enough, the report also asserted that the only effective democratic organization was a Union of Voters "controlled strictly from the bottom up" and able "to control the elected representatives of the people *at all times* (not merely on the day of an election) and through them, all of the People's governing bodies,—local, provincial and national."[91] Social credit members of the legislature could not be blamed for reading into this the imputation that their own Social Credit League was under fire, especially as it was an open secret that Byrne, who inspired the board, had never approved of the league form of organization.

Manning immediately dissociated the government and the Alberta social credit movement from what he called "the personal views of Major Douglas," while claiming that government and movement were still united on Douglas's economic principles and analysis.[92] In this Manning carried the caucus and the league executive with him. A statement issued by Manning at the close of the legislative session, in the name of the caucus and the league executive, asserted their allegiance to social credit principles and their determination to continue the fight "initiated in this province by the late Premier William Aberhart" (significantly not mentioning Douglas), and announced:

We condemn, repudiate and completely disassociate ourselves and the Social Credit movement in Alberta from any statements or publications which are incompatible with the established British ideals of democratic freedom or which endorse, excuse or incite anti-Semitism or racial or religious intolerance in any form.[93]

The statement was endorsed by the next convention of the league, in November 1947.[94]

The days of the board and the Douglasites in Alberta were numbered. Manning announced early in November that the Social Credit Board would be abolished at the end of the fiscal year (March 31, 1948), and that the political aspects of its work would be made a function of the Social Credit League.[95] He publicly denounced the "little faction of 'Douglasites' who think they have some special mono-

[90]Nov. 7 and Dec. 12, 1946, and Jan. 30, 1947.
[91]*Annual Report 1946*, p. 22.   [92]*Edmonton Bulletin*, March 22, 1947.
[93]*Ibid.*, April 1, 1947; *Canadian Social Crediter*, April 3, 1947.
[94]*Canadian Social Crediter*, Dec. 4, 1947.
[95]*Edmonton Bulletin*, Nov. 5, 1947.

poly on the basic principles of Social Credit" as representing "an attempt to undermine the Social Credit movement and destroy public confidence in the government."[96] Control of the *Canadian Social Crediter* was wrested from the Douglasites at the end of 1947. Finally, in February 1948, the premier requested and received the resignations of L. D. Byrne, Social Credit Board adviser and deputy minister of economic affairs, and of R. E. Ansley, the one cabinet minister who supported Byrne. The stated ground was that they "held views and advocated policies at distinct variance with those of the government and the Social Credit movement in Alberta."[97] The gratuitous inclusion of the movement in this citation is noteworthy.

Manning's "purge," as it was called, effectively destroyed the influence, in government and league, of those who had consistently followed Douglas in his later political teachings. It was widely said that it marked the final abandonment of social credit principles as well as practice. The government had made the name of the founder of social credit a term of reproach and contempt. At the same time it had openly abandoned or indefinitely postponed any attempt to implement social credit in Alberta; the slogan of the 1947 Alberta league convention was "On to Ottawa." The coincidence of the rejection of Douglas and the rejection of efforts to introduce social credit economic reforms in the province afforded strong presumption that the government was no longer a social credit government in anything but name. Its anti-socialist and anti-liberal orientation, and its emphasis on administration, suggested that it had come to rest in the position of an orthodox conservative government.

This was too sweeping a view. Superficially it was true enough, but beneath the surface remained a considerable legacy of Douglasism.

§ 5. The Legacy of Douglasism in Alberta

The government's repudiation of the later Douglas theories and abandonment or indefinite postponement of attempts to act on social credit economic theories was by no means a complete rejection of Douglasism. It was, rather, a reversion to the Douglas political theory and practice of the 1930's, or more accurately, to the Alberta modification of it whereby the followers accepted the function allotted to them while the government quietly assumed more power and responsibility than was its due in the Douglas theory. In essentials the government and the movement had settled down to something like the position they had reached in 1939. This, as we have seen, was

[96]*Ibid.*, Nov. 11, 1947.   [97]*Ibid.*, Feb. 21, 1948.

different from either the orthodox system or the delegate democracy that had been the legacy of the U.F.A. period.

The difference from the U.F.A. delegate democracy was most plainly manifested in the transformation of the annual convention from a working body to an inspirational meeting. The difference in practice was based on an equally plain difference in theory: the function of the U.F.A. delegates had been to bring to bear on the government the concrete wills of specific occupational and local groups; the function of the social credit delegates was merely to express a supposedly general will for freedom and plenty, and to sustain the government unquestioningly in its search for what they "knew" to be obtainable. The delegates' acceptance of this view permitted a degree of cabinet domination greater than in the U.F.A. period and different in quality.

The relation of government and followers, or of the leaders of the movement and the rank and file, was not, as in the U.F.A., rational and utilitarian but messianic. We have seen how the leaders were able to maintain this relation in spite of their failure to produce the results originally expected of them, partly by diverting the wills of their followers to the federal political field and partly by the windfall revenue from oil which enabled them to provide a high level of provincial services. But the inspirational relation between leaders and followers which was established in the thirties has remained, as has the mystique of the general will. The government is still based on the Social Credit League, and on the vague yet persistent belief of the rank and file that there is a general will and that the league and the government represent it. The league is still seen not as a party but as a movement charged with a mission of bringing a new concept of democracy to fruition.

How strongly this feeling has continued, how much of the support for the government since 1948 has been due to this belief and how much to its new-found wealth, it is impossible to determine. But it is significant that the government has continued to appeal on grounds that it represents a new and higher concept of democracy and is a unique non-party embodiment of the people's will.

That the government can take this line does not mean that the Social Credit League is still a popular movement controlled from below. On the contrary, to the extent that the standard Douglas theory is accepted in the movement, the leadership (and the government) are enabled to impose their decisions all the more easily on the people in the name of the people's own will. Thus the government can, within limits which are extraordinarily broad while the present windfall revenues continue, satisfy the bondholders while reviling the financiers.

The same qualitative relation between government and movement which makes the social credit system of government something different from the U.F.A. ideal and practice of delegate democracy, distinguishes it also from the orthodox pattern of cabinet and party governments. The social credit government is indeed closer to the orthodox pattern than to the U.F.A. ideal, both in its internal party structure and in the cabinet domination of the legislature. Yet the cabinet domination is not based on the usual exigencies of the party system, for there is no effective alternate-party system in operation. The cabinet's dominance is, paradoxically, based on the party's belief that it is not a party but the bearer of a new kind of democracy, and on its consequent submission to that station in life to which it pleased Douglas and Aberhart to call it.

The legacy of Douglasism in Alberta is not to be found in the gestures still made against finance or in any economic reform policies still enunciated from time to time, but in the debasement of the U.F.A. legacy of delegate democracy. By preaching the destruction of the party system in the name of the people's sovereignty, the social credit leaders destroyed not the party system but the tradition of effective delegate democracy which had emerged from the U.F.A. period.

In longer perspective, we may say that the non-party tradition of the west absorbed such elements of Douglasism as were congenial to it, and rejected those which were not. But in the process the tradition was itself altered. The net impact of social credit on the Alberta pattern of democratic theory and practice was, while confirming the non-party tradition and leaving the cabinet dominant, to transform the Albertan ideal type of democracy from a substantive representation of the wills of rational interest groups to an insubstantial representation of a supposedly general will by an inspired leader.

CHAPTER EIGHT

The Quasi-Party System

-»»«-

§ 1. The Pattern of Alberta Radicalism

Our survey of the theory and practice of Alberta political radicalism is concluded. It remains to consider the implications of what has been described and analysed. What is the underlying nature of the radicalism of the U.F.A. and Social Credit? Are the lines of direction it has taken sufficiently clearly related to enduring characteristics of the society and economy to allow of prediction? Is any revision of the prevailing theory of the role of parties in democracy suggested by the analysis?

We have noticed the trend from delegate democracy to plebiscitarian democracy. Attention has been drawn to the deviations from the alternate-party system: the total rejection of it in theory, and the partial departure from it in practice. Taking the whole political development and relating it to the society from which it sprang, it will be suggested that what has emerged, more or less permanently, is something new; not sufficiently described as a plebiscitary system, neither an orthodox alternate-party system nor a completely one-party system. It may be called the quasi-party system. Its existence may be seen as a natural outcome of circumstances found in Alberta, in the other Canadian prairie provinces, and less definitely, but perceptibly, in Canada as a whole.

The pattern of Alberta political radicalism is not difficult to discern: two waves of revolt, the first by the farmers, the second by farmers and townsmen, each followed by a longer period in which the government and the leadership of the popular movement, and then the popular movement as a whole, became increasingly conservative. Each revolt expressed a cumulative feeling that the existing provincial and federal governments were basically incompetent to resist encroachments on the people's standard of living and independence. The radicalism of both movements consisted not so much in the extent of

215

their economic demands (which were not extreme) as in their conviction, born of repeated frustration of these demands, that the economic subordination from which they were suffering was an inherent part of eastern financial domination and of the party system.

In each case, therefore, the people were no longer content merely to change governments; nothing short of a change in the system of government—in the methods of electing governments and of controlling them and holding them responsible—would be sufficient. Each wave of radicalism swept into office a new party intent on replacing the party system (and the concomitant domination of the legislature by the cabinet) with a more democratic system; effective sovereignty was to be returned to the people, who were to retain it by working through instructed delegates.

In other words, the people of Alberta twice reached the point of attacking not abuses but a system, or what they regarded as a system and one which was inherently exploitive. In each case, as we have argued, they mistook the system somewhat, and their action against it was not fully successful.

When each popular movement in turn got its own government into office, radicalism gave way to conservatism. In each case the conservatism emerged earlier, and became a more solid habit of mind, within the government than within the movement. But in each case the movement acquiesced and followed suit, as the limits of radical policies and radical methods of political organization were reached. The limits in each case were set partly by the limits of provincial legislative jurisdiction, and fundamentally by the dependent economic status of Albertans as producers and (as will be argued in section 2) by the limits of the small-producer ideology. The recurrent conservatism was of two sorts: a moderation of economic policies and demands to what was practicable within the limitation of the established economic order; and a return towards orthodoxy in the structure and functioning of the political system. It is with the latter that we are directly concerned.

The pattern of political theory and practice, like that of economic policy, thus appears as an oscillation between radicalism and orthodoxy, both in the thinking of the broad popular movements and in the practice of the provincial governments which they established and maintained.

It might be described as an oscillation between a non-cabinet system and a cabinet system. For it starts with a non-cabinet system in the Territorial period, followed by cabinet government from 1905 to 1921, followed by the U.F.A. attempt at "group government" which from the beginning never strayed far from orthodox cabinet government and soon reverted to it pretty completely. With the rise of Social Credit there was another swing away from cabinet government, in principle; policy (in the ordinary, not the Social Credit, definition) was to be made by experts, with the cabinet merely expressing the general will. But what was asserted in principle was denied in practice from the beginning of the Social Credit tenure of office (with the partial exception of a brief period during the 1937 insurgency), and after a few years the cabinet gave up even the appearance of anything but cabinet government.

But this description does not give the whole pattern, nor the most important part of it. For the reversion to the cabinet system was never a reversion to the orthodox alternate-party system. If we think rather of the party system than of cabinet supremacy—the two are, as we have seen, distinct and separable—we find not a recurrent movement away from and back to orthodox practice, but a persistent and mainly successful effort to stay away from the orthodox system. We find also that the effort to get away or stay away from it took qualitatively different forms in the successive experiments.

The whole sequence may be described as: (1) the fairly "direct" democracy of the frontier Territorial period; (2) with the incursion of the federal Liberal and Conservative parties into provincial politics, a period of alternate-party government (full-fledged only from about 1910 to 1921); (3) with the U.F.A. revolt against the party system, a period of delegate democracy (1921–1935) which, because of the discredit of the alternate-party system and the hegemony of the U.F.A., was in effect a non-party or one-party system; (4) with the rise of social credit ideology and the capture of office by the Social Credit movement in 1935, a further but qualitatively different non-party system. The difference consisted in the fact that the Social Credit system, beginning as a delegate democracy in its outward forms, soon revealed itself as a plebiscitarian system from which the essential quality of delegate democracy—the close and continuous pressure of local opinion and demands on concrete issues—was conspicuously absent. Popular control of the government was illusory from the outset of the Social Credit administration. When an attempt was made to reassert it after the first eighteen months, the delegate insurgency was reduced to ineffectiveness by the government allowing some of the insurgents to share with it the nugatory responsibility of finding experts to whom the responsiblity for legislative measures was in theory to be handed over. What emerged was, as in the U.F.A. period, virtually a one-party system with cabinet supremacy. But it was not a system of genuine instructed delegation modified by cabinet rule; it was now a system of cabinet rule sustained by the illusory democracy of the inspirational convention.

Thus, apart from one short period in which the alternate-party system may be said to have existed (1910–21), the pattern of Alberta political radicalism has not been an oscillation between party and non-party systems but a persistent, though qualitatively discontinuous, rejection of the party system, with a trend from delegate to plebiscitarian democracy.

To sum up, there is a twofold pattern of change in the whole course of Alberta political radicalism. The attitude and practice regarding cabinet supremacy oscillate between radical rejection and orthodox acceptance. The attitude and practice in respect of the alternate-party system persist as radical rejection of the orthodox, its place being filled by two successive sorts of non-party or one-party system, first a genuine delegate democracy, second a plebiscitarian pseudo-delegate democracy.

Some explanations appear on the surface of the phenomena we have been investigating. That a popular movement advocating radical political reform should become oligarchical and conservative by the time it has achieved office or influence is a commonplace of observation. It is, since Michels' famous study,[1] generally explained as an inherent result of the need to have a party bureaucracy to make the reform force of a mass party effective, and of the desire of those who get such power within the party to increase their power. Such tendencies were to be found in the Alberta radical movements, but they are far from being a sufficient explanation of the course of their development.

It was not any centralizing party oligarchy that turned the U.F.A. from a radical delegate democracy to a conservative cabinet-dominated party. What centralization there was, in the popular movement, was due to a falling off of constituency participation and pressure, which only revived again about 1930. As the membership became less active, decisions came increasingly to be made by a small group at the top, but the evidence suggests that this centralization was the result not of manipulation by a central leadership seeking to build a bureaucratic

[1]Robert Michels, *Political Parties: A Sociological Study of the Oligarchical Tendencies of Modern Democracy*, trans. Eden and Cedar Paul (New York, 1915; reprinted Glencoe, Ill., 1949).

machine, but of satisfaction or at least acquiescence of the rank and file in what the government was doing. The undoubted centralization within the structure of government, which we have described as cabinet supremacy, was also less a result of inherent oligarchical tendencies than of the inherent limits of U.F.A. radicalism. As we have already seen,[2] the abandonment of convention or constituency control, in favour of cabinet supremacy over the legislature and even over the provincial convention, was compelled by the exigencies of governing and administering the province within the limitations of dependence on outside capital. The significant point is that these limitations were accepted by the U.F.A. government and, though less readily, by the majority of the movement as represented in delegate conventions. The basic limits of U.F.A. radicalism are to be found in the minds of the leaders and movement alike, in their acceptance of the prevailing system of property rights.

The same may be asserted of Social Credit radicalism, though here there was a somewhat longer gap between the leaders' and the followers' recognition of the limits imposed by their own acceptance of property institutions. Aberhart, from his first day in office, preferred to placate the established outside interests. He began his premiership by accepting orthodox financial advice (being apparently unable to see that it was flatly inconsistent with social credit principles), and by rejecting in fact the political theory which required him to hand responsibility over to the experts. When pressure from his supporters compelled him to install genuine social credit experts, he did, it is true, lend himself completely to their economic devices. He was even compelled to yield his supremacy to them and their insurgent supporters, but only for a few months. After August 1937, the orthodox mastery of the premier and cabinet was restored.

From then on, even the radicalism of their economic policies was equivocal. Aberhart, and the cabinet, fell in with the apparently extremely radical proposals of the experts, but whether or not Aberhart shared the experts' knowledge[3] that the proposals were unworkable, his economic radicalism was very limited. If he did know in advance that the financial legislation of 1937–9 would be invalidated by federal agencies, he cannot be said to have intended an attack on any part of the established order. If, on the other hand, he believed that the legislation would stand, it was presumably because he shared Major Douglas's confused belief that social credit could be superimposed on the existing property structure without

[2]Chap. III.   [3]See above, Chap. VII, sect. 1, p. 178.

damaging it in any essentials. In either case, nothing that he did was in conflict with a basic acceptance of the established order.

The radicalism of the leaders of both U.F.A. and Social Credit was not so radical as to permit them to depart from the basic assumptions of the existing property structure. They could therefore neither make a complete break with the financial system in which the provincial economy was enmeshed, nor abrogate cabinet supremacy. The leaders of both movements were prepared to fight against the quasi-colonial economic subordination of their people, but not to do anything which would undermine the sanctity of property rights. They were thus compelled to take a relatively conservative position when they saw where they really stood in relation to the established economy. The U.F.A. government leaders, indeed, never concealed their conservatism; it was open and honest. Aberhart concealed his, perhaps even from himself.

Thus, in spite of the obvious differences between the course of development of the two movements from radicalism to conservatism, one common factor emerges. The radicalism of both was that of a quasi-colonial society of independent producers, in rebellion against eastern imperialism but not against the property system. And the limits of the leaders' radicalism were not fundamentally much narrower than the limits of their supporters' radicalism.

It was not that the exigencies of government, as such, caused the leaders, on attaining office, to become orthodox both in their economic policies and in their practice of democracy. Rather, the exigencies of governing a society of independent producers, in revolt against outside domination but not against property, brought out the conservatism inherent in *petit-bourgeois* agrarian radicalism.

We have argued that the oscillation between radicalism and orthodoxy in respect of cabinet government, as of economic policy, is fully explicable only by the peculiar characteristics of a quasi-colonial independent-producer society and ideology. This view is supported by a consideration (in section 2, below) of the political implications of independent commodity production in general and of western agrarian production in particular. These implications, in turn, have a bearing on the other tendency of Alberta radicalism (discussed in section 3): the persistent rejection of the orthodox alternate-party system and its replacement successively by the two types of non-party or one-party system, active delegate democracy and pseudo-delegate plebiscitarian democracy.

§ *2. Political Implications of Independent Commodity Production*

The western Canadian farmer's proverbial sense of independence has withstood and even been strengthened by all the pressures on his economic position. When he has felt his independence threatened, by railways, grain traders, mortgage companies or banks, he has fought back, by political or economic means, and in so doing has strengthened his conception of himself as an independent. This conception is not precise. Partly it is a belief that by virtue of the way he produces he *is* independent as compared with those in other occupations. And partly it appears to be a feeling that because by his own efforts he produces complete commodities for which there is a fundamental need, he should be more independent than he is, and would be so if only he were not put to disadvantage by the operations of various powerful groups outside the farm economy. Both these beliefs have some foundation, but not enough to give the farmer the real or potential independence he conceives himself to have.

He does, it is true, produce by himself, without any substantial division of labour, commodities which are basic necessities of life. In this respect he appears unique, for the primary products of forest, mines, and seas are brought forth by an extensive division of labour. But uniqueness is not a title to independence, nor does the fundamental importance of his products in the scale of human wants give the farmer a preferred position in the economy, in countries which can feed themselves, except in wartime when the operation of the price system is overlaid by considerations of need not measured by the market.

Again, the farmer is in an obvious sense independent as compared with the wage-earner or the industrial entrepreneur, and it is perhaps his recognition of this difference that makes him so tenacious of his status: he is not dependent on an employer, nor does his living, or profit, depend on his ability to employ others. But while in his own productive activity the farmer does not stand immediately in either of these relations of dependence, yet he is producing in an economy which, on the whole, and increasingly, operates by means of these relations and is dominated by the interests of those who do stand in these relations. Since he is necessarily a part, and not a predominant part, of this economy, his independence of these relations is only skin-deep. So long as the main source of capital increment and economic power remains the ability directly or indirectly to dispose of the labour of others, the farmer as an independent commodity producer necessarily remains in a subordinate position. But it does not commonly appear to him that this is the root of the matter. He more generally attributes the confines of his independence to special interests, monopoly and the like; they are more visible, and can be fought with the expectation of some measure of success. Thus his freedom from those relations of dependence which prevail in a mature capitalist economy gives him a sense of greater independence than he can in fact have.

More specifically, the farmer produces in an economy determined by the decisions of entrepreneurs of a somewhat different order than himself. If we define entrepreneurs as those who seek to increase their capitals either by the employment of productive labour or by the performance of financial or commercial risk-bearing functions, and in either case, by creating or taking advantage of favourable or monopolistic terms of trade wherever possible, then the farmer is indeed an entrepreneur. But he does not dispose of labour or capital on a scale that enables him to compete on equal terms with the entrepreneur in industry, commerce, and finance. Thus he is necessarily at a disadvantage in the markets in which he sells his produce, buys his equipment and working materials, and in some cases borrows capital.

It is customary, indeed, to attribute the prairie farmer's insecure and fluctuating position to the fact that he must sell his products in a world market and buy and borrow in a restricted eastern Canadian market.[4] The terms of trade are generally tilted against him. In an economy where manipulation of the terms of trade in favour of the large entrepreneur is a normal source of capital increment, as it has always been in Canada, and especially obviously since the marked development of monopolistic combines and mergers around 1910 and again through the 1920's,[5] it is natural to emphasize the weakness of the farmer in this respect. The farmer himself generally does so. Yet this is to overlook the still more fundamental source of his sub-ordination, already mentioned, namely his inability to dispose of substantial quantities of labour while operating in an economy in which economic power is based on that ability.

Cut off thus, by the scale of his operations and by his independence of employed labour, from the ranks of the other entrepreneurs, yet

[4]Cf. W. A. Mackintosh, *The Economic Background of Dominion-Provincial Relations*, Appendix 3 to *Report of the Royal Commission on Dominion Provincial Relations* (Ottawa, 1939), p. 29.

[5]See *Report of the Royal Commission on Price Spreads* (Ottawa, 1937), pp. 28, 331.

not generally seeing how wide the gulf is between him and them, the farmer is apt to class himself with them, or at least to feel that he has an independent position in the economy akin to theirs. He is confirmed in this belief by his clear perception of his difference from the wage-earner. The wage-earner gives up the direction of his labour; the farmer retains the direction of his, making his own decisions as to how to use his land and capital, his skill and energy. His real independence in comparison with the employee thus confirms him in an illusion that he has or can have an independent place in the economy.

He is subject to this illusion of independence whether he thinks of himself as an entrepreneur or simply as a man making a living by his own skill and energy. If he is content not to behave as an entrepreneur but simply to try to get a living from the land by his own and his family's efforts, he is perhaps less apt to suffer disappointment over a few decades of ups and downs, but he is still, one might almost say, a misfit in an economy increasingly dominated by the accumulation of capital.

To sum up, the independent commodity producer's double relation to the market—that is, his independence of the labour market either as a seller or buyer and his dependence on the price system which is ruled as a whole by the rate of profit on the productive employment of wage labour—tends to give him, as a fundamental part of his outlook, an illusion of independence. It should be noticed that dependence on borrowed capital may be part of, but is not the essence of, his position. The relation of the western farmer to eastern financial institutions, and his reactions against them, have been so prominent that they are in danger of being taken to be more essential than they are. True, the more dependent he is on borrowed capital the more completely is his whole position dependent; yet even when he is not in debt he still stands in that double relation to the market.

Veblen, in a remarkable passage too long to quote in full,[6] argued more than thirty years ago that the independence of the farmer was entirely illusory because he had been in effect reduced to the position of a wage-earner by the ability of the investment interests to "rig the market" consistently against him.

The American farmer rejoices to be called 'The Independent Farmer.' He once was independent . . . in the days before the price system had brought him and all his works into the compass of the market; but that was some

[6]Thorstein Veblen, *An Enquiry into the Nature of Peace and the Terms of Its Perpetuation* (New York, 1917), pp. 348-9.

time ago. He now works for the market, ordinarily at something like what is called 'a living wage,' provided he has 'independent means' enough to enable him by steady application to earn a living wage; . . . the market being controlled by the paramount investment interests . . . [which] are in turn controlled . . . by the impersonal exigencies of the price-system, which permits no vagaries in violation of the rule that all traffic must show a balance of profit. . . .

But in attributing the farmers' position to their inability to create favourable terms of trade for themselves, Veblen neglected the other essential of their position, their inability to dispose of the labour of others while yet producing in an economy dominated by the wage-capital relationship. Hence he oversimplified their political outlook. "The farmer constituency is the chief pillar of conservative law and order . . . ; in point of sentiment and class consciousness [the farmer] clings to a belated stand on the side of those who draw a profit from his work." This is only a partial truth. Equally one-sided was Veblen's opinion two years later,[7] that the rise of the Non-Partisan League might mark the end of the farmers' tolerance of the vested interests. In the event it did not do so.

The farmers' political outlook, through the whole history of western American and Canadian agrarian movements, has been neither a settled conservatism nor a final break from conservatism, but an uneven and probably not yet ended oscillation between radicalism and conservatism. Veblen's judgments were faulty because based on the assumption that the farmer had been reduced in essentials to a wage-earner. Only by overlooking the fact that the farmer stands in quite a different relation to the market than does the wage-earner was Veblen able to maintain his paradox that the farmers had hitherto identified themselves with their own exploiters, and to allow himself to hope that they had at last realized their error and were finally moving over to the other side. The illusion of independence had deeper roots and other results than Veblen's analysis could forecast.

This point is basic to an understanding of agrarian politics, and calls for further analysis. We have attributed the farmers' illusion of independence to their double relation to the market: independent in being at once free of direction of their own labour and free of direct dependence on others' labour, yet dependent on an economy otherwise directed and of which they are a subordinate part. It is apparent that in this respect the farmers fit the classic pattern of the *petit-bourgeois* class. By examining their position in this broader

[7]*The Vested Interests and the Common Man* (New York, 1919), p. 182.

context we may strengthen the analysis suggested above and gain a clearer idea of the roots of agrarian political behaviour.

The concept of class which finds the significant determinant of social and political behaviour in the ability or inability to dispose of labour—one's own and others'—demonstrated its value in nineteenth-century historical and sociological analysis, but has been rather scorned of late years. No doubt it is inadequate in its original form to explain the position of the new middle class of technicians, supervisors, managers, and salaried officials, whose importance in contemporary society is very great; yet their class positions can best be assessed by the same criteria: how much freedom they retain over the disposal of their own labour, and how much control they exercise over the disposal of others' labour. Nor is this concept of class as readily amenable as are newer concepts to those techniques of measurement and tabulation which, as credentials, have become so important to modern sociology. Yet it may be thought to remain the most penetrating basis of classification for the understanding of political behaviour. Common relationship to the disposal of labour still tends to give the members of each class, so defined, an outlook and set of assumptions distinct from those of the other classes.

This does not necessarily mean that the members of a class, so defined, are sufficiently conscious of a class interest to act mainly in terms of it in making political choices. Nor need it mean that their outlook and assumptions are a conscious reflection of class position or needs as an outside observer or historian might see them. Historically, while working class and bourgeoisie have both displayed this awareness at crucial periods, the *petite-bourgeoisie* has typically not done so.

The common relationship to the market by which the *petit-bourgeois* class is defined does not produce a positive class consciousness. It gives rise, rather, to a common outlook better described as the absence of class consciousness and the presence of a false consciousness of society and of themselves. It is not difficult to see why this should be so; an explanation is suggested by the way in which it is necessary to define the class. It can be defined only negatively: those whose living comes neither from employing labour nor from selling the disposal of their labour. It is the absence of all sections of the class from the market relationship on which the economy as a whole is based that indicates the essence of their position. They are all in varying degree vestigial. As capitalist enterprise expands, they become the exception rather than the rule. While the other classes may tend to become more cohesive, the *petite-bourgeoisie* cannot be cohesive. Its different elements have nothing in common except the increasing insecurity which results from their increasingly anomalous position in the economy. The *petite-bourgeoisie* is at any time a collection of different elements, all tending, with the increasing subordination of all kinds of production to the direction of large capital accumulations, to lose their original functions and position. The very cause of the existence of the *petite-bourgeoisie*, the development of capitalist enterprise which continuously renders vestigial earlier forms of enterprise in various sectors of the economy and produces new transitional groups, is the cause of the heterogeneity of the class and of its lack of any consciousness of class.

The transitional nature of the various elements of the class also appears as the cause of the tendency of them all to have a delusive understanding of the nature of society, of the economy, and of their own place in it. They conceive society in their own image, not realizing or not admitting that the day of that society is past. Their condition has characteristically generated the notion that classes are not significant entities, because their class is not an entity; that the only reality is the individual, and not historically determined relations between individuals, because each of them is, more apparently than individuals of other classes, related with others almost solely through his commodities and theirs, which appears to be a free relation between individuals in the market. That the essence of man is in his independence of others becomes a belief so strongly felt that it leads them to believe that they can be independent.

From this illusive consciousness, and from their perennial insecurity, arises the oscillation between conservatism and radicalism which is characteristic of the *petite-bourgeoisie*. They cannot entirely identify themselves, or make permanent common cause, with either of the other two classes. Yet they are repeatedly driven by insecurity to find a solid basis somewhere. So they veer between attachment to one class and to the other; or rather, different sections of the whole class veer at different rates of speed and it may be in different directions at different times, depending on changes in their own position and on changes in the political outlook and action of the other classes. In so far as they do not recognize the reality of class entities they cannot see what they are doing, and cannot achieve their ends. When several sections have been led by simultaneous pressure of insecurity to support a political programme, their cohesion has generally been temporary, for the economy rarely affords a basis for the success of a programme attractive to them. Hence the history of *petit-bourgeois* political thought and action has been a history of oscillation and confusion.

What is true of the whole heterogeneous class is not necessarily true of one fairly homogeneous section of it. At first sight the western Canadian independent farm producers do not seem to share the characteristics which we have described as natural attributes of a *petit-bourgeois* position. In the first place the western farmer, starting in a new territory, with free or cheap land, seems to have been immune from the historical process by which *petit-bourgeois* producers generally are rendered vestigial and subordinate. Yet reflection on the quasi-colonial attributes of the western farm economy indicates that the independent farmer has not been immune. He has been, from the beginning, in a dependent and subordinate position in the economy, for the family farm came into existence on the Canadian prairies at a time when the control of the economy was firmly established in other hands. Where Veblen could describe the western American farmer as having lost his independence when he was drawn into "the price system,"[8] we must describe the western Canadian farmer as never having had such independence, for the Canadian west was opened to cultivation by the railway rather than the prairie schooner. It is not that the family farm is becoming obsolete in the Canadian west; it may well remain the unit of production most suited to the requirements of the Canadian economy. It is not the existence, but the independence, of the family farm that is vestigial, and has been so from its beginning in the Canadian west.

On this score, then, the independent farmer is not to be exempted from the position characteristic of the *petit-bourgeois*. His independence is largely illusory.

In the second place, the western farmers, being more homogeneous than the *petite-bourgeoisie* as a whole, have been able to organize both politically and economically to promote their immediate interests, and in the course of this organization they have developed a vigorous consciousness of common interests. But it is an agrarian consciousness, not a class consciousness; it emphasizes the common interests of agrarian producers and their difference from all other producers, and in so doing it fails to comprehend the essential class position of the independent producers, that is, their ambiguous position in an economy increasingly dominated by capital. It is characteristic that the outstanding leader of the U.F.A. consistently confused class with occupational group.

This agrarian consciousness has no doubt a real basis, since the

[8]Veblen, *An Enquiry into the Nature of Peace* . . . , p. 348.

western farm producers have some common economic interests as against all other sections of the economy. Yet it has often been taken to explain more than it properly does. It is both too broad and too narrow to bear the weight of explanation generally assigned to it. Too broad, in that the notion of an agrarian consciousness, or an "agrarian class," conceals substantial disparities in the scale of operations of different strata of farmers. Although only a small proportion of Alberta farmers fall outside the class of independent commodity producers, there are considerable gradations in the scale of production within the class of independent producers. The concept of an agrarian class takes little account of these differences, and thus is not helpful in explaining the fluctuations in the political direction of farmers' movements, and the rise and decline of various farmers' organizations. However, this is not a serious fault, for the agrarian interpretation can readily be elaborated to show how farmers of substantially different scales of operation have different political reactions to changes in the position of farming in the whole economy. Thus, as the terms of trade have fluctuated, the different strata of farmers have found their interests now merging, now separating; have combined, dissolved, and recombined; and their organizations have undergone frequent shifts of political direction.

The more serious weakness of the agrarian interpretation is its narrowness. It does not go beyond the agrarian consciousness, but takes it on its own terms. Yet the agrarian consciousness is, by its nature, incomplete and hence mistaken; it embodies, as we have seen, the illusion of independence which is characteristic of the whole *petite-bourgeoisie*. The farmers' belief in their independence has obvious origins in the free land period, and has been maintained by the weight of established habits of thought, reinforced by their occasional ability to obtain relatively favourable terms of trade in those periods, particularly war and immediate post-war times, when the need of their products is unusually increased. But fundamentally their illusion of independence is to be traced to their continuing anomalous position in the economy, their peculiar relation to the market. The agrarian consciousness is a delusive one in that it does not penetrate to the essentials of the independent commodity producer's position. It is likely to remain so, because the independent producers' position in the productive order is such as to lead them naturally to an erroneous conception of it, and may be expected to do so for as long as the economic order keeps them in their present position.

In turn, the agrarian consciousness contributes to their being kept in their present position. The effect of the illusion of independence on the part of the independent farm producers of Alberta has been to make the whole body of Albertan producers more easily subject to exploitation than would otherwise have been the case. The *petit-bourgeois* nature of the Alberta economy has helped to keep it in a quasi-colonial position, by preventing any serious revolt against the quasi-colonial status. Almost half of the working force remain independent producers, who normally identify their interests with a concept of free enterprise which covers the operation of the arrangement by which they are subjugated. The fact that they remain independent commodity producers, subordinated only by the operation of the price system, has meant, since the price system itself gets out of hand sometimes, that when it is particularly hard on them they have a disposition to rebel. This has occasioned some inconvenience to eastern interests, but nothing serious so far, for the western farmers' consciousness of themselves as entrepreneurs has kept them and their politicians from unduly radical behaviour. Paradoxically, their mistaken consciousness is necessary to their survival as a group in the present economic order. For it is accurate enough to give them some cohesion in resisting the pressure of the outside enemy, and thus to provide some defence to mitigate the very weakness which it entails.

The agrarian consciousness is thus at once hostile to and acquiescent in the established order. It is here that we find the fundamental explanation of the oscillation between radicalism and conservatism which is characteristic of Alberta politics. It has not, of course, taken the simple form of alternate attachment to, or identification with, the classes above and below the farmers in the scale of independence, which we have described as typical of *petit-bourgeois* politics. That pattern was modified by the quasi-colonial position of the western farmers, and by the fact that the independent producers were the largest class in Alberta itself. Labour was not a potential source of any great strength because it was a relatively small part of the Alberta economy; the U.F.A. did sometimes enter into a limited and temporary electoral co-operation with organized labour, but it always emphatically repudiated any identification of interests. The modified pattern was one of alternate rejection of and reconciliation with outside capital interests; obversely this appears as alternate identification with and distraction from the interests of humanity at large. Each radical movement began with fierce opposition to the outside "exploiters" (monopolists, manufacturers' association, banks, finance) and gradually came to terms with the system of which they were a part. And each at first identified its aims with the aims of "the masses" throughout Canada (and the world), but later narrowed its vision effectively to the interests of Albertans, mainly conceived as independent producers.

§ 3. *The Deterioration of Albertan Democracy*

The same *petit-bourgeois* attributes of the agrarian outlook which we have taken to explain the oscillation between radicalism and orthodoxy help to explain also the persistent rejection of the party system in favour of a one-party or non-party arrangement, and the deterioration in the quality of democracy which we have described as the trend from delegate to plebiscitarian democracy.

We have already seen[9] how the early rejection of the party system grew out of the small-producer quasi-colonial position. Party was not needed to represent differences of interest within a fairly homogeneous economy. And, to protect their independence, the farmers did need a system of politics by which they could resist colonial subordination. The pioneer Albertans won their formal provincial independence in 1905 without having developed a party system of their own. When federal parties were introduced as the mechanism of provincial politics, they soon proved to be too closely identified with the eastern interests to be adequate for western needs.

Agrarian leaders, seeing this very clearly, deepened their perception into a critique of the party system as such. Not only was it a means of keeping the western producers subordinate to the eastern business interests; it was also a means of maintaining a class society, by dividing and ruling. This further perception strengthened the farmers' resistance to party: the crusade against the party system was justified not only by the interests of the western producers but also by the interests of humanity. The resistance to party, generated by colonial consciousness, was thus heightened by *petit-bourgeois* consciousness of the common subordination of the mass of "little men." From then on, to succeed as a party, it was necessary to attack the party system, and those who could do so most effectively got such support that they were in fact able to establish something approaching a non-party system. The quality and effectiveness of the subsequent non-party systems reflected their *petit-bourgeois* inspiration.

The first, and to the independent producer the most natural, alternative to the party system was the U.F.A. scheme by which

[9]Chap. I, sect. 4.

cabinet rule was to give way to non-party "business government," parties were to be replaced by occupational group organizations, and delegate accountability was to be enforced throughout the political structure. "Group government," as such, never amounted to anything in practice, for no substantial groups other than farmers appeared on the political scene. The idea of "business government," however, persisted, and was indeed the *raison d'être* of the U.F.A.'s delegate democracy.

"When we learn to trade right we will have largely learned to live right," Henry Wise Wood had said in 1922.[10] Democratic politics was to be a way of ensuring that people "traded right." Democratic organization as Wood conceived it, faithfully enough to the farmers' vision, was to be in the first instance, the means of protecting themselves from the wrongful trading of others—the monopolists, the manufacturers' association, the tariff lobby, and the rest of the "special interests." Ultimately it was to lead to a new society where everybody traded right and all was harmonious. How this was to come about was never well explained or well understood. But it was always clear that it was to ensure that the government would cleave to the farmers' trading interests that strict delegate control was demanded.

The U.F.A. concept of delegate democracy was thus permeated with the assumption that politics is trade. It was a peculiarly *petit-bourgeois* concept of trade: it distinguished between good trade and bad trade, and dreamed that good trade could drive out bad. Politics was seen as a means of doing this; political organization was to be designed for this purpose. This is the basic meaning of the delegate democracy of the U.F.A. The germ of its deterioration into the later plebiscitarian democracy was carried in the assumptions on which it was built. For trading assumptions in their pure form are appropriate to, and are the strength of, the party system. In their idealized *petit-bourgeois* form they lead to the rejection of party but at the same time vitiate the non-party alternative, delegate democracy.

The central weakness in the U.F.A. scheme was the attempt to replace monopolistic competition by a fully democratic system, while retaining the assumptions of competitive individualism. The farmers' movement accepted the liberal ethics of individual competition, while rejecting the ethics of monopolistic competition. The impossibility of rejecting the one while accepting the other was implicit from the outset. The farmers' insight that the party system was a case of monopolistic competition led them to reject party as a democratic

[10]Quoted above, Chap. II, sect. 2, p. 34, from *The U.F.A.*, April 15, 1922.

instrument. Yet the only alternative they could adopt was a method of political organization designed to bring them more strenuously into monopolistic competition. Business government and delegate accountability were conceived primarily as means of strengthening the position of the farmers in the monopolistic competitive order, with only an ill-defined ultimate view to transcending it.

These devices served well enough as long as they were expected to do no more than strengthen the agrarian competitive position. But when they were called upon to transcend the monopolistic competitive order by popular sovereignty they failed. In the early 1930's, when popular sovereignty would have produced a direct attack on vested property rights, the divergence between business government and delegate democracy became acute, and delegate democracy succumbed. Wood's fundamentally liberal economic ideas and accompanying individualist theory of society could provide an alternative to the party system only as long as the alternative stayed within the same assumptions as the party system, the assumptions of a competitive capitalist order.

The limitations of the business analogue as a basis for popular democracy can be seen in another respect. Both the government of the province and the government of the U.F.A. were to be in effect boards of directors furthering the common interests of the shareholders. The shareholders were to participate actively and continuously, not by taking sides for and against rival groups of candidates for directorships, but by keeping an eye on the directors whom they had chosen for their business ability, and when necessary correcting their policies by instruction. The image was that of an old-fashioned business corporation, in which the shareholders had a personal knowledge of the business. Hence the insistence of the U.F.A., manifested in the "closed-door" policy, that the occupational group was the only truly effective basis of democratic political organization. Hence also the attempt to keep the elected legislative members free of cabinet control and responsible to constituency associations, and to make the annual delegate convention supreme. By keeping the elected member independent of cabinet and party, the farmers would secure their own independence.

As an instrument for ensuring that a farmer government adhered to the wants of the farmer group, delegate democracy was fairly effective, for the farmers did have a close knowledge of the business. But it was effective only in so far as those wants did not collide with the requirements of the mature Canadian capitalist economy, of which the independent commodity producers were a subordinate part. As those requirements made themselves felt, with varying intensity from 1921 to 1935, delegate democracy was subordinated to cabinet supremacy, the more readily because its assumptions were fundamentally the same as those of the Canadian economy.

The limits of *petit-bourgeois* liberalism were reached in the early 1930's with the U.F.A.'s failure to implement the popular will when it had come into conflict with property institutions. There was no question then of the people returning to the orthodox liberalism of the old party system; that would have been to submit again to the outside forces the havoc of whose operations they were determined to resist. On the other hand, as independent producers they were not greatly interested in any socialist transformation of society or socialist vision of democracy. The remaining possibility was some other form of *petit-bourgeois* democracy. The only forms left were various kinds of plebiscitary schemes. So, in reaction against the apparent failure of delegate democracy, they swung to what is in fact the other extreme (though it always presents itself in the guise of a stronger dose of popular sovereignty)—the plebiscitary democracy in which the people give up their right of decision, criticism, and proposal, in return for the promise that everything will be done to implement the general will. From then on, the deterioration was rapid.

The Social Crediters, too, conceived democracy in the image of a business system, but, more up to date than the U.F.A., their image was that of a giant corporation, in which the shareholders are atomized, their voices reduced to proxies, and their effective rights reduced to the one right of receiving a dividend. The corporate affairs being too complex for their understanding, they could have no effective control of policies. The directors and the experts would have a free hand; the shareholders retained only a paper sovereignty: the right to change directors and experts. Freedom for the individual was freedom to give or withhold his proxy.

In the later stages of Social Credit thinking, even the model of the business corporation was discarded as savouring too much of majority rule, only to be replaced by another commercial image, the relation of seller and buyer in the retail market—an even more fragmented relation than that of directors and shareholders. "Freedom within society simply means the right of the individual to choose or refuse any proposition placed before him without interfering with the same right of every other person."[11] The relations of the market were

[11]*Canadian Social Crediter*, Jan. 25, 1945.

supposed to provide the ultimate in both individual freedom and popular sovereignty.

The individualism of Social Credit thinking, the apotheosis of a business civilization, thus passes into its opposite. Democracy is defined as the freedom of individuals, separately, not collectively, to take or leave what is offered to them. The supposed union of all voters' wills into a mass will for general results reduces each will to nullity. The individual voter has no say as to what is to be offered for him to take or leave; that is arranged for him by those who preside over the general will. Political responsibility, supposed to be restored to the individual, is taken out of his reach. Democracy is denied while it is most vehemently asserted.

The plebiscitary democracy of Social Credit has obvious attraction for a community of independent producers who have reached the limits of genuine delegate democracy. The connection between acceptance of the social credit monetary panacea and acceptance of plebiscitarian democracy is not accidental. In circumstances of desperation the one is followed naturally by the other. Products of the same assumptions, they are equally false solutions of the *petit-bourgeois* predicament. The logical connection has already been shown;[12] the historical connection may also be noticed.

In historical perspective, the social credit theory is part of a long succession of utopian systems whose authors have denounced with varying degrees of insight the evils of business civilization, and have sought to remove them without altering the essential economic relationships by which they had been produced. It is not clear whether Major Douglas realized to what extent he was following the footsteps of the nineteenth-century utopians. That he was aware of their work is suggested by his assertion in 1931 that the present generation cannot take credit for discovering the cause of the trouble, as it had been discovered several times before, notably about a hundred years ago, and in every case suppressed.[13] There was no indication to what thinkers this referred, but some resemblances are obvious.

There is in the social credit theory much of Fourier, with his rejection of the work fetish, his belief that the cause of poverty was the abundance of goods, his fascination with the laws of gravity, and his catalogue of waste. There is something of Saint-Simon, with his faith in "les industriels" who actually operate the productive and

---

[12]See Chap. VII, sect. 2.

[13]C. H. Douglas, *Warning Democracy* (London, 1931); quoted in Philip Mairet, ed., *The Douglas Manual* (London, 1934), p. 146.

distributive system, his belief that "government" would be replaced by "administration," and his assurance that diffusion of credit would save the world. Even more striking is the similarity to the ideas of Proudhon,[14] the archetype of *petit-bourgeois* radicalism. Like Douglas, Proudhon explained the source of profit as the "increment of association," and the emergence of profit as a result of a miscalculation. Like Douglas he explained poverty as due to the depredation of industry by finance, which made it impossible for those who produced everything to buy back their own products; and found the solution in a scheme of free credit for producers, along with price-fixing. Like Douglas, he found that the handing over of the nation's credit to the national bank had elevated finance to the position of an occult power enslaving the whole country. Like Douglas, he held that the destruction of this power by credit reform would remove oppression and misery without altering the labour-capital relationship; competition and private property would remain. Like Douglas, he denounced majority rule and popular sovereignty, holding that progress was always accomplished not by the people but by an *élite*. Like Douglas, he hated bureaucracy and the omnipotent state for their repression of individual liberty. His theoretical anarchism, being a rejection not of all coercive power but only of absolute state power, is essentially similar to the social credit position. Like Douglas, Proudhon was scornful of political parties, and saw a Jewish conspiracy dominating the press and the government.

In the end Proudhon's false individualism led him to conclude in favour of the dictatorship of a leader who could prevail on the masses to give him power: Proudhon became a champion of the plebiscitarian dictatorship of Louis Bonaparte. From Proudhon to Hitler, doctrines which have singled out finance as the source of social evil have led to the plebiscitary state. And not without reason, for by seeking (or pretending) to remove the evils of which they complain by credit reform alone, they fail to resolve the class tension which, if not moderated by the democratic party system, can only be covered over by the devices of a plebiscitarian state.

In Alberta, of course, the class tension was not internal; it was a tension between the independent producers within, and the pressures of the other classes outside, the provincial economy. It is not suggested that the present Social Credit administration is a Bonapartist dictatorship. Whether it would have become one, had not the new-found

[14]Douglas may have been acquainted with Proudhon's ideas indirectly through Gesell.

wealth from the oil fields enabled the demands of the whole community to be met on an ample scale, must remain a speculation.

Manning's rejection of the later Douglas theory was of course not a rejection of the plebiscitarian notion of the general will. His attempt to distinguish between the principles of social credit and "the personal views of Major Douglas," so as to reject the later and obviously anti-democratic Douglas ideas while continuing to associate his government with social credit, was well meant. Genuine detestation of anti-Semitism, as well as recognition of its inappropriateness in Alberta, led Manning to purge the "Douglasites" from the Alberta movement and government. But to jettison "Douglasism" was really to complete the rejection of all the principles that were uniquely social credit; all that was left was the plebiscitarian heritage. The Manning forces, who called themselves the "realists," in opposition to the Douglasites, were, in view of their failure to introduce social credit in practice, truly realist in abandoning social credit principles. But this kind of realism required also that they should continue to assert the principles. It is the realism of plebiscitarian leadership.

As long as the independent commodity producers retain their preponderance in Alberta, the plebiscitarian quality of Alberta politics is likely to persist. That preponderance is decreasing, and may continue to do so; but if, before such a trend should become decisive, the Social Credit administration should be displaced by another reform movement, the resulting system (a non-party one, of course) would not easily depart from the plebiscitarian pattern. The C.C.F. (the most likely contender) treasures the principle of delegate democracy as much as the U.F.A. did, but if it came to office in Alberta on the basis of yet another farmer revolt against renewed economic pressures from outside it would not be long before the limits of provincial popular sovereignty and delegate democracy would again be reached. No party which takes office as the provincial champion of the independent producer is likely to be able to transcend these limits, unless indeed it is prepared and able to do away with the capitalist basis of the whole national economy. And once the limits are reached, to the inevitable disappointment of the rank and file, there is no way to hold office but by something approaching a plebiscitarian system. The most that could be expected in these circumstances would be a swing away from plebiscitarian to delegate democracy in the first few years of the new régime.

We may conclude that deterioration in the quality of substitutes for the party system is a highly probable result of the needs and outlook of a community of independent commodity producers which forms a subordinate part of a maturing or mature capitalist economy. The deterioration is not constant; the quality of non-party democracy may achieve relative stability, with only brief deviations, for an indefinite period. Deterioration follows from the persistence of the independent producers' demands beyond the point which their governments can satisfy within the limits set by an outside economy which is yet fundamentally acceptable to them. If, owing to changes in the outside economy, the limits recede, a period of relative stability may set in; the system of government can settle down at whatever level of delegate or plebiscitary democracy it has reached. Or, without the limits receding, there may be an increasing recognition by the independent producers that the limits confronting their demands are implicit in an economic system which they do not wish to destroy. In this way stability may result from reconciliation to the limits, whose acceptance in the last resort is inherent in the *petit-bourgeois* outlook.

§ 4. The General Theory

The analysis just concluded has indicated that the most probable course of political organization in Alberta is a continued rejection of the orthodox party system and the maintenance of a fairly stable system of plebiscitarian democracy, possibly with excursions into more active delegate democracy. It suggests also that a new species of political system has come to stay. Before considering the possibilities and limits of the system it will be well to establish the usefulness of introducing the new term "quasi-party system" to describe it.

It is clear that what has prevailed in Alberta for at least thirty years is not the party system of the orthodox liberal-democratic tradition. Government has not been conducted, nor have policies been decided, by continual competition between two main parties for the support of the majority of the electorate. Nor can the reality be fitted to the orthodox pattern by treating either the U.F.A. or Social Credit as third parties. While they resemble, in structure and outlook, popular movements which elsewhere have entered into a regular party system as third parties, they have not done so. Neither of them was ever third, nor did either, starting third, become one of two fairly equal contenders; each came at one stroke to such predominance as almost to displace all others. Needless to say, there is no approximation, either, to the multi-party system typical of continental western European nations. The party system, then, in any of its usual senses, is a misnomer for what has been in existence for more than three decades in Alberta.

To describe what has actually prevailed we have been using, with or without qualification, the terms "one-party" and "non-party" system. Yet it is apparent that these categories are not adequate, and it will be better now to discard them.

In the first place, what we have is not strictly a non-party system. It may be doubted whether any political structure is really non-party. Parties, at least of a tenuous sort, are apt to be formed in any body which needs continuous government and in which the government is formally chosen by the governed. They may be found in business corporations, in trade unions, in religious congregations, and in all manner of voluntary associations. Yet the designation "non-party" may generally be allowed these, inasmuch as their governments are not elected or supported by means of regularly organized, identified, and opposed political machines, but are chosen for efficiency in administration of policies on which there is no deep and lasting division among the electorate. In this sense, Canadian local government is normally non-party. But Alberta government, except during the early Territorial period, does not qualify as a fully non-party system. Both the U.F.A. and Social Credit were parties, seeking the support of a majority of voters on a party programme, even though that programme included the aim of transcending party. They stood for certain principles and for certain specific policies in a way which makes their practice quite distinct from that of non-party municipal government. The Alberta system cannot therefore properly be described as a non-party system.

Nor can it be described with any accuracy as a one-party system. Other parties, although much reduced, continued to operate and to elect candidates in at least some constituencies. So complete was the predominance of the party in power that there was no need, from its own point of view, to attempt to proscribe other parties. Nor was there any inclination to do so. In spite of an occasional confusion between the functions of party and state in the Social Credit régime, there was no serious thought of establishing a totalitarian one-party rule. There was, indeed, no basis for an outright one-party dictatorship: such a system is only thrust up as part of a revolutionary (or counter-revolutionary) transfer of power in a strongly class-divided society.

Nor is the Alberta system adequately to be understood as an imperfect or deviant form of a two- or three-party or non-party or one-party system. For one thing, it partakes too much of the character of all three to be considered an affinity of any one of them. It shares the attributes of the ordinary party system, at least to the extent that it operates by permanently organized and publicly identified electoral machines with some opposition from other machines. It shares the attributes of a non-party system in its emphasis on "business government," that is, on administration rather than policy formation as the function of government and as the government's main claim on the electorate. It shares, too, some of the qualities of a one-party system, especially in its rejection of the orthodox notion that party is beneficial, and in its belief in a general will of the community.

More important, it lacks an affinity in the other sense to any one of the three recognized types. There is nothing in its nature, or in the conditions which produced it, to lead us to expect that it will become more like any one of them. It is built distinctly on rejection of the two- or three-party system. It developed, as we have seen, out of a provincial non-party system which early proved insufficient. And there is no basis, in present circumstances at least, for it to become an outright one-party system.

For these reasons it is best considered to be *sui generis*. A distinct category requires a new term. "Quasi-party" will serve.

The quasi-party system, as it has emerged in Alberta, may be seen as a response to the problem of democratic government in a community mainly of independent producers which forms a subordinate part of a more mature capitalist economy. It appears as a middle way between an alternate-party system which has become unreal or harmful and a one-party state which would be unacceptable and for which there is not the requisite class basis. We must now inquire to what extent the quasi-party system can meet the problem of democratic government in such a community. We may also ask whether it is suitable beyond the one province in which we have seen it.

To ask these questions about the quasi-party system is to raise two prior questions. First, what is the central problem of democratic government, or, which is much the same thing, what are the essential functions of democratic government? Secondly, what part does the orthodox party system play in the performance of these functions?

On the first question there are, in the European-Anglo-American tradition, two quite different views. One, which goes back to the seventeenth century, is a class concept; the other, which is the prevalent liberal-democratic view in the twentieth century, is pluralistic.

In the first view, democracy is an affair of the presently unprivileged; it means government responsible to and infused with the will of "the common people," those whose claim to consideration is their common humanity rather than their estates, their life and labour rather than accumulated wealth or hereditary status. This is an old dream, expressed before the modern period in peasants' revolts. It becomes more articulate and pressing from the seventeenth century on through the nineteenth, being the demand at first of the small independent producers and later of an employed working class as well. Democracy, till well on in the nineteenth century, was a revolutionary or at least a radical reformist creed, abhorred and denounced, with a few exceptions, by politicians and political thinkers alike. But neither its advocates nor its opponents were in any doubt as to what it meant. This idea of democracy is of more than historical interest; although now supplanted in the orthodox canon, it has been repeatedly revived in popular reformist as well as revolutionary movements in the nineteenth and twentieth centuries, after the popular franchise had been attained and been found wanting.

Twentieth-century liberal-democratic thought, on the other hand, has submerged the class theory of democracy in a pluralistic theory. It has assumed that with the establishment of a popular suffrage the class function of democracy is no longer significant. The primary problem of democratic government is taken to be the representation and reconciliation of a multitude of diverse and conflicting group interests—regional, occupational, racial, religious, ethical—which cut across and blur class lines. In this view the machinery of government is, in itself, neutral; it has no inherent class content, but operates in response to the pressures of all the groups.

Orthodox twentieth-century political science has in effect neutralized democratic theory while still trying to uphold democratic values. By treating the demands and pressures of all the groups as the data of the science, it has put itself in the position of treating them all as ethically equal or neutral; all, that is, except demands which would bring democracy to an end. But because the theorists have so reduced the ethical content of democracy, they have found some difficulty in drawing even that line. To the extent that they reduce politics to a sort of market which measures and equates political supply and demand, they destroy the basis for any ethical criterion of demand. There is an obvious parallel between the transformation of political economy into economics after Ricardo and that of political thought or philosophy—the term was never precise—into political science after John Stuart Mill. The change came a little later (and is not yet as advanced) in political science, but it is the same change: the humanistic substance is taken out, supposedly in the interests of more refined scientific handling of the problems. In the case of political science the removal is commonly justified, if it is noticed, by the assumption that the class problem of democracy has been solved by the attainment of popular suffrage, or that what remains of the problem can now be adjusted by the free play of the political market.

This view, largely the product of the twentieth century, had some justification in the first few decades of the century, especially in America where class lines have been less distinct than in Europe. But even while it was reaching general academic acceptance, its inadequacy was being demonstrated by the emergence of class movements which, after some experience of orthodox politics with the new universal franchise, rejected the pluralist view and resorted to political action based on the older concept of democracy. Just when the pluralist theory was being received as a solution to (or a way of avoiding) the problem that had exercised English liberals in the nineteenth century—how to reconcile democracy with the individualism and property institutions of a maturing capitalist economy—it was being made apparent, by labour and socialist movements in England and Europe, and by labour and agrarian movements in America, that the problem of democracy had again to be restated, and in something like the old terms.

The fact that the older view of democracy keeps being rediscovered indicates that it corresponds to some reality which the pluralistic theory does not adequately comprehend. The achievement of universal suffrage and the flowering of voluntary associations as political pressure groups have not erased class lines, nor is there any reason to expect that they will do so. We may conclude, therefore, that in a mature capitalist world the problem of democracy is not only the pluralistic one of representing and reconciling the conflicts of multitudinous group interests, but also (and more fundamentally) one of expressing and containing the conflict of class interests.

Turning now to the second prior question—what is the role of the party system in performing the democratic function—we find again two distinct views, corresponding to the two concepts of democracy.

In the first view, party is distrusted and denounced as part of the apparatus of rule by the privileged class. Designed to pervert or cripple the will of the people, party can perform no democratic function. In its place may be put the direct democracy of the town meeting, the local assembly of all the citizens, or, as with the

Jacobins, a single mass party which, by embracing all true democrats, transcends party. In other words, democracy requires a non-party or a one-party state. This view of party reappears, as we have seen, in agrarian reform movements in the twentieth century.

The second view of party, the orthodox twentieth-century rationale of the party system, has been built on the pluralistic view of democratic society. The party system is seen as having two main functions, both of which are held to be essential to democratic government. The first is, as a brokerage apparatus or entrepreneurial system—some such analogy from business is generally used—to sift and bring together into two or a few combinations the multitude of divergent group demands and equate them to the available supply of political goods, giving due weight to each without destroying any. The task is to produce at all times out of a very diverse series of minorities, a majority capable of supporting an effective government. On the pluralistic assumption that the really important interests of individuals are those which unite them in overlapping groups no one of which is a numerical majority, it is essential for continuous government, indeed for government of any kind, that they be brought together in political parties.

The second function is, to act as a safeguard against a permanent irresponsible oligarchy and as a check to abuse of power, by providing always an alternative body of occupants for the commanding positions. Without the agency of party to perform these functions, it is said, democratic government could not survive.

There is little question that these functions are performed more or less adequately by the party system wherever it exists, and that they must be performed if democracy is to be maintained in such societies. Whether the two functions can be performed in any modern society only by a party system, as is usually claimed, is more difficult to determine.

Whether the first of these functions can be performed only by party is a less important question than it may seem, because the first function is becoming relatively less important than it has been. If, as we have argued, the central problem of democratic government in a mature capitalist world is coming to be the moderation and containment of conflicting class interests rather than the entrepreneurial problem of sifting, weighing, and adjusting a multitude of sectional and group interests, it is evident that the entrepreneurial function of the party system is being replaced in importance by the function of moderating class tension.

The orthodox theory recognizes, of course, that the party system can operate only where class division in the society is not so strong as to prevent any class from accepting the verdict of the polls; in Lord Balfour's often-quoted phrase "our whole political machinery pre-supposes a people so fundamentally at one that they can safely afford to bicker."[15] But this is to emphasize, characteristically, not the degree of class division that does exist—this is reduced to bickering—but the supposed fundamental oneness of the whole people. If we bring back into serious consideration the problem of class tension in a democracy, as we are compelled to do by the fact of its reassertion by radical movements in our own day, it appears that the function of the party system in maintaining democracy is not only to weigh and adjust a multitude of sectional and group interests and to provide against a permanent oligarchy, but also to moderate the conflict of class interests. The party system, wherever it prevails, does do all these things.

Its capacity for moderating class conflict, within limits, is evident in its history and in its design. This function can be performed either by a pair of parties which substantially represent different classes (as the English Conservative and Labour parties), or by a pair of parties which do not represent different classes (as the Democratic and Republican parties in the United States, or the Canadian Liberal and Conservative parties) but which private organizations representing class interests seek to control or to influence in their favour. It may also be performed by the continental European multi-party system, in which the government normally rests on the support of two or more of a series of several class parties, and is thereby compelled to continual and shifting compromise. This system has at least as great a claim to be considered democratic as has either of the types of alternate-party system, and in any full investigation of the claims of the party system it would demand thorough exploration. But since the multi-party system is neither indigenous nor easily transplanted to those countries in which a two-party system has been long established, we shall disregard it here. From now on we shall use the term "party system" or (where the context suggests it) "alternate-party system" to refer to the two- or three-party system of the British and American tradition; and "orthodox" theory to refer to the prevailing Anglo-American liberal-democratic theory.

Either of the two types of alternate-party system takes some of the

---

[15]Introduction (1927) to Bagehot's *The English Constitution* (London, 1933), p. xxiv.

strain out of the antagonism of class interests by providing, if not satisfaction for one class, at least continual hope of further satisfaction for both. Of the two types the American seems better designed for containing and moderating class tension. By cutting straight across class lines, with each party appealing to all classes, it rules out class parties almost completely. Once it is established, with appropriate electoral devices, it can shut out third parties from power while allowing them to function as a useful vent for discontent. The other type of two-party system, however, is not unsuccessful. Although there the two parties are drawn up along class lines, it is not long before the necessity, in a business civilization, of running politics like a business, gives over the direction of both parties to professional politicians. The professionalized party, in or out of office, then devotes itself to seeking votes from, by appealing to, all classes. Thus the tendency is for the class content of what were built as class parties to be reduced. In this way, as long as the hegemony of parties is accepted by the electorate, even class parties do moderate class opposition.

Either type of alternate-party system, then, is competent, within limits, to perform the function of containing class opposition. And in any long view this function is more continuously necessary than the pluralistic function of adjusting diverse group interests. Historically, the latter function appears as the primary task of the party system only in expanding societies in which the prevailing economic and political power relations are sufficiently accepted that there is no strong pressure to establish a new structure of economic class relations. Since the arrival of the democratic franchise, these conditions have existed in most cases only for a few decades in the late nineteenth and twentieth centuries, the decades in which the now orthodox theory was developed. When these conditions cease to prevail, the party system can still maintain democracy but does so by virtue of its ability to moderate class conflict rather than its ability to perform the brokerage function between a multitude of groups. The two functions, of course, are commonly found together, and can indeed only be separated in abstract analysis. But we appear to be moving into a period in which the class function is becoming the more important function of the party system.

We may conclude that the party system, or something like it, is essential to the maintenance of democracy in a class-divided society. Nothing else has been found which can moderate class conflict so successfully, either by partially satisfying or by confusing the interests of opposed classes. This, of course, was the burden of the U.F.A.'s complaint against the party system.

While the brokerage function of parties may thus be reduced to secondary importance, the other main function allotted to parties by the orthodox theory—the checking of arbitrary government—still remains fundamental in a class-divided society. Where there is a strong division of class interests there is a tendency toward a government representing one class or combination of classes exclusively and permanently, or yielding so far to the demands of one class as to jeopardize the position of the other. A flourishing party system is the most effective deterrent that has been found, and may thus be considered essential to the maintenance of democracy in such a society.

Whether the party system is needed in a less class-divided society for the prevention of arbitrary government is not so clear. The need of a party system for this purpose in *any* society can be shown if it is assumed that there is always a natural conflict between the government and the people. It may be said, however, that the more homogeneous a society is, the less likely is the government to be regarded as a natural enemy. At the theoretical extreme of a society without class division, and with popular franchise, the people would regard the state's purposes as their own and the party system would not be required for the maintenance of democracy. Only in such a society is it possible to think of a general will sustaining a democracy without alternate parties. This, of course, is the meaning of the claim made by Soviet Russia and the "new democracies" of eastern Europe for their systems as true democracy. With this claim we are not here concerned, for it is appropriate only to a society where class divisions in the Marxist sense have been or are being eliminated by the elimination of capitalist relations of production.

The society we have been examining is not a "classless society" in this sense. It may appear so, because it is more homogeneous than an advanced industrial society, but its homogeneity is that of a quasi-colonial community of independent producers who are a subordinate part of a mature capitalist economy. In such a society a one-party state does not even theoretically meet the requirements of democracy; there is no more basis for it than for the alternate-party system. A one-party state will not arise unless there is a mass will for a fundamentally different society; one-party states have always been the outcome of a revolutionary dissolution of a previous class and property structure, or of a counter-revolutionary attempt to restore or maintain such a structure.

We need not venture the paradox that only a class-divided society requires a party system for the maintenance of democracy. All that is relevant to our problem here is that a class-divided society, to be a democracy, *does* require a party system, or a substitute which can perform the same functions, namely the moderation and containment of class opposition, and the provision of some safeguard against arbitrary government.

Our original question—whether the quasi-party system can meet the requirements of democracy—may now be restated in terms of its capacity to perform these functions. We now have grounds for concluding that, in the specific conditions (a quasi-colonial and largely *petit-bourgeois* society) which gave rise to the quasi-party system, it can perform the same functions as the regular party system, though in reduced degree, and that it is the only system that can do so.

Enough has been said already to show that in the specific conditions there is no basis for either a two- or three-party system, or a strictly one-party system, or a completely non-party system. It now appears that, given the unsuitability or impossibility of these systems, the quasi-party system can to a limited degree express and moderate the conflict of class interests in which such a society is involved.

The achievement of both the U.F.A. and Social Credit was to do just this. The peculiarity of a society which is at once quasi-colonial and mainly *petit-bourgeois* is that the conflict of class interests is not so much within the society as between that society and the forces of outside capital (and of organized labour). This does not mean, of course, that the conflict is expressed only in federal politics; the opposition of class interests is reflected back into provincial politics, as was clearly seen in, for instance, the U.F.A. debt legislation and the Social Credit monetary control legislation.

The record analysed in earlier chapters shows that the class conflict was expressed and contained by the Alberta radical movements, sufficiently to permit the maintenance of democratic government in greater or less degree. It suggests also, however, that there are limits to the possibility of maintaining democracy by a quasi-party system. In the Social Credit period it became possible to moderate the class tension only by a process of delusion. Whether it is thought that this was delusion of the people by the party leaders, or whether it is thought to have extended to self-delusion of the leaders, is irrelevant here. The point is that the quasi-party system shifted from a genuinely democratic delegate basis to an inspirational plebiscitarian basis. A plebiscitarian system is a way of covering over class tension which can neither be adequately moderated by party nor be resolved short of an outright totalitarian one-party rule. Thus, the quasi-party system, to the extent that it cannot moderate class tension while expressing it, contains it by concealing it. The resulting system is at best an illusory democracy.

A quasi-colonial society in which independent producers are the predominant element appears peculiarly liable to both kinds of quasi-party system. It tends, as we have seen, to reject the regular party system. At the same time, it is not strongly impelled toward a one-party state, for opposition between *petit-bourgeois* and other classes is more easily moderated than that between more completely opposed classes. Such a society does not, therefore, readily move beyond the quasi-party system in the direction of totalitarianism. But within the quasi-party framework it does tend to travel the plebiscitarian road. In so far as the maturing of the capitalist economy makes accommodation of the interests of the *petite bourgeoisie* more difficult, this class is liable to be taken in by delusive schemes. As we saw in section 3, the independent producer resists the subordination imposed on him by the capitalist economy, yet accepts the fundamentals of its property institutions.

We may conclude that the quasi-party system is capable of performing one of the main functions of the regular party system—the moderation of class conflict—but that the circumstances which bring it into existence are liable to carry it into a plebiscitarian stage which cannot be considered fully democratic but which can maintain the form and some of the substance of democracy.

The other function of the regular party system—the prevention of arbitrary use of power—may also be performed, in reduced degree, by the quasi-party system. While it does not provide an ever ready alternative government, it does generally provide an opposition group in the legislature which, with some outside backing and some access to publicity, acts as a brake on arbitrary government. There is no reason to think that the existence of such opposition would prevent a descent into completely arbitrary rule, but, so long as the circumstances prevail which led to the quasi-party rather than a one-party system, the existence of a recognized opposition performs this democratic function in some degree.

From the one case which has been examined in this volume it is not possible to say whether as a general rule a quasi-party system can avoid reaching a plebiscitarian stage, or, having reached that stage, how long it can continue to maintain any of the substance of democratic responsibility and freedom from arbitrary rule. From the example of Alberta, it appears that a quasi-party system tends to become plebiscitarian when it can no longer satisfy the economic demands of the electorate within the framework of a mature capitalist economy. It appears also that a quasi-party system can continue to maintain some of the substance of democracy if the economy enters an expansive phase (in the case of Alberta, post-war prosperity and oil) which enables the demands to be satisfied in larger measure than was possible when the shift to a plebiscitarian system took place. There is, however, no mechanical correspondence between the degree of economic expansiveness and the democratic quality of the quasi-party system. Once it has entered a plebiscitarian phase, no economic expansion is likely to restore it to a more fully democratic level, for the effect of prosperity will ordinarily be to strengthen the existing party's attractiveness without requiring it to change its ways.

The relation just suggested, between the indefinite maintenance of plebiscitarism and a renewal of economic expansion, may also hold for the maintenance of the quasi-party system as such, not merely its plebiscitarian phase. In other words, once a quasi-party state has been established in a quasi-colonial and predominantly *petit-bourgeois* society it may persist indefinitely if the economy of which it is a part shows (even intermittently) sufficient expansiveness to contain the aspirations of the electorate; yet no expansiveness can be expected to bring about a reversion to the orthodox party system. It is this which makes it probable that the quasi-party system is the new permanent system in Alberta. Close analysis of the political history of the other prairie provinces would probably show that the same system has been in effect there for some time already, although in a slightly different form.

It may be noticed finally that much that is obscure about the Canadian federal party system might yield to further analysis along these lines. We are supposed to have a two- or three-party system in Canada, yet one party has been in office, with only two intervals, ever since 1896, and continuously since 1935. This has led one observer[16] to speak of Canada as a one-party state, and to attribute the phenomenon

[16]D. G. Anglin, "Democracy and the One-Party State in Canada," *National Review*, Dec. 1949, pp. 515–18.

to the skill of the Liberal party in representing the lowest common denominator of political opinion in a country with an unusual dispersion of racial, religious, and sectional interests. The one party, it is said, has been so successful at this that it is now widely considered to be the only party able to form a government; consequently, the greater the threat that it may lose an election, the more voters rally to it from the protest parties.

Such a system, however, is closer to a quasi-party than to a one-party state, in spite of the long ascendancy of one party. Indeed, not all the characteristics even of a quasi-party system are evident. Yet some are discernible. Opposition parties, though still in lively competition with the government party, appear to be developing into regional rather than national parties, and to be unable to compete effectively for the support of the majority of the federal electorate. It is too early to say, on this basis, whether the orthodox party system is outmoded in Canadian federal government; one of the opposition parties may gain national stature and rehabilitate the alternate-party system, in spite of the enormous advantage which the party in office has in a welfare and war-planning state.

There is, however, some reason to expect that the future of Canadian federal politics may lie in the quasi-party system. The conditions that gave rise to it in Alberta are not entirely lacking in Canada as a whole. As Canada becomes increasingly overshadowed by the more powerful economy of the United States, her position approximates the quasi-colonial. And, while independent producers do not make up as large a proportion of Canadian as of Albertan society, the characteristic independent-producer assumptions about the nature of society are very widespread in Canada, a legacy of the not distant days when anyone could set up in business or farming for himself. Our analysis has suggested that when these two attributes—quasi-colonial status and independent producer outlook—are combined in one society during a period of maturing or mature capitalism, we have the conditions for a quasi-party system. That system appears to be the most satisfactory answer that can be found, within such conditions, to the problem of maintaining the form and some of the substance of democracy.

It is only a partial answer, as we have seen. The circumstances which give rise to a quasi-party system are apt to carry it into, and keep it in, a plebiscitarian stage which cannot be considered as democratic as a vigorous two-party system. But beggars cannot be choosers: it is only when the conditions for a two-party system have disappeared that the quasi-party system emerges. The only requirement for its indefinite continuance is the continuance of a degree of economic expansion which can accommodate the aspirations of those who have become disillusioned with the orthodox party system. The quasi-party system may thus be considered either the final stage in the deterioration of the capitalist democratic tradition, or a way of saving what can be saved of liberal-democracy from the threatening encroachment of a one-party state.

Index

->>><<<-

251